# AH SUH ME SEE IT,
# AH SUH ME SAY IT.

# AH SUH ME SEE IT, AH SUH ME SAY IT.

## COMMENTARY ON THE SOCIAL AND EDUCATIONAL ISSUES IN JAMAICA

**By Esther Tyson**

XULON PRESS

Xulon Press Elite
2301 Lucien Way #415
Maitland, FL 32751
407.339.4217
www.xulonpress.com

Printed in the United States of America.

First Published by The Gleaner Company Limited, Jamaica

ISBN-13: 9781545619582

# TABLE OF CONTENTS

**Part 1 Education In Jamaica**

## Part 2 The State Of The Family In Jamaica

## Table Of Contents

### Part 3 Societal Values

## Part 4 The Impact Of Dancehall On The Jamaican Culture

## Part 5 The Church In The Jamaican Society

## Part 6 The Abortion Debate In Jamaica

## Table Of Contents

### Part 7 The LGBT Agenda In Jamaica

### Part 8 Government Leadership In Jamaica

# PREFACE

I served as the principal of Ardenne High School, Kingston Jamaica, my alma mater, from January 2000 to August 2011. After a few years, I began to send letters to the Editor of The Gleaner, one of Jamaica's newspapers, to comment on issues that impacted students in the country. One letter commented on the then ministers of government attending the funeral of a known 'don' associated with crime whose funeral was given permission to be held at the National Arena. Government ministers in their party colours were seated at the very front of the attendees. My concern was the impression that this would have on the students who might see this action as tanta-mount to the government's approval of this don's lifestyle. This letter resulted in discussions being aired in the media about the appropri-ateness of those actions.

Subsequently, in 2007, I was asked to accept the role to be a monthly columnist for The Sunday Gleaner to comment on social and educational issues. One seminal article that I wrote was called 'Rampin Shop —musical poison' Part 4 No. 70. This article helped to snowball the discussion on the impact of violent and raw sexual dancehall music on the youth. The Broadcasting Commission would later place a ban on such music on the public airwaves. In spite of the backlash I received from some academics, I was gratified to see the outcome of the article.

I wrote this column from 2007 – 2016. In early 2016, I realized that some issues had not changed and that if I were to comment on what was currently happening, I would be repeating myself. I, however, wanted to leave a documentation of my perspective on the matters about which I had written. This book, Ah Suh Me See It, Ah Suh Me Say It, is that documentation.

The articles are compiled in a thematic format while indicating the date they were originally published in The Gleaner. There are eight themes organized as eight parts. Although the book is not formatted in a chronological order, each part is arranged by date. Many of these articles have been used in tertiary institutions to inform discussions on educational and social issues. I trust that this publication will continue to be useful to students, lecturers, and readers concerned about the social fabric of the Jamaican society.

# INTRODUCTION

The book, **Ah Suh Me See It, Ah Suh Me She It**, by Esther Tyson, contains the reflections and studied opinions of one of the nation's celebrated educators. Her career as educator for over 40 years included an eleven-year tenure as principal of one of Jamaica's top ten high schools. She is therefore eminently qualified to speak and is deserving of being heard.

The book is a compilation of articles published in the Jamaica Daily Gleaner over an eight-year period (2007 – 2015). As indicated in the book's sub-title, it offers commentary on a range of issues topical in the Jamaican society, with the expected emphasis on education. She offers views on the status of education in Jamaica and what is needed to achieve the educational goals outlined in the nation's Vision 2030 document.

Another area of emphasis is family life. While indicating the well-recognized decline in family life in recent years, she offers hope for improved family life, pointing to significant and successful initiatives by various organizations to arrest this decline.

She is bold in highlighting societal ills and challenging those responsible for perpetuating them to effect needed changes, including leaders in government as well as the private sector.

She discusses, inter-alia,

- Politicking that undermines nation – building
- Children's rights versus responsibilities
- Culture of indiscipline in schools
- The roles of church and state in national development
- Impact of crime and violence on children's ability to learn
- Importance of proper parenting practices for improved family life
- Abortion
- Influence of music and the entertainment industry in shaping the values and attitudes of youth

The reader will find, however, that the Commentary is not only a litany of woes – it also showcases success stories of young people who have achieved academically despite daunting personal challenges as well as innovative strategies that have been successfully used by Jamaican educators and school administrators to overcome obstacles and achieve gratifying results.

Mrs. Tyson expresses hope in the future of the nation, citing the annual Inter-schools' Athletic Championships and the annual Schools' Challenge Quiz aired on national television as examples of excellence in administrative leadership and as arenas in which admirable values and attitudes are honed and consistently displayed by our youth.

With the practiced eye of the seasoned educator Esther Tyson has identified critical challenges facing the Jamaican society and has offered insightful solutions that the nation would do well to apply/ would make a difference, if applied.

Barrington Davidson (Dr.)

Founder, Executive Director

Family Life Ministries, Jamaica

# DEDICATION

This book is dedicated to my husband of 38 years, Rawle Tyson.
He has supported me in all my endeavours in spite of being shot
and paralyzed in 1997 at the age of 39 and later suffering a massive stroke that resulted in Broca's Aphasia in 2004 after completing his doctorate.

In spite of being confined to a wheelchair and not being able to
speak clearly and fluently at this time, his response when asked
how he is doing, is that he is healthy and he is happy. God broke
the mould when He made him.

He is my inspiration.

# ACKNOWLEDGEMENTS

This book would not have been completed without the involvement of various organizations and persons who assisted me in one way or another. First, I acknowledge the inspiration of Almighty God in guiding my thoughts as I sought to comment on what was happening in our society from a Christian worldview. Secondly, I thank The Gleaner Company for affording me the opportunity to express my views freely within the confines of the law and for granting me the licence to use the articles in this publication. In addition, I am grateful to the Ardenne High School Board of Management that supported me in my role as a columnist while I was principal of the school.

My family: my husband Rawle, children, Mikaela and Jaquan Levons, Jonathan and Kaydene Tyson, Sara and Sheldon Campbell, my sisters Janeth and Carol have all been very supportive of my role as a columnist and encouraged me to write this book. Thanks especially to Sheldon who assisted in editing some of the articles for this publication and to my mother-in-law, Ruby Tyson, who did a detailed editing of the typeset. My close friends have provided moral support along the way. I must thank Karl and Marcia Chambers in Atlanta who provided a conducive environment for me to work on this book.

I must express my appreciation to so many persons who gave me positive feedback while I wrote the column. Many thanked me for being the voice of Jamaicans who had similar views but who were not able to express them publicly. Thanks to Shirley Richards who has encouraged me to give voice to the voiceless and who champions Christian values before the policy makers of our land.

The photographs included were done courtesy of Bruce T Photography and those that were taken at Robert Lightbourne High School were included with permission of Jamaica National Foundation and Stuart Reeves, photographer. I am grateful to the principals of Robert Lightbourne High School, Tarrant High School and Mona Primary for being willing to have me include the photographs taken at their school in this book.

# PART 1

# EDUCATION IN JAMAICA

# TEACHERS: SOCIETY'S BUFFOONS?

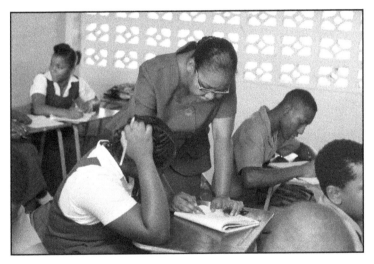

**Teacher in Jamaica**

The teacher enters the classroom believing that by doing her job with excellence, she will be compensated decently. [The gender of the teacher is feminine since the greatest percentage of our teachers is female.] The situation, however, applies to both genders. The teacher expects that after being in the classroom for some years and being wise in saving, she will be able to have a car and a home of her own. She is sure that she will receive society's respect for the significant contribution that she will make to the development of productive citizens for the nation.

These are the normal expectations of someone who has chosen the profession and who feels called to make a contribution to society. She expects to be rewarded for her training and the work she does. Society, however, sees these expectations as laughable. We know this because of the reality that exists in the teachers' world – a reality that makes it clear that teachers are the society's buffoons.

**The Reality**

On entering the classroom, in this case at the secondary level, the teacher sees a room packed beyond capacity with many students who are ill-prepared to learn. There are students who are sleeping because they live in areas where gunshots are so prevalent that they cannot sleep; then there are others who have been abused at home that their eyes are glazed over and they are unaware of what is happening around them; additionally, there are those who are out to prove that they are in control of the class and who work to undermine the teacher's control. There is general laughter and mayhem. The teacher takes half of the class time to get the students settled. The lesson that has been planned has not been completed. The teacher leaves the class feeling frustrated. The frustration is further exacerbated by the lack of resources. Added to this is the recent physical threat to the teacher's person from the students whom she is seeking to influence to be better persons.

The teacher goes home with many books to mark and realizes that because of the number of errors, the task will take three times as long. She goes to sleep after midnight and wakes up a few hours later to catch the bus before the crowd descends to arrive at school for 7:00 a.m. The teacher recognizes that she is required to play many roles in the classroom for which she is not prepared. She is expected to be, not just a teacher but a mother, a big sister, a counsellor, a mediator, a lawyer, a nurse, a provider of lunch money, bus fare and also a security guard. The teacher tries to deal with all these roles while trying to figure out her own personal issues.

There are times when she finds it difficult to come to school because there is no bus fare left after paying all the utility bills and the rent. The teacher feels that perhaps she could work a second job but because of the amount of preparation and marking that has to be done, she finds that she has little time left to do this. If the teacher gets a second job then the first will suffer.

The teacher finds out from the landlord that the flat she is living in is going to be renovated and that he needs the place to be vacated. She tries to find other accommodations but she feels disrespected because potential landlords do not want to rent their places to teachers because their salaries are too low.

**Expectations A Joke**

This same teacher who left university feeling that teaching was a profession which would enable her to give back to society, who felt that she would enjoy seeing others learn and that society would surely compensate her for her hard work, now finds that society thinks that these expectations are jokes to be ridiculed. She finds herself unable to make ends meet as she takes home J$40,000 per month. She finds herself thinking that she has made a mistake when she had set teaching as her professional goal. When are we, as a society, going to realize that our educational output will not improve unless we begin to treat the teachers who have the care of our children for the greater percentage of the day with dignity and respect? When are we going to realize that giving adequate remuneration to our teachers with decent working conditions will pay off in exponential terms to our children and our nation?

There is a natural law in the universe which says that we reap what we sow. As a nation, we are sowing frustration, discord, disrespect and abuse to our teachers. What should we expect to reap from such seeds but discontentment, lack of productivity, inertia, lack of motivation and absence of zeal and passion?

How many persons in other professions could perform at their best under such negative circumstances?

**Sacrifice**

Yet, I am thankful that there are many teachers, who, despite the situation within which they must function, do so with grace, professionalism and great sacrifice. Yet it should not be this way. I contend that our government needs to put the education of our young first. They should see that the needs of the primary functionaries in the system, the teachers, are taken care of in a way that will enable them to operate at their optimum. I assert that the Government needs to see that teachers are continually assessed and upgraded, earn a decent salary and create working conditions which are commensurate with the requirements of their job.

**Published April 1, 2007**

# ON POLICE SHOOTING, EDUCATION AND IRRESPONSIBLE POLITICKING

There has been a lot of attention paid to the police shooting at Ardenne High School at the end of June. This attention was not solicited by the school but is the result of the embarrassment and shame that the police high brass and the Government felt about the apparent reckless and irresponsible behavior of an officer of the law who is sworn to uphold justice and to defend life in this country. To have an officer, in plain clothes, running through a school compound with gun out, among students, shooting an unarmed man in a staffroom without even identifying himself to the staff is absolutely reprehensible.

As a school community, we speak on behalf of all the citizens of this nation who have suffered from such atrocious behaviour from the police. This should not ever happen again in this country. As a school community, we wait to see the outcome of this situation. The insane man has been arrested, the injured prep-school student is traumatized but recovering and the officer has been pulled from front-line duty, but justice needs to be served. We look forward to seeing this situation dealt with thoroughly and not ignored and left to be lost in the short memory of the Jamaican people. If Jamaica is to believe that there is indeed reform taking place in the police force and that justice can prevail, then this situation must be resolved and resolved speedily.

**What Is Free Education?**

Elsewhere, the term 'free education' is being bandied about in the media by many and is being used as a political gambit in this general election. My question is, what does free education mean? Does it mean free approved school fees? Approved school fees are charges established by the Ministry of Education. These have not been increased since 2002. These approved fees are most unrealistic. No school operating a programme to benefit its students can function effectively on these fees. This is the reason that many schools ask parents to pay additional fees. Does free education, therefore, mean the economic cost of educating a student? Does it mean that whoever is intending to give Jamaicans free education will be willing to give the schools the full cost of educating each student under their care so that parents will not have to pay additional fees? This question needs to be answered.

As a nation, all are aware of the continuing increase in the cost of living since 2002. How realistic is it then to expect schools that have to pay the forever-rising utility costs to function on the approved fees? Schools get no exemption or discounts from utility companies. Light bills are exorbitant, water rates remain the same for all citizens and telephone rates are not discounted for schools. The maintenance costs for operating schools are astronomical. The Ministry of Education gives traditional high schools J$20,000 per year for maintenance.

**Administrative Costs Increase**

The cost of simply running the schools' administrative offices increases yearly. The Ministry of Education tells us repeatedly that there is no money for capital infrastructural development. Where are we to get this from? Principals and teachers are forced to spend much of their energy and time fund-raising in order to keep the schools afloat. We have become professional beggars within the school system. This way of operating needs to change. We need to be able to focus on the academic development of our students, not on fund-raising. Free education must, therefore, mean freedom for teachers and administrators of schools to focus on educating the nation's children, and freedom from the burden of fund-raising, freedom for parents from paying any fees at all. Anything less is not free.

I was heartened when at the beginning of the intense period of political campaigning both major political parties agreed to control the irresponsible use of language and personal bashing of their opponents. Therefore, my distress was great when within the last week both parties were back at the mudslinging and name-calling. How can we expect the people on the ground to respond to each other in a peaceful manner if the leaders do not have the self-control that it takes not to use belligerent tones to describe each other and not to respond as if they are involved in 'cass-cass'[1] and 'tracing'[2] when something is said about them?

## Disgraceful Conduct

I find it absolutely disgraceful the way that our political leaders have been conducting themselves in the past week. When one party candidate is going to refer to another party as "rapists" and in turn the offended party responds that if the opposing member has his virginity he would be able to keep it since nobody would want to rape him, is a reflection of how low we have reached in this nation. I am ashamed of the behaviour that these leaders have displayed to the nation. Our leaders need to sincerely pray the Prayer of St. Francis of Assisi – "Lord make me an instrument of thy peace/Where there is hatred, let me sow love/Where there is injury, pardon ..."

Do we think that nation changers such as Nelson Mandela, Mahatma Gandhi and Martin Luther King Jr. changed their nations with mud-slinging? What image are we holding up for our people to mirror? What do we want for ourselves as a nation? "Cass-cass" and "cuss-out?"[3] What is even more appalling is that this type of degrading behaviour does not stop there. Many of the followers in the parties will pattern this behavior and move further from mere words to violence. Isn't this the country where a man kills his uncle over ackee?

**Published August 5, 2007**

# TEACHERS AT RISK

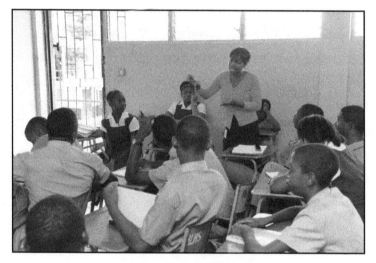

**The Jamaican Classroom**

The raft of incidents of teachers being attacked and students injuring each other that has been reported in the media in the past two weeks gives a frightening picture, albeit an incomplete one, of a downward spiral of the discipline in our schools. What is even more frightening is the image of parents supporting students in disrespecting their teachers. It was reported that a parent had a teacher arrested for using a bamboo switch on a student to prevent him from cutting another with a razor blade. Now that is the limit. Apparently, the teacher trying to stop the student from injuring another is now regarded as breaking the law. It has reached to the place where teachers need to consider their own safety when teaching in our school system. Teachers have to realize that they are teaching in a war zone. This war zone has students on one side, with some parents aiding them, while the teachers are on the other side, with some parents aiding them. Our teachers have little resource or protection from the attacks they endure with the provisions made by the Ministry of Education.

**Senseless**

We are told that teachers are no longer allowed to search students in school; you must, instead, ask the students to turn out their pockets, to reveal to you what they have. Does this seem senseless to you? No wonder they want to train the teachers as police, since only the police can do searches. Many persons are pushing children's rights, which I support; however, not many are pushing the students' responsibilities. As much as we emphasize the right of the child to care and protection, we must also emphasize the responsibility of the child to self-discipline, hard work, respect for authority and concern for others. There must be balance in the message being projected.

Teachers are now feeling even more stressed than they were before because of the threat to life and person which is becoming a part of the Jamaican school reality. We suffered first from a measly pay package, next from the general disrespect felt in the society, now we add a third: a threat to life and limb. I foresee that we shall once more have a large number of our teachers opting to take up the opportunity of teaching overseas where they will get better pay and get less attacked. I noticed agents from British Columbia scouting for teachers and that other recruiters from overseas are once again on the hunt. They will have willing prey with the threatening environment in which teachers are now operating in our country.

This situation actually is the outcome of what is happening in our society generally. After all, the school is a microcosm of the wider society. We do not choose the students, apart from transfers, who come to our schools.

**No Home Training**

Students are allocated to public schools by the Ministry of Education. We get students from homes and communities which are disciplined and orderly and who are properly socialized, and we also get students who have little or no home training, who are left to parent themselves. It seems that some parents have abandoned their children or else the parents are no more disciplined than an out-of-control teenager. You see the "chickens are coming home to roost".

The question is, how are we going to change this? When I say that our family life, as a nation, needs to be restored, persons say that it is an idealistic thought. They say that we must accept the fact that the family structure in the Jamaican society is by and large non-functional, therefore, the schools must be depended on to socialize the children. How can schools do this if teachers fear for their lives, fear to correct students, or to discipline them? Parents are taking the side of students to 'boo' their principals, arrest the teachers, come into the schools and "beat up" the teacher who has dared to correct their children. Which school administration, which teacher is going to be willing to take on the challenge of re-socializing out-of-control children coming from an out-of-control society with little support from the parents?

It might be that the Ministry of Education has seen the end of this mad road we are travelling on why the thought of training the teachers as police has come up. Is that the solution? If so, we should turn the schools into military training camps. That probably is a good way of utilizing the soldiers at Up-Park Camp since the war we are fighting is internal and the poor teachers are ill-equipped, lacking the resources and the expertise to deal with this war zone.

## Culture of Indiscipline

When are we going to realize that the culture of indiscipline, slackness and violence is pulling us downward in this spiral of mayhem? In the same way that we have negotiated a memorandum of understanding (MOU) about the pay package for Government workers, the Government needs to negotiate an MOU between parents, private-sector organizations, the police, the media, the DJs and singers, the transport authorities, students and teachers, on what is acceptable and expected of our children. Many of them are out of control. Why? Because they are products of an out-of-control society. The culture must change.

John Milton, the English poet, tells us, "He who reigns within himself and rules passions, desires, and fears is more than a king." We need to promote that message to our people. Right now, the opposite message is ringing like a loud, clanging bell in the ears of the nation. We, are suffering the effects of that message being played out tragically on the roads, in the communities and in our schools.

**Published May 4, 2008**

# UNFAIR SCHOOL COMPARISONS?

**Robert Lightbourne High School**

The analysis of the Caribbean Examination Council-Caribbean Secondary Education Certificate (CXC-CSEC) examinations compiled by Dr. Ralph Thompson and now Bill Johnson, which were published in The Gleaner recently, has highlighted the disparity between the results of the upgraded high schools and the traditional high schools. (Thompson 2006) People complain that the upgraded schools are no good and that they are not producing good enough CSEC results. One writer to The Gleaner suggested that principals of such schools should be ashamed of themselves. The question is, with all the views and judgements being spouted about these results, are we aware of what is happening in many of these schools?

This article focuses on the results of interviews with the principals of three 'upgraded' high schools – Cynthia Peart of Papine High School, Angela Chaplain of Vauxhall High School, and Claney Barnett of Haile Selassie High School. The interviews focused on the communities that these schools serve, the Grade Six Achievement Test (GSAT) grades of the students whom they receive, the academic and social challenges that the schools face, and the interventions implemented to address these challenges.

First, however, I need to look at the history of the upgraded high schools. Wesley Barrett, retired chief education officer in the Ministry of Education, wrote an article published in *The Observer* in response to the cry for the principals to be ashamed, entitled, "Don't try to shame them, help them." (Barrett 2008) He pointed out that the "new secondary schools" or upgraded high schools were developed to focus on vocational education. From the beginning, these schools received students who were not able to gain a space in the traditional high schools through the Common Entrance Examination. Although the Grade Six Achievement Test (GSAT) replaced the Common Entrance Examinations, it maintained one similarity: the GSAT was still used as a placement examination for high schools. In this regard, the upgraded high schools continued to receive those students who were performing below a satisfactory standard. In an attempt to remove the stigma attached to the new secondary schools, the Ministry of Education decided to name all secondary schools, apart from technical schools, high schools. It is general knowledge that some of these schools were changed from all-age to high schools without the infrastructural changes and additional resources required.

## Comparison Began

Mr. Barrett noted that immediately after the name change was made, the comparison of the results of the CXC-CSEC Examinations sat by the new high schools to the older high schools, began.

These three schools, Papine, Vauxhall and Haile Selassie high schools, were ranked, out of a total of 84 upgraded high school with the quality score being out of 100, in the Education 2020 feature published by The Gleaner on April 8, 2008. See Table 1 below. All three schools receive some of their students from communities which include some of the most volatile areas in Kingston and St Andrew: Papine, from Mud Town, Land Lease and August Town; Vauxhall, from Rockfort, Mountain View, Central Kingston, Franklyn Town (areas such as Bryden Street and McIntyre Villas); Haile Selassie, from Payne Lands, Majesty Gardens and Waterhouse.

Many of us associate the names of these communities with violence and crime. The children who have been socialized in this atmosphere of fear and violence take with them the effects of this exposure to school. What are some of the observable effects?

When shootings begin in some of these areas, the parents remove their children out of fear. This, in turn, affects the students' attendance. Children who do not attend classes regularly will not be exposed to the teaching that they need to get. In addition, when families in certain communities are targeted, they have to move with their children and this has an impact on the children's education. The teachers are affected by shooting that occurs nearby and they become jittery and, therefore, they cannot focus on teaching in this kind of situation. One of these schools has no circumference wall and when violence erupts, it spills over into the school grounds. Then, there are the attendant problems of students coming from sometimes warring communities and bringing the war into the school, as in the case of Haile Selassie some three weeks ago. Furthermore, when violence starts in places such as August Town, buses stop running, and so do the taxis. People cannot cross borders and, therefore, the children become traumatized and are unable to attend school.

**Aggressive Behaviour**

In all cases, the principals complain of the general aggressive, loud and violent behaviour of the students. Fights erupt either on the school compound or on the streets among students. These principals must deal with all of these anti-social behaviours. How can we expect children who operate in an atmosphere of fear and violence to learn as well as students whose environment is stable and peaceful? How can the principals change the reality of the violent communities from which their students come, when the police, the army and the Ministry of National Security cannot? There are many other social challenges which these principals face in seeking to educate the students from these communities, such as the lack of parental presence and guidance in these children's lives; students registering months after school has begun; students without birth certificates; students sent to school without uniforms, shoes, lunch money or food; students coming to school with old wounds needing attention. In short, all the maladies associated with parental neglect.

This article cannot review all of the issues related to the students' inadequate social upbringing. The general consensus is, however, that the social issues have a great impact on the students' ability to perform at an academically acceptable standard.

**Interventions**

The principals have made valiant attempts to address the effects of violence and social maladjustments in these students' lives. At Papine High, there are partnerships which have been built with the students and staff of both the University of Technology and the University of the West Indies to assist with behaviour-modification programmes. Psychology students and clinical psychologists participate in programmes to help students who have been identified as "At Risk." All students do guidance and counselling classes. There is also a dean of discipline in place. In addition, students who become difficult to handle are referred to the Ministry of Education's Programme for Alternative Student Support (PASS).

At Haile Selassie, the problems seem to require more personnel than is made available by the Ministry of Education. There is a social worker-guidance counsellor, but her hands are full and she is unable to manage the number of cases with which she is presented at any one time. In addition, there are two school resource officers working there. These officers have a presence in all school activities and have even started a cadet corps. Many varied attempts have been made to address the social issues, such as bringing in representatives of the Registrar General's Department to register students so they can receive their birth certificates. In spite of doing this, however, some parents still do not turn up to make use of the offered opportunity.

Haile Selassie's principal, Claney Barnett, brings in a dental clinic to check the students, and also the Heart Foundation. This is in an attempt to address the students' health issues. She has also used the Egg Project to teach students what it means to be a responsible parent. Under this programme, students are given an egg to represent a baby that they must take care of in order to show them how fragile a baby is and how difficult it is to care for one. She reported that for the three years that the programme was in place, there were no pregnancies among the students. Unfortunately, because of the lack of financial and human resources, the programme had to be discontinued and pregnancies have again become a feature of the students' lives.

The fees collected by the principal are startlingly inadequate to pay the utilities used by the school, much less to bring in paid human resources to address the needs of the students. The principal says she has become known for her begging. Monies donated are deposited at Leder Mode and students who need shoes are taken there to be outfitted by the principal. The principal makes cornmeal porridge on Tuesdays and Thursdays for the students who come in without breakfast in a personal attempt to alleviate the hunger of some of them. The principal tells me a story of a boy whom she had given a pair of shoes in grade nine and who is now in grade 11, coming to say, "Miss, you know is de same shoes dis? Guess what? A still wearing it."[4]

At Vauxhall, the teachers work together to assist in the re-socialisation of the students under their care. Parents are brought in as a part of the intervention to improve students' behaviour. At-risk students participate in the Success camps organised by the National Youth Service. In this camp, held during the summer, the students spend three weeks in training and rehabilitation. In spite of this, sometimes students have had to be removed from the school.

**Grades Not Made Public**

As the GSAT grades are not made public in the same way the Caribbean Examination Council –Certificate of Secondary Education Certificate (CXC-CSEC) results are, people might be wondering, what grades do the students who go to these schools achieve?

Haile Selassie receives students whose scores are generally below 20 per cent, with all scoring zero for communication tasks. Papine receives students ranging between 40-50 per cent, with an upper range in the last two years of 60-65 per cent and a lower range below 30 per cent. The complaint from principal, Cynthia Peart is, however, that usually, the parents of those scoring at the upper end transfer these students to other schools. In addition, there are the students who enter the school through the Grade Nine Achievement Test (GNAT). Many of these students come in illiterate and innumerate.

Vauxhall receives students with averages between 55-65 per cent. Some 30 per cent of these students come in reading below the required level. To assist students who come in illiterate, special reading programmes are put in place.

The Ministry of Education provides a reading specialist in these schools. At Haile Selassie, more needs to be done because of the widespread need for remediation among the students. The funding for this is lacking. In all the schools, more needs to be done in the area of numeracy. This is a general problem in Jamaica. This stems from many teachers of mathematics not being trained to teach the subject let alone provide remediation to those who are challenged in this area. The schools need to be given the assistance they require to address the demands of the students sent to them. All these schools require special educators who are trained to deal with assessment and remediation of students who are academically challenged. It is unfair to expect schools to produce results without resources. In any comparison that is being done of the 'traditional' high schools and the upgraded high schools, all the variables need to be taken into consideration.

**Timar Jackson's Story**

Fortunately, in every situation, there is a light that shines, and the story of Timar Jackson provides one such light.

## Unfair School Comparisons?

Timar entered Ardenne High School's sixth form in September 2006 from Vauxhall High School. He had passed nine CSEC subjects with six distinctions and three credits. There are students in Ardenne's sixth form who had earned more distinctions at the CSEC level, but Timar outperformed them at the Caribbean Advance Proficiency Examination (CAPE) Level. In CAPE Unit 1, he earned four distinctions in pure mathematics, economics, accounting and communications studies. At the Jamaica Association of Principals of Secondary Schools (JAPSS) National Awards ceremony he placed first island wide in Accounting Unit 1 and second in Economics Unit 1.

Timar was born in Bull Bay, St Andrew, and has three older brothers and a younger sister. They were raised by their mother. Timar's brothers are all tradesmen. Only one of them completed high school. His sister is now in high school. Timar said that his mother told him that she wanted him to be something other than a tradesman and he had that in mind when he went to Vauxhall. Timar recounted that in grade seven, he was an average student getting in the 60 per cent range. He faced challenges at school. There were many fights at school involving weapons. He recalls that he was robbed three times while at Vauxhall. The first time was extremely traumatic. It was while he was in first form. Men from the community held him up with knives while he was on his way home and robbed him. He did not want to go back to school but his mother told him that he had to learn to overcome his fear. She taught him strategies to deal with the community into which he was going.

When asked what motivated him to start achieving at a high level, he told of the strategy that his principal, Angela Chaplain, used:

That of posting the grades of the top 10 students in each grade in the school. Timar said that in grade eight, he determined that his name would be on the list. That became his motivation. Timar did not only do well academically, but he also participated in rugby, cadets, speech and drama, and he did a stint in track and field. Timar felt that his greatest challenge being at Vauxhall were the disadvantages that he faced because of the shift system. Classes were for 30 minutes each and the longest period allocated to a subject was two sessions. The teachers were not able to complete the syllabus because of the limited time. Timar said that he had to work on his own to ensure that he completed the syllabus. His mother could not afford extra lessons, therefore he had to read his books and study on his own. He later gained entry into the highly competitive sixth form at Ardenne High School. He became a prefect and earned the respect of the school through his academic excellence and humble and calm demeanour.

**Top Student**

At the recent Sixth Form School-Leaving ceremony, Timar was named the top student in grade 13. Timar has already gained the Open Scholarship from the University of the West Indies to pursue his tertiary education there. He wants to be an economist or an accountant. Timar has overcome the odds and he is achieving his goals despite his humble beginnings. His home and his school worked together to help him make his dreams come true. He credits his motivation to his mother and his principal, Ms. Chaplain.

*Unfair School Comparisons?*

It can happen, but parents and teachers must work together; the community and school must work together. When is the Government going to begin to hold parents, and not only the schools, responsible for their children's performance?

Table 1: Gleaner-Thompson

**Ranking of Schools**

|  | English | | Math | |
|---|---|---|---|---|
|  | Rank | Quality Score | Rank | Quality Score |
| Vauxhall | 20 | 4.5 | 46 | .8 |
| Papine | 57 | 2.1 | 63 | .6 |
| Haile Selassie | 8 | 1.0 | 60 | .6 |

**Published May 18, 2008**

# LESSONS FROM CUBA

The Jamaican Association of Principals of Secondary Schools (JAPSS) held its biennial retreat in Havana, Cuba, from Wednesday, May 21, to Sunday, May 25. Thirty principals participated in this retreat, the aim of which was to view for ourselves the Cuban educational system. Arrangements were made with the Ministry of Education in Cuba, which developed an itinerary for us to speak with officials of the ministry and to visit schools ranging from secondary to pre-university and university levels.

What we were exposed to was a system that was developed in response to the needs of the people of Cuba and which keeps evolving even as the needs continue to be identified. The education ministry engages in ongoing research and uses the results to refine the system. What I found most impressive were the recent changes made at the secondary level since 2000. The Ministry of Education realized that the students did not do as well at the secondary level as they did at the primary level. The research pointed to the fact that the students found it difficult to adjust to the secondary level with its myriad teachers and large class size. The ministry, therefore, decided to make drastic changes to address this problem.

## Ratio of Students to Teachers

First of all, The Ministry of Education reduced the ratio of students to teachers at the secondary level to 1:15. This means that there are classes with only 15 students or where a class has 30 students, there are two teachers. Second, it sought to minimize the number of teachers teaching each class. It revamped its teacher-training practices and instituted a system which saw each teacher at the secondary level being trained to teach at least four subjects. Third, through research, they identified the subjects the teachers thought to be most difficult and they developed a system to deliver those subjects to the students. They did this by videotaping expert teachers teaching subjects such as science and mathematics and these were delivered to the students through television.

How is this delivery organized? In Cuba, there are four educational television stations. These are used to air educational programmes which are seen by all the students at a particular grade level throughout the school week. The ministry ensures that each classroom is equipped with a television and a video player. Teachers are there to supervise the students and to assist them. Why am I impressed? Because the government uses research to assess what the educational needs of the students are. These results are used to address the needs as they arise. This is because they are convinced that education is the means by which they will achieve the advancement of the people of Cuba. Now, although I do not agree with the communist ideology, I am struck by the passionate commitment to education which the nation has.

**Priorities**

The priorities of that nation are health and education. The buildings need refurbishing and many of them need a coat of paint. Those people spend money on what they are passionate about. The question is: What are we, in Jamaica, passionate about? Is it education, or 'bling bling'? Is it show or reality? An editorial in The Gleaner of Thursday, May 29, said that although education was a

> "critical part of the foundation upon which Jamaica can expect to build a successful, safe and functional society ... it is an area in which we have not done particularly well." The editorial added: "Many of the problems in the Jamaican society can be traced to this failing." (The Gleaner Editorial 2008)

These failings were then outlined.

What should this assessment lead to? Shouldn't it lead to drastic measures being put in place to remedy this malady? The private sector, including the media houses, which undertake to have polls done for all sorts of reasons, needs to initiate and fund research on the ills of our education system and how best to address them. The private sector and the Government then need to unite to implement these remedies. The transformation-in-education vision is a wonderful one, but the team lacks the necessary funding to do all that needs to be done. One area that the team is seeking to address is the area of special education.

It is clear that the special-education needs of our nation are overwhelming. The organization and funding of this area are sadly lacking. As a result of the poor family-life culture which exists in our nation, many of our children have wound up with serious learning problems. Special Education needs funding to be properly researched and to have solutions swiftly and efficiently implemented. Do we have the will to address this disease in our nation?

## Serious Condition

The Gleaner editorial outlined this serious condition as stated below. In its current state, the education programme needs immediate and widespread remediation. Let us look at this disheartening picture:

**Two-thirds of our children** are not ready to enter primary school.

**Over 40 per cent of grade-four students** do not master the literacy/numeracy requirements.

**A third of all students** leave primary school illiterate.

At grade six, the **mean average test score in the national exam hovers not much over 50 per cent**.

At the end of high school, **no more than a quarter of the students** have the requisite qualifications to matriculate to tertiary institutions or to get meaningful jobs.

**No more than 40 per cen**t of Jamaican students pass math at CXC and a similar percentage fail at English.

We can continue to pay lip service as a nation to education or we can, as the Cuban people did in eliminating illiteracy between 1958 and 1961, put in place the drastic measures needed to deal with this alarming situation. We are now at the point of 'to will or to die'.
**Published June 1, 2008**

# THE AUXILIARY FEES DEBATE

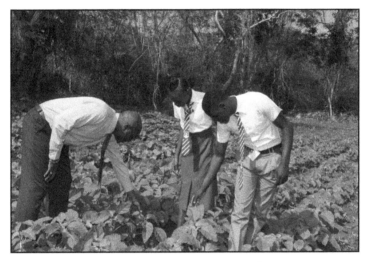

**In a school's vegetable garden**

I agree with the position of the Prime Minister and the Minister of Education that no child should be denied access to a secondary school education because of the inability of parents to pay auxiliary fees. Where the problem lies is in the fact that no increase has been made to school fees since 2002 and in some instances, 2003. Therefore, the increase of J$2,000 is far from being sufficient in real terms. This means, however, that only a basic classroom education can be provided for our children. To provide a holistic education product, it would be necessary to make up for the Government's inability to pay the full cost of educating each child by asking parents to make a contribution to the education of their child. Each school develops its curriculum depending on its philosophy and vision of education. The end result is that the costs may differ according to the programme being offered.

**What 'Agreeing' Would Mean**

Agreeing with the minister's position to operate within the strictures of providing an education on the less-than-sufficient funds allocated by the ministry and the auxiliary fees paid by only 60 per cent of parents, would mean that I agree that Ardenne High School would, therefore:

- No longer provide an after-school programme which covers sports, with a total of 20 teams and coaches who have to be paid each month, even though such programmes are the feeders for national teams. We will do only what the money raised by the sports department's fund-raising can cover, i.e. J$1.5 million out of J$4.5 million.

- No longer provide a vibrant and active co-curricular programme of 30 clubs and societies. All these need transportation, entry fees to competitions, costumes or uniforms, meals provided during training and competitions, payment of some coaches of the performing arts, among other requirements.

- No longer employ three additional cleaners to clean a building which houses 16 forms; the Government does not provide funds to pay them.

- No longer provide security for our students during the days and for the compound on weekends: it is not provided for in the Government's budget, only for the week nights.

- No longer ensure that there is a cyclical maintenance schedule that is carried out during the summer to make the facilities liveable; it cannot be done with the J$50,000 the ministry provides for maintenance.

- No longer provide celebration events for our students' performance during the year; it takes money to provide certificates and trophies.

- No longer employ part-time teachers where there are not enough full-time teachers to cover all classes. This is usually paid from the additional funds.

- No longer seek to obtain the electrical supply necessary to have the E-learning labs functioning since the Government has not provided the money to do so; we would convert those two labs into traditional classrooms.

## Implications

Instead, we would have the parents who have money to pay each coach enter into an agreement with the coach to train their child in whatever activity he or she offers. We would not have teams which represent the school entering national competitions, since this would mean we would have to take the responsibility to pay the implied costs. We would have to manage with the less-than-clean environment, since the labour union would object to our giving the government-paid ancillary workers more work than they already have. We would have to have the gates of the school open in the days, since there would be no one to man them. Both students and the public would be free to come and go as they please. We would have $50,000 worth of maintenance done in the summer, since this is all that is allocated in the budget. We would go back to the days of not celebrating at grade levels our students' academic performance, or at the end of the year their co-curricular achievements. We would have to eliminate the use of air-conditioning in the computer labs because this adds to the electricity costs of the school. In addition, when the Government's tuition grant runs out before the end of the school year and there is no money left to run the school, we would have to close the school, because it is the auxiliary fee that has now become the operational fee.

I agree with the Government's approach if there is the under-standing that this is how we would operate. I disagree with the Prime Minister that we should be doing more fund-raising. Teachers are trained to teach, not fund-raise, although we have always been doing fund-raising. The Government has not given money to the school to build any structures on Ardenne's compound in the last 40 years. It has assisted with fixing the roofs of three classrooms and the hall. The school is currently in major fund-raising mode to build a much-needed science block at a cost of over J$30 million. This work is under way. All our stakeholders have been involved in fund-raising for this project. Our major partner in this process is the NCB Foundation.

## Big Challenge

There is a big challenge at Ardenne, however; we have a town gully that has been channelled through the school. This gully is dangerous in the rainy season and needs to be covered. We have been asking various government entities to do this, but we get the same response – estimates are given, but no money is available. This gully threatens the land that is available for us to build on in order to improve our infrastructure. Not only does it threaten the land, it also threatens the lives of students who have to cross over it to go to the industrial arts centre. Should this not be fixed by the Government?

The Prime Minister says we are to raise funds. We are fund-raising, we have fund-raised, and we will continue to fund-raise, because that is the only way we have been able to make the school progress. But, Mr. Prime Minister, if we are to achieve academic excellence, fund-raising cannot be the focus of our teachers; we then would be accused of not only being extortionists, but also hustlers.

**Published August 3, 2008**

# CONDOMS IN SCHOOLS?

In response to the (Ministry of Health Jamaica 2007), which revealed that AIDS is the "second leading cause of death in persons 15-24" while HIV infection "doubled in the age group 10-24 between 1995 and 2006", students have been calling for condoms to be distributed in schools. I am sure that the fact that the age group that has "the highest number of non-regular sex partners in 12 months," is ages 15-19 would seem to justify this call.

I have an issue with this proposal on various levels. First, I agree with the Minister of Education when he says that "The Ministry of Education is not in the business of distributing condoms in schools". Schools undertake the task of educating our students about sex, not facilitating sexual activity. This is a matter that the homes and health centres should undertake.

Second, the information that HIV has doubled in the age range which includes children ages 10-15, who, according to our law, are under the age of consent to be having sex, points to a serious legal issue. When these children report to hospitals or clinics, what mechanism is there to prosecute the usually older adults who have had sex with them? If we are serious about the Child Care and Protection Act, then measures need to be put in place to prosecute adults who are having sex with children. The information required to do this can be gained from the young pregnant 'girl-child' coming into the clinics, along with those children who are infected by HIV. Let us begin to get serious with the predators and perverts in our nation who are preying on the young. They need to be held responsible under the law for their perversion. The answer is not simply to issue condoms, because to do so would be against the law.

## Biological Implications

Third, apart from the legal implications of issuing condoms to children under the age of consent, are the biological implications for children of this age who engage in sexual activity. Children having sex early with multiple partners means that they are exposed from very early to the human papilloma virus, which is associated with cancer of the cervix. We need to note that the use of condoms does not protect against this virus. It means that young women develop cancer of the cervix at a young age. In addition, early sexually activity in young girls leads, many times, to their having blocked tubes, being more prone to ectopic pregnancies and also to infertility.

In all of this discussion looms the moral issue. Is there going to be a point when we stop and think about whether sex is simply to be treated as an animal appetite to be fulfilled, such as the need for food? Is it, therefore, that if our six-year-olds, who are now being sexually overexposed because of the music, cable-TV offerings and generally heightened sexualized culture in which we exist, want to engage in sex, that we are to simply offer them a condom so they won't get infected with HIV? What is the standard? Who determines the standard? We need to understand that the thinking of convenience which now exists is taking us down a dangerous, slippery slope. There have to be standards that we abide by as a society that are based, not simply on what is craved by the majority, but by what is best for the majority. What is best is not always what is desired, but what is needed to maintain a healthy, civilized society.

**'Dat A Foolishness'**

I propose that in the same way that in Uganda the promotion of abstinence helped to decrease the level of AIDS infection, that it can be done in Jamaica. I already hear the voices clamouring, [5]"Dat a foolishness." It worked in Uganda because the government there was willing to do a widespread campaign called ABC – Abstinence, Be Faithful, Use a Condom. (Ross 2005) In the schools in Uganda, thousands of teenagers are part of the 'True Love Waits' campaign. This has helped to promote the concept of abstinence among the youth. Those who want to cry down the suggestion that this can help us in Jamaica need seriously to question why they would be against such a campaign.

In Jamaica, a movement called 'Passion for Purity' has been started among young people by a teacher at the Wolmer's Group of Schools. I believe that the Ministry of Health and the Ministry of Education should endorse and promote this programme right across schools in Jamaica. We need to help our young people to hear another voice, a voice that speaks to self-control, self-respect, respect for others and for God. That voice needs to also come from the churches. Our churches need to speak more intensely to this issue. We need to counteract the voice of slackness, 'gal in a bungle",[6] if you feel it do it, and 'man a ole dawg'[7], that rings consistently and stridently in our nation.

Let us take a page out of Uganda's book. It is reported that in downtown Kampala, Uganda, a large billboard with the image of two cranes, which is the Ugandan national bird, has the message, "The crested crane sticks faithfully to one partner until death. Abstinence and faithfulness – 100 per cent guaranteed." (Ross 2005) Not even condoms are that successful.

As a nation, we seem to fit the description of the persons being described by Paul in Ephesians 4 and verse 19 (The Message Bible):

"They can't think straight anymore. Feeling no pain, they let themselves go in sexual obsession, addicted to every perversion." (Petersen 2002)

**Published December 7, 2008**

# THE JAMAR HAMILTON STORY

I n ninth grade, some boys were playing cricket in the classroom, using the broken wooden back of a chair as a bat. The ball flew and hit another boy, who was sitting talking with a friend, in his mouth. Two teeth were broken, leaving this teenage boy of 15 with a smile displaying broken front teeth, which did not add to his attractiveness. In spite of this, the young man continued to be friends with the boys who had damaged his teeth. He continued with his humble, affable demeanour to assist his classmates with their work. This young man's name is Jamar Hamilton. It is a name that you will be hearing more about in the years to come.

Jamar is the top student in the CXC-CSEC 2009 examinations. He is a student of Ardenne High School. He passed 10 subjects, all with distinctions. In each subject, he attained a straight- 'A' profile.

Who is this young man? What is his background? What has influenced him? What separates him from the typical young Jamaican male who only sees success in 'cutting a chune'[8] or 'mekking duppy'?[9]

Jamar hails from Portland. He first went to Portland Preparatory School then to Shebian Preparatory School. He passed the Grade

Six Achievement Test (GSAT) from Shebian Prep and was awarded a Jamaica National Building Society scholarship to Ardenne High School. He was the head boy of Shebian Prep.

Jamar had adults who influenced his life positively. Jamar recalls that Miss Cunningham from Portland Prep encouraged him to write stories and articles in spite of the fact that he hated it. He was motivated to continue writing when he wrote an article that was published in the Children's Own that was thought to be so good that it was published again. He, however, still found English to be his most difficult subject until 10th grade, when Miss Aiken got him to see the subject in a different way and he began to like it.

Another great influence on his life was his principal at Shebian Prep, Dr Williams-Allison. Jamar recounts that she never allowed her students to settle for second best. She made sure that she provided the material for her students to excel. He recounts how, to prepare them for GSAT, Dr. Williams-Allison took her students on a four-day retreat to provide them with a period of focused, saturated study. She also made sure that they learnt to assume responsibilities, with the older students helping and caring for the younger ones.

Dr. Williams-Allison said that 'Shebian' was an old Coptic word which meant 'house of learning'. The concept is essential to her vision of learning in which she takes the term 'school' and transforms it into an all-encompassing idea which includes: How do I learn as a person? What is my relationship to my community? What is my relationship with God? What do I turn my back on? These are clearly magnified in Jamar's life.

**Good Support**

At high school, Jamar's greatest motivators were his teachers and his friends. He could go to his teachers after class and ask them to explain what he did not understand. He felt that he had great teachers and friends at Ardenne High School.

Jamar learnt to look out for others from home. His family consists of his father, mother, grandmother and his elder sister, Joy, who was born with brain damage. Jamar's mother relates how as a child, he would take his sister outside to play and when others passing by would say hurtful things about her, he would get very upset. He was protective of his sister. This caring attitude characterizes Jamar's life. He portrays it at home and also at school. He is known to be humble and extremely willing to assist his classmates to understand any area that is difficult for them.

Jamar's parents instilled positive values in him. In spite of the fact that they never got a high-school education, they ensured that he received that opportunity. His mother would stay up with him in the nights to assist him with his work. She would ask others for help when she did not know the information. In addition, he learnt from his parents not to look for excuses not to achieve, but to persist in the face of obstacles to do well. Even though his father works away from home, he still encourages Jamar and lets him know how proud he is of him. Jamar's parents taught him not to allow his circumstances to determine his outcome, but to use hard work and perseverance to accomplish his goals. His parents brought him up in Church, and this has had a positive impact on his life. He is prayerful. Prayer, he says, is a source of comfort to him.

## 'Bad-Man' Mentality

When asked what he thought accounted for the 80:20 female to male ratio at university level in Jamaica, Jamar felt that many Jamaican young men wanted to live by the 'bad-man' mentality. This mindset has been bred from music, television, and even parents. This attitude, he felt, will only change with a commitment from the society to the wholesome development of our young men. Jamar has no formula for academic success. Each person, he says, learns differently. What might work for one individual might not work for another. What is important is to be motivated and determined in one's goals to succeed.

What are Jamar's future plans? He wants to be an aeronautical engineer. In pursuing this dream, he has enrolled in the newly opened Caribbean Aerospace College in Jamaica. He will go on to further studies abroad to equip himself to achieve his goals.

Jamar displays integrity. According to his guardian, "The Jamar you see is the Jamar you get." I know that he will go far and the characteristics of humility, gentleness, thoughtfulness of others and prayerfulness will go with him.

Jamar, Ardenne High, Shebian Prep, Portland Prep and your family are proud of you.

**Published February 7, 2010**

# WHITHER FREE EDUCATION?

**Tarrant High School**

The Government has declared free education for all up to the secondary level. Based on this declaration, government-funded schools are given school fees annually for each child by the Ministry of Education. This year, the funds from the ministry should have been disbursed three times in the year. Schools expected to receive the third disbursement at the beginning of the second term. This has not happened. The Ministry of Education has since sent out communication to the effect that because of the financial constraints that the Government is experiencing, the ministry's payment to the schools has been delayed. There is no indication as to when the schools will receive these funds.

This delay is having a serious impact on schools that depend solely on the funds from the ministry to operate their institutions. There are schools that now have to send their utility bills to the Ministry of Education to be paid. All of this is happening in the context of the Government advising parents that the auxiliary fees that schools charge to assist in meeting the expenses of running the institutions are not compulsory. Since this announcement, school administrators have seen a decline in the number of parents who are paying auxiliary fees. Contrary to the perception that this is because of the inability of parents to pay, some of the parents who do not pay are non-compliant simply because they have declared that it is "free education" time now. On the other hand, there are parents who are domestic workers and labourers who come in to make arrangements with the school to pay even $1,000 a week until the fee is paid up. These parents take pride in the fact that they can contribute to their children's education. They have not bought into the 'freeness mentality' which is prevalent in our nation.

Some questions therefore arise: Can the country, in its present financial crisis, afford to fund 'free education' for all? Can the country afford to pay for the education of the children of parents who can afford to pay school fees? What quality education will be delivered to the students of schools where the funds are not forthcoming in a timely manner from the Ministry of Education and which do not have supplementary funds from auxiliary fees? How can the Minister of Education be requiring improved education output with reduced resources?

**Cannot Continue**

I believe that the Government needs to acknowledge that it is not able to continue to fund free education up to the secondary level. It needs to return to the cost-sharing arrangement which was previously in place in the secondary schools. Under this arrangement, parents who needed financial assistance from the ministry would apply for it. These applicants would be interviewed by the school's guidance counsellors and their application forwarded to the Ministry of Education. The approved assistance would be forwarded to the school. This arrangement seems to be more suitable to our present financial crisis. Let those parents who can afford to pay, do so.

In, The International Handbook on the Economics of Education, (Johnes 2007)Jamaica was cited as one of the countries in the World Education Indicators survey that compared to countries such as Greece and France, spent a significant per cent of its gross domestic product on education. Whereas in 1999, Jamaica spent 7.5 per cent, Greece spent 2.6 per cent and France 4.4 per cent. I think we have to look again at the practicality of the 'free education' policy in light of our current realities.

As it now stands, a number of schools have to be relying on the auxiliary fees paid by parents to keep the schools functioning. Yet, our Prime Minister called principals, who require parents to pay additional fees, "extortionists". This was a most unfortunate position for him to have taken and it will forever be etched into the minds of the hard-working principals who are required not only to be instructional leaders, but finance solicitors of their schools.

With the cost of utilities steadily increasing, for example, electricity, schools are now required to pay an astronomical amount of money for these services. Another prohibitive cost is that of security. The Ministry of Education has issued a Safety and Security Policy document to the schools but there are no accompanying resources to implement the policy. It is the auxiliary fees once again that have to be used to cover much of the security costs. Yet again, The Ministry of Education is encouraging the increased use of technology in the schools. The E-Learning Project supplies the schools with equipment, yet there is no technical support provided to maintain the system. It is the auxiliary fees that are used to provide the needed technical support.

**Co-Curricular Activities**

The global current trend in secondary education is to produce students who are not only academically educated but students who are rounded by participating in co-curricular activities. These activities, such as sports, service clubs, academic and performing arts clubs, are not financed by the Ministry of Education but are supported by the auxiliary fees paid by the parents. Yet, when students who do not pay these fees are told that they cannot participate in these activities, there are accusations of unfairness and exclusion. We need to become realistic with regard to the true cost of educating the Jamaican child at the secondary level. This assessment needs to include the cost of producing the rounded student many parents and employers want to see.

The Government produces policies and edicts without the supporting resources. This approach might result in political mileage but it does not result in an improved education system. We need to be realistic. We need to acknowledge that, as a nation, we are not at the place to implement 'free education'. We need to set a standard of education and allow the parents who can afford to assist in providing this education for their children to do so.

**Published March 7, 2010**

# SETTING STANDARDS AND A DEEPENING WATER CRISIS

The performance of our youth at the 100th staging of the Inter-Secondary Schools Sports Association (ISSA) Boys and Girls Championships (Champs), and in the finals of the 41st Television Jamaica (TVJ) Schools Challenge Quiz Competition gives me hope for our nation. My hope lies not only in the excellence of the performance of our students but in the attitude that they portrayed in the competitions – that of good sportsmanship and camaraderie, of selfless giving and mutual respect.

The student of Wolmer's Boys School, who, because he had already gained a gold medal and wanted his teammate to share in that victory, slowed down to allow his colleague to win the race, reflects a selflessness which needs to be lauded in our nation. Why? Because it is becoming rare among us.

The opening ceremony of Champs displayed the talents and gifts of our students in a manner which was well-organized and disciplined, in spite of the late start. The scintillating performance of the mass choir reminded us that there is still an appreciation of clear harmony, good pitch and tone among our young people. The colourful array of the costumes of the performers combined with their precision and skillfully choreographed movements created a kaleidoscope that stimulated our senses.

My disappointment came when in the midst of such high-quality performances, the organizers allowed some dancers who accompanied the former female lead singers of the Dragonaires to cavort on the stage in 'b-riders' that left little to the imagination. Their attire was inappropriate for an event which catered to our youth.

I want to encourage educators and parents to set high standards for our young people and expect them to live up to them. We need to put in place rewards and sanctions for when our students attain or fall short of these standards. We need to model for our youth the behaviour and attitudes that we expect them to display. Therefore, when the writer of a letter to The Gleaner seeks to castigate the editorial which abhorred the behaviour of an athlete who gave a gun salute at the end of a high jump competition, it shows that we have begun to settle for what is base and undesirable as the norm among us. I will repeat that old saying from 'Desiderata' – "Children live what they learn." As adults in the nation, we need to clean up ourselves, so that we will not be embarrassed to set high standard for our youth because we are not living up to them ourselves.

In both competitions, Champs and Schools Challenge Quiz, students are held to high standards of performance and behaviour. There are rules that they must abide by in order to succeed, and they adhere to these. It means that it is possible in the schools and wider society to set standards reinforced by the attendant rules and sanctions and exemplified by those in authority in order for us to train our youth to be productive citizens of this nation.

As an educator, I have seen repeatedly that about 90 per cent of the students who display antisocial behaviour develop their behaviours because of the lack of parental guidance and support. This antisocial conduct is further reinforced in a society that has developed a culture of violence and indiscipline as its norm. If, as a nation, the leaders, the adults begin to set high standards and reflect these in our conduct, our young people will begin to positively "live what they learn". This must begin with our political leaders, in how they conduct themselves in Parliament and in how they conduct the affairs of state.

**Water Crisis**

Another matter of immediate importance is the impact of the water crisis on institutions of learning. The National Water Commission (NWC) has informed the public that the situation is getting dire. We know this at Ardenne High School since, whereas we used to get water for half the day when the water lock-offs first began, within which time and overnight the tanks could be filled, we are now getting water for three hours in the mornings at a pressure which is not high enough to replenish the tanks. Formerly, when we contacted the NWC they would assist us by sending a truckload of water; this practice is no longer the norm. This has resulted in the administration having to close school early on some days, cancelling school on two occasions and also purchasing water at a cost of $20,000 per truckload to ensure that we can have classes on other days. This is not a tenable situation.

**Two Options**

With the new school term approaching and the water situation worsening, combined with the Caribbean Examination Council's examinations (CXC) beginning in the first week of May, we are left with two choices: purchase water at a cost of $20,000 per day, which will cost $1 million for the term in order to have full school for the term; or have only those students who are sitting external examinations come in for the new term to try to manage with the three hours of water we get each day. The school year is winding down and funds are limited. Unless parents are willing to contribute to purchasing water for $20,000 each day, we will be forced to choose Option Two. Not having all our students in school for this summer term, however, will have implications for their course of study in the new school year. Syllabuses which normally would have been completed for the students of grades 7-10 will be left unfinished. This in turn means that in the new school year there will have to be a change in the number of days students and teachers go off on holidays, etc.

Once again, as administrators of public schools, we need direction and intervention from the Ministry of Education on the matter. Sadly, this has not been forthcoming. This situation is unprecedented in my lifetime and the leaders of our nation need to determine the way forward in this new paradigm in which we are operating.

**Published April 4, 2010**

# MISSING FACTORS IN EDUCATION 2020

B ill Johnson's ranking of secondary schools based on their performance in math and English in the Caribbean Examination Council - Caribbean Secondary Education Certificate (CXC-CSEC) Examinations 2009 has once again been published in The Gleaner's Education 2020. (Johnson 2010) The article was titled 'Education system gets Grade F'. In addition, the announcement that the Grade Four Numeracy Test reveals that less than 50 per cent of the students who did that test accomplished mastery, has dismayed the Ministry of Education officials. Our education system, as we all know, is in trouble.

Once more, we will be looking at the schools' performance in terms of classroom preparation and delivery, assessment and feedback, yet underlying all of this are bigger issues which, as a nation, we are failing to address. This is the impact of crime and violence and the abandonment of parental responsibilities on the academic achievement of our students.

Baker-Henningham H., Meeks-Gardner J., Chang S., Walker S., sought to explore the effect of violence on academic achievement and published their findings in 2009 in a paper titled 'Experiences of violence and deficits in academic achievement among urban primary school children in Jamaica'. (Baker-Henningham Helen 2009) The findings showed that,

"there was a – relationship between children's experiences of violence and academic achievement, with children experiencing higher levels of violence having the poorest academic achievement, and children experiencing moderate levels having poorer achievement than those experiencing little or none".

This report establishes what we know as educators in the classrooms: the clear correlation between students who are exposed to violence and crime in their communities and violence in the homes and low academic achievement. In many instances, the students who act up come from situations where there is abuse, violence, and sometimes, exposure to criminality. The students reflect attitudes of defiance of authority, lack of motivation to learn, unwillingness to believe that they can achieve success through education and lack of control over their negative emotions, such as anger. These students become disruptive in class and affect the learning process of other students. They seem not to value what education has to offer and make little effort to adapt to normative patterns of behaviour.

Baker-Henningham also has done research that shows that another primary reason for academic underachievement is ineffective parenting. Again, this is confirmed with what we see happening in our schools. Students who are underperforming academically, if they do not have a learning disability, are not getting the parental super-vision and support those students who are doing well are receiving. In Jamaica, ineffective parenting is becoming endemic. Add to this then, the children's exposure to crime and violence and we see that we are condemning ourselves to a generation of adults who will not be educated enough to be able to move our country forward eco-nomically and socially.

## Cognitive Abilities

Many of our youth do not know how to reason. Their cognitive abilities have not been developed by their parents reading to them, encouraging early stimulation through play, and exposing them to activities which help to develop their minds. The point is, that we have many people who are too young and/or too irresponsible in how they live their lives becoming parents. They treat babies as toys, and as soon as these children become too demanding, they are abused, mistreated or abandoned. This is happening all across our nation. Anyone who reads about what affects learning positively, knows that this type of upbringing will blight the academic future of such children.

If at grade four we are finding that less than half the students assessed have achieved mastery of numeracy, it means that we need to go back even earlier and intervene in the lives of our stu-dents. I believe that more than 60 per cent of our children need spe-cial-education intervention from as early as grade one. In order to change this dismal condition, which predicts a gloomy future for our people, strategies and resources must be put in place to affect and change the outcomes. The Government must aggressively deal with the horrific crime problem in our nation. If they are not managing on their own to change the situation, they must bring in outside assistance. In addition, they must begin to clean up their own involvement with the criminal elements in our nation.

**Accountable**

Furthermore, parents must be held accountable for how they perform their parenting responsibilities. Training in parenting needs to be mandated for every girl/woman who gets pregnant and goes to a clinic or doctor for prenatal care. Fathers must be identified on birth certificates and be held responsible for the upbringing of their children. They, too, should be mandated to go to parenting classes. The Government should establish community organisations that provide a system of trained home-care supervisors who visit homes in the early years of children's lives to help to train parents and supervise the children's care.

No amount of implementing performance management in the schools or data-driven curriculum delivery and assessment will improve our academic performance nationally in a significant way if these social problems are not addressed.

In addition, the Ministry of Education needs to deal with the immediate crisis by recognizing that each school should have equipped and trained special-education personnel to implement strategies which would help to alleviate some of the learning problems our children are experiencing because of the deprivation and abuse they have experienced in their early developmental years. The training of special educators needs to be fast-tracked in our colleges and universities. These persons need to be added to each school's establishment instead of principals trying to be creative in having a teacher who has not been appointed for that purpose doing 'a little thing' to help some students.

We are in a crisis and we need critical care.

**Published May 2, 2010**

# JAMAICA AND ITS EDUCATION SYSTEM

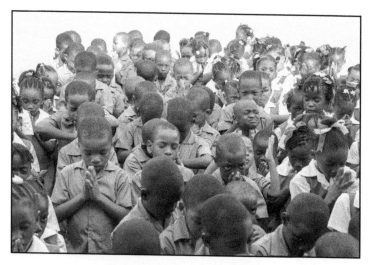

**Children at school prayers**

The debate as to whether the National Education Inspectorate's (NEI) Report should be made public rages on. The question we should all be answering is: Are all stakeholders in education working together to ensure that our education system is overhauled to become effective in training our youth for the 21st century? Is the

Ministry of Education working to supply schools, from the early child-hood to the secondary level, with the necessary resources for student learning? In order to achieve the status of a developed nation by 2030, this is absolutely essential.

The Government has promised free education up to the secondary level. If this is a serious commitment, then the attendant actions must reflect this approach. There are basic tools that are needed for learning. Textbooks and writing materials are some such. In spite of this, there are stories of primary schools not receiving textbooks. This situation must be addressed with urgency. Such schools cannot be expected to produce the anticipated results in the Literacy and Numeracy Assessments.

One of the key factors in the education process is the environment in which learning takes place. If we are serious about developing our citizenry into an educated force, this aspect of learning must be addressed. Having teachers attempt to teach multi-grade levels in one classroom with a total of 60 or more students, for example, indicates that we are giving lip service to our intent to improve out educational outcomes.

Furthermore, in order for effective learning to take place, teachers must be trained so that they are competent in their field and at the same time able to guide their students in their educational development. One area that is becoming increasingly problematic in our search to achieve an educated populace is the matter of communication. For us to be competitive in the global economy, our people need to be able to communicate with the outside world. Here is the problem, Jamaican Creole is not spoken by any other nation, whilst Standard Jamaican English is understood by other English-speaking persons. Many of our teachers are coming into the classroom being unable to master Standard English. Our children, therefore, are finding it difficult to learn Standard English. There are not many opportunities for them to be immersed in the language. For many, it is not heard at home, or in the public space, or through the media and neither in the classroom. It should be clear then, that English must be taught as a second language in our classrooms, yet the teacher-training institutions are not training our teachers to teach English this way. Hence, the basic competence of communicating with other nation groups is not being shaped in many of our students.

**Lagging Behind**

Another area in which the teacher-training institutions have been lagging behind is in the development of information technology (IT) competence in the teachers. According to Dr. Didacus Jules, registrar of Caribbean Examination Council, "Our teacher preparation processes have not kept pace with ... challenges and in too many countries, an insufficient proportion of the teaching service is neither trained nor prepared to successfully deliver instruction to the new generation student in distinctly different conditions such as we face today. The teaching service needs to be re-energised." (Jules, Rethinking Education for the Caribbean 2010) This statement is applicable to the outdated mode of preparation taking place in our teacher-training institutions. Teachers must come into the classroom, not only knowing how to use IT to enhance learning, but they must have developed the skills to recognise learning difficulties in students. In addition, they must have been given help to deal with their own emotional issues so that they can be emotionally well enough to deal with the myriad of problems facing our students in today's Jamaica.

An important stakeholder group in education that has to be highlighted is our parents. More and more parental responsibility for the social, spiritual and emotional development of our children is being demitted by parents and left to the schools. This responsibility primarily belongs to the home, yet more and more the schools are being expected to perform the parents' role in the upbringing of their children. Research continually shows that children who do well are those who are given the support at home by their caregivers and who are allowed to play and learn through play, yet we have a culture where many times the children are told that "unnu play too much"[10]. Children's cognitive development is enhanced by parents who read to them regularly when they are quite young, yet many of our parents are unable or unwilling to read to their children. They see little value to this practice. Studies also show the impact of abuse on the learning capacity of children, yet in Jamaica, our people continue to practice physical, verbal and sexual abuse and expect our children to perform at the level of those who live in supportive environments.

Our government, private sector and media practitioners need to develop a plan to educate our people on their responsibilities as parents. Since our society is not an extremely literate one, it needs to be done through audio-visual means. We must change our culture, which sees children as a bother or as a workforce.

Publishing the results of the literacy and numeracy tests might expose what is happening in the schools, but it certainly will not address the serious problem with which we are faced. In speaking with the Jamaica Teachers' Association (JTA) on this matter, they have indicated a commitment to accountability and transparency in the education system whilst the Ministry of Education is seeking to carry out the programme of Transformation in Education. The JTA and the Ministry must now work together in this transformation. All stakeholders must be united to achieve this goal.

Unity is strength, so much so that God, knowing its power, destroyed the Tower of Babel.

**Published January 2, 2011**

# DEMORALISING SECONDARY-SCHOOL PRINCIPALS

Here is my question: Has the Government of Jamaica developed an agenda to demoralize the principals of secondary schools?

I have started to wonder because of a series of actions carried out by the Government.

First, they implement a policy of free education for all up to secondary education, then ignore the economic cost of educating each child and send to the schools less funds than what is needed for running a school efficiently. In the meantime, when the principals arrange with parents to pay additional fees to cover the cost of the quality education that they require for their children, the leader of the nation declares that these principals are "extortionists". This is while the Government is, at the same time, putting forward goals that are to be achieved, but without the necessary funds. For example, principals have been sent a document outlining the Ministry of Education's (MOE) policy on safety and security in schools. This document states: "As the chief executive officer of the board, the principal must ensure that school infrastructure is safe and secure for students and staff

65

wherever they may move about or gather." In addition, "principals are expected to develop a programme of routine maintenance of the school premises, paying particular attention to littering and garbage disposal, defacing and graffiti, immediate replacement and restoration of doors, locks, windows, grilles and furniture." (Education 2010)

Now place those goals against the following realities: The Ministry of Education gives each principal J$50,000 per year for maintenance of schools. The provision of security by the Ministry of Education is two watchmen, who are paid to watch the school in the nights. There is no provision made for security guards to be employed during school time. How do principals, therefore, accomplish the mandate sent from the Ministry of Education? Many principals depend on the profits from canteens or tuck shops and auxiliary fees from parents to carry out the task of, for example, putting in perimeter fencing, employing security guards, replacing damaged windows, etc. Yet in the very act of seeking to carry out our mandate, we are accused of being "extortionists".

Furthermore, when tragedies occur in schools, our government leaders issue statements that principals will be held accountable because they are to ensure the safety of their staff and students. These are the same leaders who decry the principals for seeking to get the funds to pay the security guard, to repair fencing, and to replace doors. When our Government declares that parents are not required to pay additional fees, there are some parents who take this as an opportunity to verbally abuse the principal and the staff when they ask about the auxiliary fees. Therefore, the Government continues to create opportunity for parents to abuse the principals by these politically motivated pronouncements.

## No Clear Governing Structure

In addition to demanding that principals attain the MOE's goals without the accompanying resources, the Government expects that principals will be good managers of their schools. Being a good manager requires that you employ and assess staff and ensure that they are working to meet the stated goals of the school, as agreed by the school board. Carrying out this mandate might require that some persons be terminated from their posts. When the MOE authorizes an investigation because of the written complaint of a dismissed employee without the board's involvement, while at the same time making its actions public without completing the investigation, the minister's intention seems to be to demoralize principals.

When a principal finds ways and means to develop his school while under the direct supervision of his board, and a government ministry oversteps the authority of the board and orders an investigation into the school's canteen without going through the MOE, the Government is sending a  clear message to principals:  there is no clear governing structure in place to which you report, and you are an open target to any politically motivated government official who is intent on destroying your career and your good name.

Are we aware of the environment within which principals are operating in modern Jamaica?

Many of our secondary-school principals have to face the constant challenge of leading schools with children who are the product of an increasingly coarse, uncivil, violent, and lawless society. Principals do not produce these children. The adults, the parents, the wider society have produced them. "Children live what they learn." (Desiderata)

Compounding this is the fact that principals are confronted with young teachers, many of whom are unable to deal with the trials which they face in the classrooms. Many are products of our ravaged communities and homes and are not even able to help themselves, much less the children. Principals are, therefore, confronted with the necessity to find ways to help these teachers overcome their own problems and train them to help students.

Principals are increasingly faced with the possibility of physical harm because children are being taught by example and precept that "unnu nuh fe tek nuh diss fram nobady".[11] Correcting a child these days is perceived by some as a "diss."[12] Many teachers are becoming afraid of correcting students' misbehaviour.

Yet our leaders, who should be encouraging the principals to deal with this daunting task of educating the children of this society, seem intent on making their jobs more difficult. When there is no clear line of authority, when decisions seem to be politically motivated without just cause, when pronouncements are made which make you vulnerable to abuse by those you attempt to lead, when your best intentions are misconstrued and deliberately misinterpreted, when your integrity and good reputation are destroyed by unproven accusations, there seems to be little motivation for principals to remain in the system or for bright young minds to aspire to such a role.

If our Government, therefore, has accomplished nothing else, it seems it is becoming quite accomplished in this area: the demoralizing of secondary-school principals.

**Published February 6, 2011**

# LEVELLING THE PLAYING FIELD?

The Government and people of Jamaica are indebted to the Inter-Secondary Schools' Sports Association (ISSA) for the service it has provided Jamaica in creating the cradle to foster the development of the sporting talent of our youth at the secondary-school level. Without the vision and organisation of ISSA, our nation would not have developed the talent now being displayed in track and field globally. It is the staging of Boys and Girls Championships (Champs) that has provided the opportunity for our stars such as Usain Bolt to be discovered.

But how did Usain reach Champs? He entered Champs as a student athlete from William Knibb Memorial High School. Now, some persons might have asked, "Where is William Knibb High?" or "Which school is that?" before Usain Bolt became the most well-known athlete in the world. Because of Bolt's success on the national and international scene, this question is now moot. Usain's success has helped to put William Knibb High on the map of sought-after high schools in Jamaica. Another such school is Charlemont High, where Asafa Powell attended.

**Talented Students Wooed Away**

These institutions have had the chance to showcase to the nation and the world the students they have nurtured for five years of high school. There are other schools that have had students with latent talent in the sporting field that have had these students wooed away from them by schools with larger budgets, well-endowed alumni, and ambitious coaches who are determined to maintain top billing in track and field and football.

Anecdotal evidence points to ambitious coaches who want to make a name for themselves and their schools, backed by wealthy alumni who scout talent from other schools. They zero in on the parents and guardians of such students and design hefty and attractive financial packages to lure students and parents to leave the schools in which they have been placed through the Grade Six Achievement Test (GSAT) or the Grade Nine Achievement Test (GNAT). There are stories which abound of students, some of whom have not attained the grades at GSAT required for entry to some schools, being transferred into such institutions simply because of their sporting talent. They are unable to maintain the average deemed satisfactory by the school, and yet are made to go through the system without passing even one subject. On the other hand, there are others who are allowed to repeat grade levels to keep them in the school, not to strengthen their academic performance, but more to strengthen the track or football team.

The question is: Is this practice helping to level the playing field, or is it tilting the field further in the direction of schools that are prestigious and well-established, with strong backing from wealthy parents and alumni? Should such practices be allowed by ISSA, the cradle of the sporting talent of Jamaica? Should ISSA put in place guidelines that govern the wholesale buying of students from one secondary school or schools by others in an attempt to win a competition by gaining an unnatural advantage for themselves at the expense of other schools? Another question is: Are we about winning at the cost of weakening and undermining other schools? And, what message are we sending to our students when we bring them into our schools simply because of their sporting talent without emphasizing the development of their academic capacity?

When our students realize that they are being transferred from one school to another because their parents or guardians have been offered attractive financial packages by the school, what moral authority do school administrators have to help that student develop his or her character? How does the school speak to such students about hard work and integrity and commitment when they are allowed to skip classes and no consequences are meted out because they are the star athlete or footballer?

Dr. Lascelves Graham, writing in The Gleaner on January 5, 2011, on this same issue, made the following astute comments:

The practice of recruiting youngsters into our high schools for the purpose of influencing the outcome of sporting events is symptomatic of a larger problem which seems to be running amok in the society – the erosion, the slow, silent, imperceptible but apparently inexorable eating away of the integrity of our people and our systems.

He continues:

Jamaican, like English high schools, believe that sports is one of the developmental tools (others include religion, music, drama, etc) that can help youngsters develop character, mental toughness, and discipline .... (Graham 2011)

We believe sports can play a key role in helping to teach values, attitudes, and life skills to youngsters who have satisfied the academic admission criteria and who deserve, as shown by their demonstrated academic potential, to be in the school.

**Time to Re-Examine Role of Sports**

I concur with Dr. Graham's assessment of the situation. As educators, we need to look again at the purpose of sports in high school and not seek to ape the politics of the intercollegiate sports in the USA. Even in the USA, this practice of luring high-school students from one school to another is frowned on. In an article published in High School Today on January 11, 2011, titled 'Standards for Measuring Success Not Based on Number of Victories', the following observations were made:

The measuring stick for success at the high-school level must remain different from the NCAA Division I model. While winning as many games as possible is a goal for all high-school coaches, the final outcome of a contest – in the long run – is not the all-determining factor for judging success. Success at the high-school level has more to do with preparing students for their lives after sports than the number of victories or state championships. (Gardner and Van Erk 2011)

Let us ensure that we model to our young people the importance of positive character development and the need for acquiring morals and values not based on winning at all cost; but rather, values that reflect hard work and commitment to working with the raw material that you are given.

**Published March 6, 2011**

# OUTDATED EDUCATION CODE

larm bells are going off all over the island at the increase in incidents of violence in the schools. Students are suffering serious injuries and even losing their lives at the hands of other students. Teachers are feeling threatened by students' behaviour and principals are legally left with limited options as to how to deal with students whose antisocial behaviour threatens the well-being of the school.

The way schools in Jamaica function is governed by The Education Regulation, 1980 which is part of The Education Act. (The Ministry of Education 1980) This regulation, hereafter called 'the code', is 31 years old. It is outmoded and does not address many of the realities being faced in the classrooms of Jamaica in the 21st century. For instance, although the code states that "a student shall obey the rules of the school he is attending", the code indicates that "a principal may suspend a student for a period not exceeding 10 days" if his or her behaviour has a detrimental effect on the discipline of the school. Now this, in itself, may sound satisfactory. The problem lies in the fact that at the point where a student has to be suspended and referred to the board of management, the course of action outlined by the code becomes impracticable.

Within the period of 10 days or less, depending on the length of the suspension, the board of management is expected to call a meeting of its voluntary members; review the case presented, and determine if the matter warrants being investigated by an appointed personnel committee of the board; the personnel committee is required to carry out investigation in the case; having investigated the matter, then they conduct a hearing into the matter; having conducted a hearing at which students and parents are to attend, they then take the findings back to the board of management, which determines further course of action. The course of action provided by the code is:

30.3. a. Reinstate the student with or without reprimand or a warning to the student, and where appropriate, to his parent or guardian;

b. Suspend the student for a further period not exceeding five school days beyond the period of suspension already given; or

c. Instruct the principal to exclude permanently the student from attending that institution and shall inform the minister of such action.

This procedure outlined in the code has resulted in a number of students whose behaviour is detrimental to the school still being kept in the institution. It is extremely difficult for the procedure that has been outlined above to be completed in 10 days or less. These 10 days include weekends. During this time, documentation must be prepared by the principal to be presented to the board; board members have to be contacted and a meeting held; investigation must take place, which includes interviewing students and teachers; documentation of such interviews must be done. In addition, a second board meeting must be called to determine the outcome for the student. Keep in mind the fact that board members are persons with full-time jobs elsewhere. It sometimes becomes difficult to get a board together at a moment's notice. This system needs to change.

**Additional Constraints**

Added to this onerous system is the fact that the police will not take students into custody unless they have been seen doing an injurious act, or with a weapon in their possession. If students or teachers report that a student has been acting suspiciously, or a principal has reason to believe that a student's behaviour is of such that it will cause injury to another student or students, the police will not take such a student into custody to investigate the matter. The police, when called, will talk to the student. The police are constrained by the fact that the student is underage.

The Jamaican reality is that many violent acts are being committed by underage students, particularly male students. The present code was created for a school scenario where students were assumed to be involved in largely mischievous teenage pranks which sometimes got out of hand. This is no longer our reality in the schools. In many schools in Jamaica, both teachers and students are living in fear and operating under a great level of stress caused by students whose presence in the schools is having a negative impact on the teaching-learning process and on the well-being of the majority of students. In some schools, teachers have become afraid for their safety that they simply ignore the students whose behaviour is out of control.

For many years, principals have been advocating that the Ministry of Education set up time-out centres for students with persistent antisocial behaviour. This would allow for students who are identified with such conduct to be referred to these centres. They would be placed there for a period of time within which they would be interacting with psychologists, social workers and other persons trained to modify antisocial behaviour. These students, having satisfied the team that their conduct has been adjusted, would then be readmitted into the normal school system. The present system, in which overwhelmed guidance counsellors are expected to solve the level of dysfunctionality of students, is impractical. Calls to address this crisis have been unheeded.

The present system cannot work. The schools are repositories for what our society produces. There are increasing reports of irresponsible parental behaviour, students who are suicidal, mental disorders being exhibited, violent and aggressive behaviour being displayed from a young age, and age-inappropriate sexual conduct, among other activities.

Teachers have, by and large, been trained to teach an academic curriculum. Teachers are not police officers. Principals are not lawyers, nor are they trained as psychologists. These competencies seem to be what are now required in the Jamaican classroom. The resources to deal with the present realities in the Jamaican classroom are lacking. The society needs to pressure the Government to provide the schools with the resources, human, physical and otherwise, to deal with this crisis.

**Published May 1, 2011**

# WHITHER FREE EDUCATION (2)?

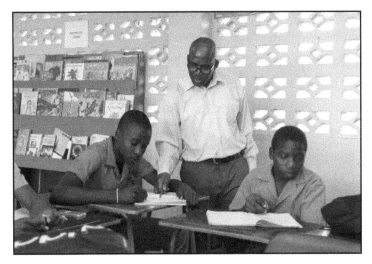

**Male high school students**

Indeed, as wise King Solomon said, "The borrower is a servant to the lender." (Solomon n.d.) It seems that the plans to lift our education system to a higher level of efficiency and accountability are being threatened by the requirements of the International Monetary Fund, to which Jamaica is bound.

Is it possible that the much-needed pull-out centre in Potsdam, albeit far from being sufficient to fulfil the country's needs, might not be completed for lack of funds? The Jamaica Teaching Council, according to the news, will not be established. The plans to build three much-needed schools will have to be scrapped. The amount of money normally allocated from the national Budget to education has not been adequate to meet all the demands of the Jamaican situation, yet we are being required to slash even that allocation to an even smaller figure. How then can we claim to be a nation that offers free education? It is clear that we cannot afford it.

UNESCO research indicates that for education to develop the way it needs to in most nations, there has to be partnership between the public and private sector. (UNESCO 2011) In Jamaica, this need has become even more urgent if we are to progress as a nation by educating our people. Our leaders need to face the stark reality that the national Budget cannot carry the full cost of educating our youth. They need, therefore, to look to ways to engage the private sector in assisting in providing education to the children of our nation. Furthermore, I believe that the Government would do well to reconsider the whole matter of cost-sharing. Under this system, persons who could not afford to pay approved fees to the schools would apply through the schools for assistance from the Government. There was a process to determine the applicants' level of need, and this information was sent to the Ministry of Education. The ministry would then approve the assistance to each applicant, and this money would be sent to the schools. Persons who could afford to pay the full fees did so.

It seems then to be the proverbial 'shooting ourselves in the foot' to be paying fees for parents who can afford to pay, and yet not being able to establish much-needed alternative facilities to deal with many of our at-risk students because of the lack of funds. During the last school year, the increase in violence in schools, antisocial behaviour and general disrespect for order has been alarming. Schools do not have the resources to deal with students who are the perpetrators of this type of behaviour. Since the schools do not have the financial, human or physical resources to deal with this phenomenon, the Government needs to establish these facilities right across the island with a concentration of such centres in Kingston and St Andrew, St Catherine and St James. Establishing one centre in St Elizabeth is a small start in this direction. Potsdam can accommodate only 40 students. St James alone will yield more than 40 students in one year alone, much more the numbers from Kingston and the other parishes. Alarmingly, even this one facility might not be completed.

## Disturbing Behavioural Issues

We cannot continue to speak about 'failing schools' without addressing some of the disturbing behavioural issues that are plaguing many of these institutions. This is not to deny the reality that principals and teachers do contribute to these schools performing below par; however, in some cases, the issue is much wider than the non-performance of these educators. If, as a nation, we are serious about lifting the standard of education in our country, we will need to look at the reality of what is taking place in the schools. Schools reflect the state of the society. Students are coming into schools from homes rife with abuse and neglect. When these children come into school from homes and communities where violence is an everyday occurrence and abuse is the norm, the behaviour they display at school is simply a reflection of what they have absorbed from their living conditions. In addition, many Jamaicans do not view education as valuable. After all, there are many students who have left university and are unable to find jobs. The question is being asked, "Why bother?" Instead, the thinking among some is that it is better to hustle and try to 'cut a chune'[13] and 'mek a money'.[14]

**Teach Entrepreneurship**

There needs to be a shift in our thinking in education where we begin to teach entrepreneurship to our students encouraging them to understand that they will have to create a livelihood for themselves, instead of expecting a job to be waiting on them. We need to give our young people the tools to survive in this new national and global climate. Also, the business environment in the country needs to change to facilitate young, upcoming entrepreneurs making a success of any viable venture. Jamaica is known to be bogged down by bureaucracy. This red tape stymies the initiative of some who would have otherwise ventured into manufacturing or the service sector. We need to ensure that our education helps our graduates to make a living in a way that is more than 'hustling'.

Times are changing; our thinking needs to change with the reality that is facing us. We cannot afford 'free education', even if the proclamation gets votes for the political candidates. We need to begin to look at ways in which the private sector can partner with the public sector to provide quality education for our children. In addition, the education product needs to change. We need to ensure that our students leave school with the skills of innovation, creative thinking and entrepreneurship in order to have a good quality of life as adults.

**Published September 4, 2011**

**Change of Culture**

The culture of school being a place which provides a holding area for students needs to change. Teachers need to be motivated to see themselves as agents of change. They need to believe that they can make a difference. Teaching while having no motivation to see students excel, despite their seemingly low starting point, is simply holding on to the job to get 'a money'. This is not acceptable. The transformation in the schools must be given urgent attention. To strengthen this culture change, systems need to be put in place to hold teachers accountable for their performance in the classrooms. Teachers should understand that they are answerable to the students and parents, as well as the principal, board and the Government. Students should not live in fear of repercussions from a teacher because they complain about a teacher's absence from class or lack of preparation. After all, this would be similar to a constituent speaking out about an MP's lack of performance and being targeted for harassment because of doing that.

Other than being held accountable, teachers should be required to update their training on an ongoing basis. If the Government is serious about the development of our nation, it must focus on the continuing training of our teachers as a priority. Education has changed rapidly with the advancement in technology. Our students' learning requirements have changed, but many teachers' knowledge base has become antiquated. The Jamaica Teaching Council needs to be made a legal body so that it can develop and implement training programmes that are needed for our teachers.

Our education system can change, but it can only improve when the systems that have been proposed under the transformation programme are implemented effectively. It cannot take another four or five years before we see the recommendations made earlier this decade begin to take effect. It would mean that we have lost another generation of students to the slipshod education process that exists in some places in this country. Overall, then, the culture of transparency and accountability that we are pushing for in Government needs to become part of the culture of the schools of Jamaica.

Nations such as Singapore that do not have the natural resources we do, were able to move their countries forward because they understood that their greatest asset is the developed minds of their people. Singapore has become a prosperous nation because it was not fearful to invest in its people and develop its knowledge capital. I hope that in the same way we have seen progress in our political process, we will see similar advancement in how we view and value education in our nation. We have found ways to invest money in the roads in Jamaica. We need to find ways to invest the money needed into education. Even more, we need the people of Jamaica to value the education process and to push for a world-class system for our children.

**Published January 1, 2012**

# EDUCATION TRANSFORMATION STILLBORN

T he reports prepared by the National Education Inspectorate (NEI) are published on the Ministry of Education's website. (The Chief 2011) Currently, only reports of those schools inspected in 2010 have been published. These reports are informative and give an overview of what is happening in the schools inspected. Twenty-three of these reports are on primary and all-age schools. Of the 23, only one school's performance was ranked 'good'; nine were 'satisfactory'; and 13 were unsatisfactory.

The NEI has five levels of judgements: Level 1 – failing, quality is low; Level 2 – unsatisfactory, quality not yet at the level acceptable for school in Jamaica; Level 3 – satisfactory, the minimum level of acceptability required for Jamaica; Level 4 – good, the expected level for every school in Jamaica; Level 5 – exceptionally high quality of performance or provision. If out of 23 schools catering to primary education – some situated in rural St Andrew and Portland, others in inner-city communities and two in Harbour View, St Andrew – only one is considered to be performing at the expected level for every school in Jamaica, it begs the question of what is being done to bring the other 22 schools up to the level of 'good'.

It was heartening to see the school that was deemed good. It was Shirley Castle Primary School in rural Portland. It is a small school with 36 students and three teachers. The size is not the only factor determining its success, since there is a school that is performing below par with 18 students and three teachers.

## Common Thread

An analysis of the summary of the judgements on the unsatisfactory and even some satisfactory schools reflects common features. One such is the teachers' knowledge of the subject and how best to teach the students. In quite a few instances, even where it is determined that the teachers' knowledge of the subject is satisfactory, the teachers' knowledge of how best to help the students to learn is lacking. This is particularly disturbing since in many instances these schools have a small pupil-teacher ratio. What is seen is that many teachers do not know how to stimulate the students to learn. Their use of appropriate methodology is lacking.

Look at some excerpts from these reports:

"While teachers have satisfactory subject knowledge, many lack a clear understanding as to how students learn best. Teaching lacks variety and innovation and seldom takes into account the needs of students with differing levels of ability."

"The quality of teaching is inconsistent across the school. Although most lessons are satisfactory, there are too many failing lessons and too few lessons where teachers use a range of effective teaching strategies. Teachers lack a clear understanding of how children learn and rarely use creative teaching methods to enrich students' learning experiences."

"The quality of teaching is unsatisfactory across the school, with too many lessons deemed as failing. There is a considerable lack of understanding among teachers about how students learn. Teaching methods lack variety and attention to the differences in levels of ability among students. In some lessons, poor planning, unclear objectives and inaccurate teaching methods undermine student progress."

"Teaching and learning are unsatisfactory. Most lessons rely on a narrow range of activities, with too much teacher talk and too little focus on how students' thinking can be developed. Few resources are used beyond the blackboard, Ministry of Education textbooks, and student notebooks."

A common thread running through the reports is that where schools have multi-grade classes, teachers display a lack of knowledge on how to teach in this context. The following comments reflect this.

"Teaching and learning (are) unsatisfactory, and many teachers have insufficient knowledge of how best to provide for the needs of the different abilities and grade levels in one class. Questioning techniques are frequently too narrow to develop the students' own thinking."

"Teaching provides unsatisfactory support for students' learning throughout the school. Although there are pockets of good teaching, most teachers employ ineffective teaching methods which fail to challenge the needs of all their students, both the high achievers and those students who have learning difficulties. This is especially obvious in multi-grade classes where teachers fail to differentiate between these two groups in lessons, both in the teaching of the planned activities and what is expected of students; this particularly limits the progress of the upper grade-level students and the high achievers. Teachers are qualified but lack the skill to successfully make an impact on the learning of all their students."

**Improve Faltering System**

Teaching is at the core of the education process. If there is a consistent problem with the teaching methodology that seems to be affecting students' learning outcomes, the Ministry of Education needs to fast-track the plan to have education territorial officers who are specialists in their subject areas assigned to schools that need assistance. It is ill-advised to spend millions of dollars establishing the NEI without putting in place the support structures needed to improve the faltering system that now exists.

The Transformation in Education Report was done from 2004. It is now 2012. That means that we have had almost two generations of students going from primary to high school in this system, which in many places operates schools as simply a holding area for children whose parents are at work or who need a break.

Transformation has become a stillbirth. The work being done in early childhood is commendable, but it is not enough. This system needs serious surgery for the needed improvement to take place.

The other organizations involved in the training of teachers need to do a detailed assessment of the reports coming out of the NEI to see the context within which they are preparing teachers to operate. In this case, the colleges need to address the whole matter of teaching student-teachers' appropriate methodology for the Jamaican class-room in this 21st century.

I will be looking further at other factors that are impacting the performance of our schools in other articles.

**Published March 4, 2012**

# THE IMPACT OF LEADERSHIP ON THE PERFORMANCE OF PRIMARY SCHOOLS

I N LAST month's column, I reviewed the reports prepared by the National Education Inspectorate (NEI) that are published on the Ministry of Education's website. Currently, only reports of those schools inspected in 2010 have been published. These reports are informative and give an overview of what is happening in the schools inspected. Twenty-three of the reports are on primary and all-age schools. Of the 23 schools, only one was determined to be performing at the level of good, nine were satisfactory and 13 were unsatisfactory.

The NEI has five levels of judgements: Level 1 – Failing, quality is low; Level 2 – Unsatisfactory, quality not yet at the level acceptable for school in Jamaica; Level 3 – Satisfactory, the minimum level of acceptability required for Jamaica; Level 4 – Good, the expected level for e school in Jamaica; Level 5 – Exceptionally high quality of performance or provision. If out of 23 schools catering to primary education, some situated in the rural areas of St Andrew and Portland, others in inner-city communities and two in the Harbour View community, only one is considered to be performing at the expected level for every school in Jamaica, then it begs the question of what is being done to bring the other 22 schools up to the level of 'good'. It was heartening to see the school that was deemed good. It is the Shirley Castle Primary School in rural Portland. It is a small school with 36 students and three teachers. The size is not the only factor for its success since there is a school that is performing below par with 18 students and three teachers.

An analysis of the summary of the judgements on the unsatisfactory and even some satisfactory schools reflects common features.

Last month, I reviewed the impact of teaching on students' performance. This month, I will look at the impact of governance and leadership on the performance of the reported schools; this will include the boards of management and the principals.

**Significant Observation**

The most significant observation that I made in assessing leadership and governance in the 10 schools deemed satisfactory to good is that they all have strong principals. These principals sometimes are supported by boards that are committed to the school, but in some cases there is little mention of the board. These are some extracts which reflect the judgements on the principals and school boards:

"Leadership and management are satisfactory. The school benefits from a committed principal and has an effective school board with a hard-working chairman. The board is holding the school increasingly accountable for its performance."

"The school is satisfactorily led by a confident principal who provides a strong sense of direction to the school, and an active board that has a positive influence on the work and development of the school."

"The principal provides strong leadership and all staff are committed both to the school and to further improvement. Overall, teaching and learning are satisfactory." "The principal's firm, focused and inspirational leadership motivates the staff to meet the students' instructional needs and make good progress. The inexperienced board provides limited advice for the development of the school but supports the programmes implemented by the principal."

There are three factors seen in these assessments which determine whether a school performs positively – a strong, committed principal, an effective school board, and a culture of accountability. Unfortunately, in some of the schools that are judged to be unsatisfactory, while there might be some committed principals, there are usually non-performing or weak school boards, or a lack of communication of the vision from the principal to the staff. In many cases, the principals, although being well-intentioned, do not hold the staff accountable for students' performance, nor do they provide strong instructional leadership. There is no evidence of a school performing unsatisfactorily where there is a culture of accountability and robust instructional leadership. The following extracts reflect this:

**Unsatisfactory Management**

"The leadership and management of the school are insufficiently rigorous in focusing school improvements on student achievement. The principal holds teachers accountable for the quality of their teaching in a limited manner. Leadership and management are unsatisfactory." "The acting principal is a dedicated professional who has the care and welfare of all students at heart. However, there is little evidence that teachers are held to account, or that actions from the school development plan are followed through or monitored by the board. Consequently, the school is not moving forward and students are not developing as they should, either academically or personally." "The leadership and management of the school are unsatisfactory. The principal has made several improvements focusing on the students' well-being. However, insufficient attention is given to improving learning and students' attainment. Teachers do not receive effective guidance as to how to improve their teaching skills and their students' learning. "

This important factor that determines the health of our education system must be addressed with haste. The practice of persons being appointed to school boards without receiving training in their responsibilities needs to become a practice of the past. Even though school board members serve voluntarily, they must be selected carefully to ensure that they will add value to the schools that they serve. The National College of Leadership, as a part of the Transformation in Education, needs to be established post-haste so that principals in our schools can receive the training that they need to ably equip them to lead the schools with efficiency. The days of teachers simply moving up the ladder from classroom teacher to vice-principal to principal must be put behind us. The job requires a strong character and specific training to develop the competencies needed.

Michael Fullan in The Moral Imperative of School Leadership (Fullan 2003) makes the point that: "Leading schools ... requires principals with the courage and capacity to build new cultures based on trusting relationships and a culture of disciplined inquiry and action. That school leaders with these characteristics are in short supply is the point." For Jamaica's educational system to improve, we must find a way to develop such leaders. This is our imperative.

**Published April 1, 2012**

# EDUCATION THEN AND NOW

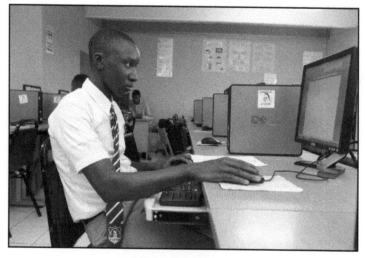

**In the Computer Lab**

As a nation, Jamaica has come a long way from where we started with our education system in 1962. Then, the norm was that children were sent to infant school, then to primary school. Many children did not go to school on Fridays because they stayed home to help their parents or went to the fields to help. Some parents felt that Friday was a play day. Furthermore, not many children went to high school, because you had to pass the Common Entrance to go to high school, and if you did not get a scholarship through the Common Entrance, your parents had to pay fees. However, not many persons could afford the fees. The idea of a teenager moving on to tertiary education was even more unthinkable for the average Jamaican in 1962. Then, there was only one local university, and the teachers' colleges. Some persons were able to send girls to England to do nursing, but only the fortunate few. Tertiary education was perceived as being for the elite, not ordinary Jamaicans.

Based on this overview, one would get the impression that our educational system has made great strides in the last few decades. Indeed, we have come a long way, but there is much room for improvement. While we have increased access to education, we still need to improve the quality of education being offered.

**Demands of Education**

The demands of education, both globally and nationally, are now quite different from what they were in 1962. Then, our people felt that completing secondary education was a great milestone. Now it is seen as simply a stepping stone to higher education of one form or another. Then, if you completed secondary education, it was possible to find a job in the commercial sector or the civil service. Now, most entry-level jobs in banking and the civil service, for example, require a first degree. Then, if you passed five GCE O'Level subjects, you would be able to enter sixth form in a traditional high school; now, the demands are for eight or more CXCs with grade one. Then, you had more than one opportunity to take the Common Entrance Examination; now, you take the GSAT once. Then, not many Jamaicans were leaving to pursue tertiary education in the United States and other foreign countries; now, it has become commonplace. In other words, the stakes have gotten higher. We now compete not only with ourselves but with the world. We need to be aware of what the demands are in the global marketplace and what the acceptable standards of education are at each level.

The poor results of our secondary education system need to not only be discussed, but also addressed. First of all, we need to realize that grammar-school education is not sufficient to prepare our students for the 21st-century, knowledge-based economy. Students need to be leaving the secondary level with their cognitive skills developed; their ability to manage conflict intact; their capacity for teamwork, well-practiced; their ability to research and access information fully engaged; their understanding of the demands of multiculturalism aroused; and full competence in the use of information technology. There are various ways through which this can be accomplished, not only through a grammar school education. With the many advances being made in technology, it has become even more important to equip our students with a skills-based education. Have we realized that students who leave high school and college with skills are the ones most likely to be employed, compared to students who are studying the grammar subjects?

Therefore, using the results of only the CXC examinations is not enough to determine if the students are ready to go out to the world of work or further education. There are other assessment programmes being used in schools.

To be fair then, we should be assessing our schools on what is being done through skills-based educational assessment tools, such as The City of Guilds and HEART examinations. Furthermore, right across the board, our students need to be taught how to be courteous and civil and to develop positive work ethics. The lack of positive work ethics and courtesy in our nation has now become an economic block. Companies are choosing to go to other countries with their businesses because we have become infamous for our rude behaviour and poor work ethics. This does not rule out, however, the issue of accountability, which is sadly lacking in many of our schools. Parliament needs to fast-track the legislation to allow for accountability structures to be put in place in schools. The Jamaica Teaching Council, which has, on paper, the remit to oversee registration and training of teachers, is well past due.

The establishment of The Leadership College, which has been touted for so long to train principals and senior management of schools, is going at an alarmingly slow pace. The much-proclaimed plan to decentralize the operations of the Ministry of Education into regional bodies that will give specialized support to schools and that will be manned by educators who are skilled in their particular fields has all but been forgotten. We cannot afford to have another generation fall through the large cracks in this system.

I am sure that we are aware of examples of countries such as Singapore that are way ahead of us economically, even though they have fewer natural resources. Singapore's economy is a knowledge-based one. How did they move ahead of us? By taking the challenges they faced with their education system seriously. They looked at it, assessed it and fixed it. Now they are reaping the benefits of making hard decisions.

When are we going to have leaders of government who are bold enough to realise that using short-term programmes to patch our educational system will not fulfil Vision 2030?

**Published August 5, 2012**

# HAS THE SALT LOST ITS SAVOUR?

"You are the salt of the earth, but when the salt has lost its savour, how can it be salted again?" (E. H. Petersen 2012) So, said Jesus Christ to his disciples. I say to the teachers of Jamaica at the beginning of the 2012-2013 school year that you are the salt of the education system, and the savour needs improvement. Teachers, you have the most powerful influence on the development of this nation's children, apart from their parents. You have the awesome power to make or break a life. Society would have us teachers feel that we are failures, but that is a false message. There are many teachers who are doing excellent work in the field. Even in the most disruptive school environment, you will find a small pocket of teachers who are making a difference in their class. There are many teachers who are surrogate parents for many students. They, sometimes, are the only positive adult figure that a child has in his or her life. There are teachers who are being creative, innovative and who have excellent teaching skills. Their students thrive under their instructions. If this were not so, our national results would have been worse than they are now. So many students are lacking proper parenting that it seems that if some teachers were not in fact playing their role well, in loco parentis, Jamaica would have been in a worse condition than we are.

There are, however, too many teachers who are incompetent, lacking training and lacking passion for the job. They are in the classroom with a negative attitude towards the students, believing that many of them cannot learn. They have bought into the negative attitude that we tend to have in this nation. They blame the children for their own failures. They do not seek to examine their practices to see how they can improve. These teachers take all the praise when the students do well, but place the responsibility at the feet of the students when they fail. These teachers, however, cannot take all the responsibility for the condition of our education system. It is the system itself that allows such teachers to be proliferating in the classroom.

First of all, the standard for matriculation to teaching colleges is too low. Countries that have successful educational systems, take students who are the cream of the crop, academically, and train them extensively to become competent, efficient and respected teachers. Furthermore, background checks need to be done on teachers before they are allowed to enter the classroom to interact with vulnerable children. In the same way that the police force has now begun to do background checks on applicants, so too should the Ministry of Education and the board of management of schools for teacher recruits. This would help in reducing the number of pedophiles and perverts who are using the classroom as a contact point with the intention of molesting students.

## Awesome Responsibility

It is distressing to hear the reports that many cases of child sexual molestation and abuse are perpetrated by teachers. Teachers have an awesome responsibility and power over the lives of students and, therefore, the Ministry of Education needs to be vigilant in screening persons who are allowed to go into the classroom.

In addition, all teachers need to be properly registered and held accountable for their professional development. The Jamaica Teaching Council, under whose mandate this job would fall, is still not fully operational because the legal framework for its function has still not been finalized. Meanwhile, the cat naps, the mice play. Therefore, a teacher can be fired from one school and simply move on to another without there being any follow-through on their misconduct. The Ministry of Education does not have the structure in place to monitor such teachers, even though reports have to be sent to them when a teacher is dismissed from a school.

Even though the Transformation in Education team had recommended that more responsibility and authority be divested to boards of school for the management of schools, this has still not been done. The present Code of Education Regulations 1980 (ibid) is long outdated and does not address many present realities. It is difficult for boards to dismiss those teachers who are non-performing or behaving immorally or unethically. This is because, many times, teachers are returned to schools after they are dismissed because the Jamaica Teachers' Association, whose officials are experts on the code, use technicalities to have them maintain their tenure.

I repeat my call for a College of Leadership to be established for school administrators. The requirements of leading a school in today's Jamaica are much more complex than they were 10 years ago. The practice of having a teacher going through the system and later becoming principal, without receiving training in financial management, human resource management, instructional leadership, interpersonal relationships, project management and plant management must change if we want our education system to improve. Furthermore, we need to ensure that our school leaders are persons of integrity and moral rectitude.

The system, as it exists, is not promoting the development of a cadre of bright, passionate, morally positive, academically qualified, and fulfilled teachers who will ensure that the students of Jamaica receive a world-class education.

How then are we going to fulfil Vision 2030 with a system that is in serious need of restructuring?

**Published September 2, 2012**

# HONOURING AN EXTRAORDINARY EDUCATOR

**Dahlia Repole**

Today, I honour Dr. Dahlia Repole who dedicated her life to the development of education in Jamaica. She made an indelible stamp on St Andrew High School for Girls, her alma mater, and Excelsior Community College (EXED) in her role as leader of those institutions. However, she was not only an educator, but a wife and mother.

I worked with Dahlia Repole, 'Mrs Rips', as vice-principal at St Andrew High while she was principal. I regard her as one of my mentors in education. She encouraged me, as a teacher of English, to develop my leadership capacity and to further my training in education. She was a good team leader. She knew how to share her authority with her vice-principals. She quickly adopted any programme that we suggested that she saw would be valuable to student development. She was not afraid to share power. Furthermore, it was while working with Dahlia that my husband was shot and left paralyzed. She reached out to my family and worked with the school board to ensure that I was given paid leave to be with my husband abroad during his rehabilitation. This time extended beyond the period for which I was paid by the Ministry of Education. She was a compassionate and thoughtful person.

She has been honoured by both St Andrew High and EXED for her sterling contribution to their development. These are some of the words that her alma mater used to tell the story of her accomplishments (much of it my paraphrasing):

Dahlia Repole received her secondary education at St Andrew High School for Girls, excelling not only in academics but in sports such as netball and hockey. She represented the school and Jamaica not only in hockey but also as a coach. After graduating from St Andrew High, (Dahlia) pursued a Bachelor of Science degree and earned a distinction in the postgraduate diploma in education at the University of the West Indies, a Master of Education degree from Georgia State University, USA, and a Doctor of Philosophy from the University of the West Indies. After teaching at St Andrew High, in

1975 she was appointed as the vice-principal, a position she held until 1978. During her tenure, she was an outstanding administrator and produced a seven-year school plan which served as an invaluable guideline for the institution's development. She then served as director of EXED from 1982-1986.

In 1989, Dahlia returned to St Andrew High to serve as principal for more than 11 years. Dahlia's love for young people and her deep concern for their total development resulted in her founding the St Andrew Business College in 1991 to prepare students who wanted to enter the world of business.

**Effective in Solving Problems**

Dahlia also recognised the importance of having a highly qualified staff and encouraged her teachers to pursue continuing professional development. Her personality as a natural counsellor made her effective in resolving problems occurring at all levels of the school. A true pioneer, Dahlia led EXED to become the first community college to offer accredited bachelor degrees in several academic programmes. Her visionary leadership motivated her to open off-site campuses in the neighbouring community of Woodford Park and in St Thomas. She also responded to the needs of several communities in proximity to the main EXED campus by designing special adult education and outreach programmes for their residents.

Dahlia's expertise as an educator has extended beyond the shores of Jamaica leading to her serving in many capacities. Dahlia's daily testament, in her own words, was that "helping others makes life worth living". This has been manifested in her energetic community involvement, including her development and management of a small business programme for 30 youth community projects, in her capacity as project officer for Jamaica/Western New York Partner of the Americas.

**Most Outstanding Achievements**

In recognition of her outstanding achievements and dedicated service Dahlia was conferred with the national honour of the Order of Distinction, Commander Class. Perhaps her most outstanding achievement has been that of devoted wife, loving mother of five children and a proud grandmother. Her daughter, Anika, expresses her regard for this remarkable woman, in these words:

"My admiration for this woman knows no bounds. She knew the secret to a balanced life, never having any one aspect sacrificed for the other. She was an amazing educator and put her all into her profession and studies towards her career, yet found a miraculous way to also devote her heart and soul to her family.

"I remember vividly, upon the confirmation of her being approved for her PhD. after her final presentation, that she sat there in front of the examiners with her head in her hands and cried. It was at that moment that all her life's work in education had reached its pinnacle and both a cry of relief and pure joy leapt from her being and into the room. She was so proud and I was honoured to have witnessed this moment.

"However, despite her continuous efforts in the area of her studies, she never shirked her duties as wife, mother, sister, aunt, grand-mother or friend. She always had time to listen, to offer her objective advice without judgement. She was the fireside of our family, where we came to be our authentic selves. There was no pretending.

"She was so much to so many, and still she was my mommy, my friend. My proudest moment will always be when she told me I was her friend and confidante, and if there is one thing for me to value for the rest of my life, it would be that I could have been that to this woman who was everything to everyone else. She will be forever missed, but her presence still lingers in the kiss of the wind on the cheek, the sight of a beautiful flower and the sound joyful laughter."

**Published February 3, 2013**

# ARE CONDOMS IN SCHOOLS THE SOLUTION?

T he recent report that Dr. Sandra Knight, chair of the National Family Planning Board (NFPB), has called for the revival of the debate on schools distributing condoms, (K. Thompson 2013) in light of the discovery that one Corporate Area high school has some 60 per cent of its students in one grade being parents, leads back to the question of whether we will continue putting Band-Aid on our problems or deal with the wider issues that they point to.

The news report points out that Dr. Knight is concerned because of the conflicting relationship between Jamaican law and the rights of children under a United Nations (UN) convention. The report states that the UN prescribes that children have the right to sexual reproductive-health services, while Jamaican law defines anyone under the age of 18 years as a child and, as such, is prevented from accessing sexual reproductive health information and/or services, even though the age of consent here is 16 years.

There are many issues embedded in this statement. At first glance, there is confusion between the age of consent for sexual involvement and access to sexual reproductive health information and services. The law gives consent for children to have sex at age 16, then another law prevents them from having access to sexual reproductive-health information and services before age 18. This conflict needs to be addressed.

**Children Having Sex**

The second source of confusion is that we are saying that it is fine for children to be having sex. Being sexually active, however, means that you are ready to be a parent, since no contraceptive, especially the condom, is foolproof. How can we legalize children having sex when they cannot support themselves economically, nor are they mature enough to be parents?

The concern that we are not obeying the UN convention indicates that we are not examining whether the UN's position is the correct one for our nation, where we need to focus on strengthening our family structure, building parental involvement in the lives of their children, and developing a sense of responsibility among our people for their sexual conduct. This push for children to have access to sexual reproductive health services without their parents' consent contradicts that focus. Furthermore, are we saying that only children aged 16 and over are to access these services? Are we aware, and I am sure Dr. Knight is, that the ages of the young mothers at the Victoria Jubilee Hospital, span from age 12? In other words, as soon as they have passed puberty, girls are having babies. Are we saying, therefore, that once children pass puberty, they are to be given condoms, since they are having sex at younger and younger ages? Is this the solution to the wider issues? What about parents who want to supervise their children's sexual development up to age 18? Will this supervisory right be taken from the parents?

Recent neurological studies on the teenage brain, using magnetic resonance imaging, show that teenagers are controlled by the emotional centre of the brain while the prefrontal lobe that controls mature decisions is largely developed by age 25. The PBS-produced 'Frontline Report' of January 2002 indicated the following: "Despite all the new scientific research, 'Inside the Teenage Brain' suggests that there is a consensus among experts that the most beneficial thing for teenagers is good relationships with their parents." (PBS 2002)

## Deflowered by DONS

In light of the outcome of this research, how do we reconcile the push for children to be independent of their parents when making sexual decisions when, in fact, what they need is a closer relationship?

Another implied issue is whether the men with whom these girls are having sex are all teenagers like themselves. We know, in Jamaica, that in a number of communities ruled by dons, the young nubile girls are expected to be deflowered by these men. Will distributing condoms in schools deal with this? Has research been done to find out who the fathers of these children are who are born to girls under 16 years of age?

The law needs to have teeth to deal with these older men who are illegally having sex with young girls. Where is the drive to get our fathers to be responsible for bringing life on this earth? Although the law has been proposed for fathers' names to be on birth certificates, it has not yet been passed. Will distributing condoms in school, address the cultural mores that say that if young girls do not have a baby in their teen years, they are 'mules'? Will it affect the established practice of incest, which is so embedded in our culture? Will it heal the widespread emotional scars inflicted on our young women by early sexual initiation, many times forced?

## Campaign for FAMILY Planning

Will providing condoms in schools change the culture of 'a nuh nutten,[15] a little sex', when jurors fail to convict rapists in the courts or judges simply give them a slap on the wrist? We need to push an aggressive campaign for strong family life practices, not purely a strong campaign for condoms in school. We need to address the destructive cultural practices that promote irresponsible sexual behaviour, focusing on not only the young girls who are mothers but also the young men who are fathers, and older men who father children with young girls. We need to challenge the widespread incestuous sexual practices in our nation. We must change the belief that sex 'a nuh nutten'. It clearly is something if, in response to so many young mothers in one grade level in a school, our NFPB is raising an alarm and pushing for condoms in schools as a solution.

Jamaica is faced with harsh economic realities, a high level of crime, widespread family dysfunction, and a high level of mentally disturbed persons. There is an underlined problem that we are not dealing with. We need to look to that and stop the Band-Aid treatment.
**Published April 7, 2013**

# IS JAMAICA READY FOR VISION 2030?

Vison 2030 (Planning Institute of Jamaica 2010) has set out ambitious goals for Jamaica to achieve. The theme of this vision is 'Jamaica, the place of choice to live, work, raise families, and do business'. This plan outlines that in order to transform our country, many of us will need to change how we think and view life. It states that, "As a society, we will need to have a shared set of core values which will allow us to achieve Vision 2030 Jamaica." What are these core values? Honesty and truthfulness, respect, trust, forgiveness and tolerance, discipline, punctuality, responsibility, love, compassion, cooperation, national pride, good work ethic. (Values and Attitudes Secretariat, 2002) There are four goals that are outlined, the first being that Jamaicans are empowered to achieve their fullest potential. The four national outcomes of this goal are to have: 1. A healthy and stable population. 2. World-class education and training. 3. Effective social protection. 4. Authentic and transformational culture.

**Possible Outcomes**

There are various strategies that have been outlined to achieve these outcomes. The outcome of world-class education and training will be attained by, among other actions, ensuring that every child has access to proper early-childhood development, improving the learning environment at primary and secondary levels, and ensuring that graduates from the secondary level are ready to go on to higher education, training or work.

The Vision 2030 document admits that there are challenges to achieving its goals. These challenges include poor performance of learners, especially boys, at different levels of the education system; the need for better-trained education personnel; inadequate parenting; insufficient attention to positive values such as truthfulness and respect for each other and inadequate support for the vulnerable in the society.

The document also gives the reason why the year 2030 was chosen. It states, "By 2030, our children will be adults, and many of us would have joined the ranks of senior citizens. The world is changing around us, and we want to position our country to use these changes to our advantage." It also states, "Our investments in education, particularly early childhood development, will lead to better performance of our children at all levels, and better-qualified and more productive citizens in the future."

All these are laudable goals. The problem is that we are 17 years away from this target and I am faced with a grim reality in many primary schools. The majority of our primary-level children, who will be

23-25 years of age by 2030, are beginning their educational journey with grave deficits and disadvantages.

Many students enter school with cognitive deficiencies because of the lack of stimulation to develop their visual and motor coordination, among other things. Many are living in homes where there is no one who cares to spend time with them to help them develop these basic skills. They are left on their own, and some are constantly abused. This abuse, in addition to poor nutrition, affects the development of their brains.

Furthermore, many parents lack the positive values and morals that are needed to teach their children so that they can develop to be socially well-adjusted, compassionate, contributing members of the society. Therefore, the efforts to assist with the basic needs of the students, such as clothing, food and shelter, have to be given greater focus. Many students are not registered on Programme of Advancement Through Health and Education (PATH) because they lack birth certificates. Increased efforts must be made to ensure that we have our children registered at birth. Anecdotal evidence, however, indicates that although births are now being registered at the bedside in the hospitals, some of the women who do not want to name the fathers slip away from the hospital before the process can be done. This problem needs to be addressed.

**Social Development**

In addition, there are the issues related to the social development of the children who are being reared in homes and communities where adults and parents behave in direct opposition to the core values that have been outlined in Vision 2030. They are violent in dealing with conflict; they steal and are dishonest as a matter of course; they retaliate at the slightest provocation; they show little respect in dealing with others, especially the elderly, children and women; and they want handouts or quick, ready cash, even if it is obtained unlawfully. Children brought up in such environments are adversely affected psychologically. Therefore, they go to school and in the event of conflict their first response is to retaliate violently. If they do not have what they need, they find it no challenge to steal what belongs to someone else. They find it difficult to concentrate for any extended period of time. They find it hard to understand simple instructions.

In the primary schools, many times the classes are large, especially at the lower grades, and teachers are not allocated assistants. Imagine conducting a class with 30-40 children who are behaving the way I have described above? How is effective teaching to take place in this environment? There are so many schools that need special educators who are trained to assess students who are suspected of having learning challenges. Unfortunately, this is not a policy that the Ministry of Education has. Many schools have to depend on MICO Care Centre to do the assessments. This institution, in turn, is overwhelmed by the number of applications for such assessments and there is a long waiting list. Furthermore, guidance counsellors and principals will tell you that even when they make arrangements for MICO Care to come to their schools to do these assessments, many parents are not willing to send the children to be evaluated, whether because they lack the minimum fee or because they are in denial that their child might have a learning difficulty.

This is simply one area that glaringly highlights the difficulties in our attaining Vision 2030. We are a resilient people, but we have become mired in accepting a culture that many times highlights the negative aspects of our nation so that it becomes the norm. Vulgarity, 'badmanism', violence, paternal and maternal irresponsibility must become matters at which we become outraged and seek to change, so that our children can be given a fighting chance to indeed be "socially aware and responsible, conscious of what is good for society, committed to a sustainable lifestyle, spiritually conscious and mature, tolerant of diversity, rooted in his/her Jamaican 'smaddiness'"[16] (Task Force on Educational Reform Final Report).(ibid)

**Published May 12, 2013**

# THE LANGUAGE OF INSTRUCTION: JAMAICAN CREOLE OR STANDARD JAMAICAN ENGLISH?

By 2030 every child in our country will have the best learning environment. Each person will leave school at the secondary level with at least five (Caribbean Secondary Education Certificate) CSEC subjects including English, mathematics and a foreign language (grades 1-3), and will have a working skill. (Vision 2030) (ibid)

Amid the present debate and controversy concerning the outcomes of our education system and the benefits accrued to teachers, is a concern that I have. This concern relates to the decreasing thrust to teach Standard Jamaican English (SJE) at our tertiary institutions and rather to focus on the use of Jamaican Creole (JC) in the classrooms. It is generally acknowledged that the world is a global village. The possibility of travel to various nations has exceeded the expectations of Jamaicans even 20 years ago. Jamaicans are working in diverse corners of the earth. This means that we need to prepare our people to live and work in different nations. Added to this is the reality that we do not have the ability, in our present economic situation, to provide jobs for many students who are leaving our tertiary institutions. One of the essential ways to prepare our students to compete globally is to teach them a language that is the acknowledged language of business and commerce globally, which is English.

Our training institutions acknowledge that our children coming into school at the early childhood stage and primary level will use JC as their first language. Our teachers, however, need to be trained and become adept at helping our children to acquire SJE as a second language. This should become the language of instruction. In this way, our students will become immersed in the language.

## Immersion Situation

This is particularly important since there are many homes where children are not exposed to hearing SJE spoken. The schools, therefore, need to provide an immersion situation, along with formal instruction, to make the successful acquisition of English possible. Even though this approach should be self-evident, it is not happening in many of our schools. Why? Many of our universities and teacher-training institutions are not ensuring that all teachers of English are trained to teach English as a second language. Therefore, as I go into some classrooms, I hear many teachers conversing with the students in JC freely. On one occasion, a young English teacher at the secondary level was asked why she did not use SJE. Her response was because the students said they would not understand her.

In other situations, I have heard primary-school children correcting teachers' use of JC instead of SJE. It seems, then, that we can no longer depend on the teacher to be a standard of how SJE should be spoken. If homes, therefore, do not provide the environment within which SJE is learnt; if the media cannot be depended on to present models of how to use the language; and if schools cannot provide examples of how the language is to be used, how do we expect our children to be prepared linguistically to compete in the global market?

How do we expect to meet the target of Vision 2030? How do we expect the CSEC English results to improve?

This comment from the Report on Candidates' Work in the CSEC Examination May/June 2012 English A General Proficiency Examination sheds light on some of the issues:

"It is clear that large numbers of students across the Caribbean have not mastered the use of Standard English. There continues to be interference from dialects and patois used throughout the region; to these have been added the slangs originating from dancehall music and the North American ghettos and the abbreviations familiar to users of the messaging media of modern technology. For students who almost abhor reading, some methods must be found to encourage correct use of the language."

We know that only 46 per cent of the students that sat the English A Paper in 2012 achieved a passing grade. We need to be reminded that this is not the percentage of the complete cohort of grade 11. This percentage is based on those who were permitted to sit the examinations. There are many students who were not allowed to sit the examinations by schools that screen students. This means that the percentage pass rate for the grade 11 cohort is much lower.

## Assist with English

If we are serious about preparing our students to compete in the global marketplace, we must begin to address this problem of no other country being able to communicate with our students who have the facility to only speak Jamaican Creole upon leaving secondary school. Our universities need to not only invest money in the study of Jamaican Creole but also assist such students in being competent in speaking and writing English.

One sad testament to how off track we are in this matter is reflected in the state of what used to be a useful and dynamic Writing Centre at the University of the West Indies, Mona. This centre catered to UWI students who needed help in preparing their assignments for submission to their teachers. Postgraduate students would be paid a stipend to dedicate some time to meeting with undergraduates to guide them with their essay writing. I thought this was a well-needed service since complaints were often heard about the insufficient competence of university students in writing Standard Jamaican English. Yet this centre was closed because of lack of financial funding.

As a nation, we need to take another look at the currently popular approach to teaching our students in Jamaican Creole without assisting them to transition from our native language to SJE. There are too many teachers in the classrooms who have adopted the view that it is not necessary for them to be competent in SJE and, therefore, do not make an effort to set a standard for the children in speaking the language. In addition, our teacher-training institutions need to place a strong emphasis on the teachers of English, learning the rules of JC, and how to help our students move from using our native language to understanding the rules of SJE and becoming adept at using it. Furthermore, we need to become a nation where reading is encouraged. That discussion, however, is for another time.

I recommend that all teachers, especially teachers at the primary and secondary levels, use Dr. Velma Pollard's book, From Jamaican Creole to Standard English: A Handbook for Teachers, (Pollard 2003) as a guide in teaching students to understand the rules of JC and how to move to understanding and using SJE. It will help our students to improve their outcomes in the CSEC English A examination.

**Published June 2, 2013**

# A STORY OF GRIT: TWO GIRLS AND A BLIND MOTHER

A ngela Lee Duckworth, at the University of Pennsylvania, studies intangible concepts such as self-control and grit to determine how they might predict both academic and professional success.

Lee Duckworth, in TED talks Education, made a presentation on 'The Key to Success? Grit'. (Duckworth 2013)

She related that when she was teaching, she realized IQ was not the only difference between her best and worst students. Some with the highest IQs were not doing so well, and some with lower IQs were doing better. She realized that there was the need to understand about learning from a motivational and psychological perspective. Duckworth needed to research whether doing well in school and life depended on much more than the ability to learn easily and quickly. She then left teaching to pursue postgraduate work, studying which students and professionals would be successful, and why, in varying contexts.

This is what Duckworth found the predictor of success turned out to be – grit. "Grit is passion and perseverance for very long-term goals. Grit is having stamina, sticking with your future, day in, day out, for years and working hard to make that a future a reality. Grit is living life like it is a marathon, not a sprint."

She found that this matters especially for children at risk for dropping out. Talent, she says, does not make you gritty. The best idea she heard about building grit is called 'Growth Mindset'. This was from Dr. Carol Dweck of Stanford University. Growth Mindset says that the ability to learn is not fixed, that it can change with your effort. Dr. Dweck has shown that when students read and learn about the brain and how it changes and grows in response to challenge, they are more likely to persevere when they fail because they do not believe that failure is a permanent condition.

**This Is A Story Of Grit.**

Kelliciann McLean, 17, and her sister, Niomi Brown, 18, are both members of the Tarrant High School lower sixth form. Their mother is Pauline Smith, who has six children with six different fathers. The girls are the youngest of the six children. Pauline, their mother, became blind while she was attending Norman Manley High School. She did not finish high school. She became pregnant at age 16 with her first child.

Pauline's mother did not take her vision impairment seriously, and later when Pauline was properly diagnosed, she was deemed to have retinitis pigmentosa. She was blind.

The sisters have different experiences with their fathers. Niomi's father is the most supportive, while Kelliciann describes her father as a 'sperm donor'. Life has not been easy for these girls; however, they do not complain about the only life that they have known. They speak with pride about their mother, who, in spite of her disability, has been their guide and has taught them to have grit. Both girls attended St Jude's Primary School where Niomi was ahead of Kelliciann, as she was the older sibling. Their mother had no money for them to do the Grade Six Achievement Test (GSAT) extra lessons when so many other of their classmates where being prepared in this way for GSAT. It was financially difficult for them.

**Selling Sweets At School**

Niomi danced for St Jude's Primary and so was given the privilege of selling sweets at the school so that she could pay for her graduation expenses. Kelliciann says she believes her mother still owes money to the school for her graduation fees.

The sisters sat GSAT a year after each other. Niomi passed for Tarrant High, and said that this was a disappointment to her mother, who had wanted her to be placed in a more traditional high. After all, she said, throughout primary school, she had always been in the top classes. When she came to Tarrant and performed well, some teachers wondered why she was at Tarrant. Because of her good academic performance in grade seven, she was awarded a scholarship from M&M Company to cover her expenses for school for grade eight. Niomi continues to dance for the school. Both girls are proud of the fact that they sat Caribbean Examination Council (CXC) home management: Niomi in grade 10, and Kelliciann in grade nine. Both scored grade two.

How did they manage at school financially? The girls were registered with the Programme for Advancement Through Health and Education (PATH) and were able to get lunch. Their mother, a member of the Jamaica Society for the Blind and the Council for Persons with Disability, went to the council to get assistance to pay the girls' fees. The council provided assistance for a percentage of the school fees. Otherwise, the girls came to school without money. They also had to face the mockery that some students made of their mother's blindness when she came to school. It was hurtful for them when the children made fun of their mother. This did not stop them from feeling proud of their mother's strong spirit. They were seeing grit in action.

The sisters both sat the Caribbean Secondary Examination Certificate (CSEC) examinations: Niomi passed six subjects and Kelliciann passed seven. Both girls had already passed home management before. In addition, Kelliciann, who wants to be a dietician or a pastry chef, passed the National Council on Technical and Vocational Education and Training (NCTVET) food preparation Level 1 examination and is now awaiting her results for Level 2. Both girls tell the story of Ronald Townsend, a blind man who worked with the Ministry of Labour but who is now retired. He would help them with money for stationery and other things and paid their fees to sit home management at CXC.

## Wants To Become A Teacher

Niomi's ambition is to attend The Mico Teachers' College and become a teacher. She realized, however, that she could not afford the fees. This made her discouraged. While preparing to do her CSEC examinations, Niomi discovered in February of that year that she was pregnant. She hid this from everyone. Mom, on knowing, was disappointed because she had great hopes for Niomi and Kelliciann. She wanted better for them. She wanted them to break the pattern in the family. The girls pointed out that one of their older sisters, who gives some support to Kelliciann, is an exotic dancer. The girls are aware of the dangers of that lifestyle and are clear that they will not be following that path. Their sister, however, encourages them to make better of themselves.

Then there is a brother who is in prison, the result of following a life of crime. He also encourages them to do better for themselves. He wants them to do well so they can help their mother. Niomi's mother encouraged her not to give up preparing for her examinations when she found out she was pregnant. She found it difficult to complete her School Based Assessments (SBA) but she persevered and was able to do so. The school did not know that she was pregnant, apart from her home economics teachers, whom she describes as being her second mothers. They figured it out but said nothing about it until later on.

Niomi did her examinations, participated in graduation and even danced while being pregnant. She had her baby in November 2012. At the start of this school year (2013-2014), her teachers encouraged her to apply for sixth form and complete her education. They encouraged her not to give up. They were helping her to develop grit.

Being in sixth form is a challenge for both sisters, as PATH, a welfare programme, does not provide lunches for students at that level. Their mother has applied for a school grant from PATH to help with the school fees. She is still awaiting the response to her application. The girls say there are many days when they do not eat. One of their brothers sometimes gives their mother some money. Niomi says that she is disappointed to be at the same grade level as Kelliciann. She, however, uses her son, Jaden, as a motivation to excel in her studies so that she can provide a better future for him.

**Great Influence**

This is what Niomi says:

"Our mother has been our greatest influence. She shared her experience with us and told us to learn from her mistakes. She always said that she wished she had the mother that we had. When I fell down, she taught me not to give up, not to make a baby stop me from pursuing my dreams.

"The elders in the community encourage me. When they ask about my academics, they encourage me to go back to school and achieve what I want. We have a sense of belonging in our community. We grew up there, so everyone knows us."

"Seeing the path my sister is taking, we want to change that pattern."

These girls have grit. In spite of living in a house provided by Food for the Poor, having no indoor bathroom, having no father to support them, having no food to eat for many days, having a mother who is blind, having no money to provide for their needs, one getting pregnant, they are overcoming to achieve their goals.

This is a story of hope and encouragement. It is a story of grit.

**Published October 13, 2013**

# VALUES, STANDARDS AND EDUCATION

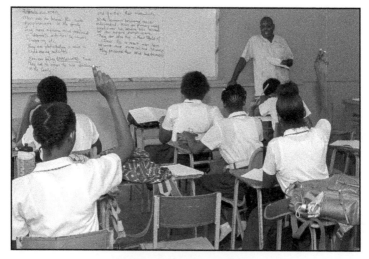

**Social Studies Class**

In a report in The Gleaner of October 9, 2011, Jamaica was ranked among the worst in the Americas for poverty, unemployment and inequality. Jamaica was said to have the second-highest unemployment rate at roughly 11.8 per cent and the country also had the fourth-highest poverty rate at 43.1 per cent compared with

23 regional neighbours. (The Sunday Gleaner 2011) We are now in 2013 and there are news reports of companies frequently laying off their employees. It seems that the level of poverty is increasing. This is extremely worrying for those of us who work in the field of education.

It seems that across Jamaica where school populations are derived from the inner-city and deprived rural communities, the social challenges facing students are greater. The need for deans of discipline in schools over the last decade reflects a growing problem with indiscipline among students. Attendant with this reality are the various deficiencies that many of our students from a lower socio-economic background display. This is not only because of poverty, but because in situations of poverty, many parents are not giving the children the cognitive stimulation, nutritional provision and social skills that they need to do well in school. When you combine this with the lack of resources in many of our schools, we have an equation that results in less than success.

**Challenges**

As a nation, then, we need to face the realities that we are dealing with in the schools. The situation at the Half-Way Tree Transport Centre, the raunchy Maggotty High video, the behaviour of children right across this island are increasing cause for concern. It is a reflection of a society that has lost its way – economically, socially, morally and spiritually. Many in the society quickly condemn teachers. Yet many of these persons would not last one day in the classroom of an inner-city school. The challenges that teachers face daily are tremendous. The schools should have a cadre of not merely one or two guidance counsellors and a dean of discipline but social workers and psychologists to deal with the myriad emotional, psychological, social and spiritual problems those students present with every day. In addition, because of the cognitive problems these students have developed, each school needs to have a supply of special educators who can help these children fill the gaps and be re-engaged in the mainstream.

There are too many children who are angry or withdrawn because of the physical, psychological and emotional abuse that they face in their homes. There are too many children without the support from nurturing adults to guide them in their development to adulthood. There are too many: absentee mothers and fathers; grannies, who are ill, raising children; young siblings bringing up younger siblings; girls who live with men for support; children who live on their own. These children, who have lost their childhood too quickly, come to school emotionally scarred and act out their anger and disillusionment in confrontations in the classroom. They are combative and see the slightest infringement of their space as a reason to fight. They are resistant to authority. They do not know how to socially adapt to situations that require them to practice self-control and take instructions from persons in authority. They are not being parented.

**Socialisation**

The school, then, is our children's only hope of proper socialization. How do we do this with inadequate resources? How do we do this with teachers who are also emotionally wounded and need help, who, therefore, find it difficult to handle these challenging students in front of them? So many young teachers are themselves products of a society that has lost its way. I am glad that the Government has implemented the Programme for Advancement Through Health and Education (PATH) which provides lunches for the students. For many students, it is the only meal they have for the day. There are some schools that have more than 80 per cent of their children on the programme. Principals find that children are eager to come to school on the days when they know they will receive their PATH lunches. There are some schools that have implemented breakfast programmes, but many others cannot afford it. It is well-known that children's brains need good nutrition in order for them to learn. How do we expect to improve our educational output with so many children lacking adequate nutrition?

I am thankful that the Parenting Commission has been put in place. We need to look at having mandated parenting sessions for pregnant mothers who come to the prenatal clinics. The fathers should be required to participate in these sessions, too. The Parenting Commission should partner with churches in the communities to develop community-based parenting programmes. There are so many children having children who do not know what to do. There has been such a breakdown in values and standards in our

137

society that many parents do not have such values to pass on to their children. These parents need to be taught.

The parenting handbook written by Faith Linton and Barry Davidson, Answers to Questions Parents Ask, is a good resource to be used in such a programme. (Davidson and Linton 2012) I need to ask what is being done with the many mothers who are having babies before age 16? Who are the baby fathers? Why are they not being arrested and mandated to take responsibility for their actions?

We need to change our culture to one where education is seen as important and beneficial. Unfortunately, there are too many parents who do not have this view. For this change to happen, we must engage the media and the entertainment industry. We must partner with the private sector to develop visual and audio promotions of healthy parenting habits. We must show why education is important to us as a people.

This can be done, since it is this same media and entertainment industry that has promoted a culture that decries family, marriage and good order. Unfortunately, there has been a promotion of 'man fi dead if im diss yuh'[17], 'gyal in a bungle',[18] and a general disregard for law and order. If we are to change our culture from where slackness reigns to self-control, respect for law and order and where good sense prevails, we have to work together as a society to make this happen. We have little choice. The path we are currently on – the road that we have carved out for our children – leads to inevitable destruction.

**Published November 24, 2013**

# MAKING SCHOOL A SAFE PLACE

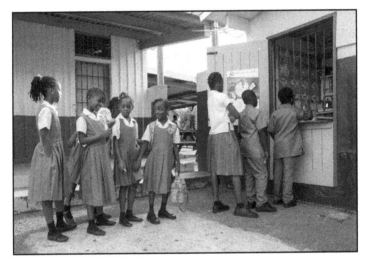

**Students at Lunch**

This article is a follow-up to what I had written and was published in last Sunday Gleaner of November 24, 2013, 'Values, standards and education'. We cannot deny the reality of our Jamaican classrooms that see many students coming in with many deficiencies because of their economic and social backgrounds. Yet we cannot give up. We must find solutions that can help.

In our society, where dysfunctional parenting seems to be the norm, it is the school that has found itself with the responsibility of giving our students hope. Studies have shown the importance of the first five years of a child's life in developing their brain. According to Eric Jensen, in Teaching with Poverty in Mind: "Chronic exposure to poverty causes the brain to physically change in a detrimental manner." (Jensen 2009)This statement, if it stands by itself, will support the hopelessness some teachers feel in the classroom. However, it does not end there. Jensen maintains, based on research, that: "Because the brain is designed to adapt to experience, it can also change for the better. In other words, poor children can experience emotional, social, and academic success."

What then are some of the ways we can give our students positive experiences that will help them to succeed against the odds? I will put forward one main point in this article: That we should make school a safe place – physically, emotionally, mentally and spiritually. In order to make our schools safe physically, we must have perimeter fencing enclosing the schools. This is to ensure that we keep persons within the school grounds safe from those in the community who would want access to the school to do our students and staff harm or to damage the compound. Many students come from areas where they do not feel physically safe. It is important that they feel that school is a bastion of safety from the physical threats they face in their communities. We must ensure that students do not take weapons to school. This means that where we have reason to believe that this is happening, students must be searched for weapons using the Ministry of Education's Security and

Safety Guidelines which give the principal and designate permission to search where a threat is perceived.

## Use Metal Detectors

Furthermore, where it is deemed necessary, we need to employ the use of metal detectors to deter those whose thinking have not yet been transformed to a peaceful mindset. In addition, where it can be obtained, security cameras need to be put into our schools to give close supervision to students' behaviour.

School should also be safe emotionally. The classroom needs to be a safe place for the students, so they can learn by expressing themselves, make mistakes, and learn from said mistakes.

Nan Henderson, in an article, 'Havens of resilience', in Educational Leadership, September 2013, (Henderson 2013) speaks to the importance of schools helping students to develop resilience in order to overcome the challenges of poverty and abuse. She articulates that "a student's resilience is fostered when his or her internal and environmental protective factors are strengthened". Henderson points out: "All caring adults in a school are potential agents of protective factors. First, they can notice and reinforce students' internal protective factors – such as easy temperament, good reasoning skills, self-esteem, and internal locus of control."

In addition, teachers can help students to recognize and grow these traits by "engaging students in conversations and other interactions".

141

Second, educators can "create classroom and school cultures that are infused with environmental protective factors (such as) regular structures, routines, civility, and caring". We know, as Ms. Henderson acknowledges, that teachers cannot "eradicate poverty, remove neighbourhood gangs, stop cultural violence, heal parental addictions, or prevent the myriad of other types of stress, risk, and trauma that many students face daily". Yet, many times, it is a teacher who makes a difference in the lives of children and makes school a safe place for them. Children who are brought up feeling emotionally safe at home are not the ones who challenge us in the classrooms. It is those students who come from places where they experience neglect and abuse that usually present defiant and disrespectful behaviour. These students are the ones who need us to reach out to them.

Allison Warshof and Nancy Rappaport, in 'Staying connected with troubled students' (Warshof and Nancy 2013) advise teachers to build relationships with such students. Building relationships begins with "empathetic listening – the ability to tune in to what the other person is actually saying, instead of what we want to hear". They continue by explaining that "empathetic listening can be developed and practiced. It starts with being attuned – being aware of the changing needs, feelings, and states of another person, and shifting our response accordingly. Teachers who are empathetic listeners consider the students' point of view without neglecting their own."

## Attitude Important

One attitude that is tremendously important to Jamaicans, more so to students, is respect. Teachers have to be careful to not only demand respect of our students, but to give them respect. One of the most significant ways that we as teachers can do this is to listen to our students. Let them give their point of view.

Many students complain that teachers do not listen to them; they do not allow them to give their side of the story. To gain our students' confidence and respect, we must listen to their stories. Even when we are upset with them, listen to their stories. This is one way in which we can make our classes a safe place emotionally for our students.

How do we make school a safe place for our students, mentally? As teachers, we need to carefully diagnose our students' strengths and weaknesses and deliberately design strategies to address these. It means we must differentiate our teaching. This is a lot of work, but it will be more beneficial in the long run to both the teacher and the student. Do not expect a student who is weak in a skill that is needed to deal with a topic to perform optimally. When such a student is called upon to respond, and feels hopeless, the student becomes embarrassed in front of his or her peers. Embarrassment leads to a feeling of being disrespected, the student then begins to act out to maintain power and status. If we use groupings and individual coaching to assist our students, we can help them to develop at a pace that will encourage them and infuse them with a sense of hope that they can learn.

I can hear the teachers complaining about class sizes and the lack of space for grouping, but our creativity will assist us in finding ways to make it happen. In addition, it is important that we inform our students of what we will be teaching ahead of time, set standards for them, and give them ready feedback. The more predictable our classrooms are, the safer the students will feel. They will make an effort to learn and not be embarrassed because they make mistakes, since it is through trying they realize that they can learn.

Last, we must not forget that we must provide spiritual guidance for our students. We still have the freedom to express our faith and beliefs and to encourage our students to develop their own. Ensure that students participate in meaningful devotions at school. Infuse your classes with the teaching of soft skills and life lessons that will help students to develop. Remember, many of our defiant and challenging students are hurting and confused and need to be shown a clear path and to be guided in making wise choices. Many homes are not providing this; it is up to us, as teachers, to do so.

This is by no means the only solution to our problems of defiance, violence and disrespect in the Jamaican classroom, but it is a beginning. In spite of our lack of resources, difficult personal issues, and sense of inadequacy, let us, teachers, rethink the way we approach our students. Let us understand the powerful impact that the power of one can have on even one student. Let us start the ripple effect.

**Published December 8, 2013**

# FIRST POINT OF SOCIALISATION?

' P rison schools – Gov't study says poor-performing institutions produce most inmates'. This article published in The Gleaner on Wednesday, January 22, 2014 has elicited outcry from many quarters, with some agreeing with the conclusion drawn from the study.

The article indicates the following:

"The research unearthed evidence to suggest that the names of some schools were more likely to be featured than others. There is also overwhelming evidence to infer, with a high degree of confidence, that at least seven out of 10 inmates in our adult prisons have had some association with a non-traditional high school," the study said. (Luton 2014)

I need us to examine the language the writer uses. The evidence "to suggest"; evidence to "infer"; "have had some association" with a "non-traditional high school". This language tells us that while it is possible to derive correlation between criminals and non-traditional high schools, the schools cannot be determined to be the cause of these men becoming criminals. It is important, then, to recognize that although we look to our schools to mitigate the effects of the failure of our homes and communities to instill positive values and attitudes in our children, the focus must first be on the core areas.

Professor Anthony Harriott, in a report titled 'Crime Trends in the Caribbean and Responses' (Harriott 2002), outlined the causes of crime in the Caribbean to be the following:

"The motivating forces (unemployment, immiseration, relative deprivation, etc; the opportunities (the affluence that is one side of the coin of inequality, etc.); poor guardianship (weak and ineffective law enforcement, weak informal control by disorganised communities and families, etc.); the means and facilitators (firearms, corruption)."

Therefore, when The Gleaner places a bold headline on the front page of its newspaper that declares 'Prison schools', it is being misleading, sensational and less than honest. This headline gives the impression that the schools are the cause of these young men being in prison. I was heartened to see two principals of schools that were named responding to this claim.

We know in Jamaica that some of our young men who end up being incarcerated attended some non-traditional schools, yet we need to recognise that they did not come to the schools with minds that were blank slates. By age 12-13 when our students enter high school, their minds have already been stamped by their experiences coming from their homes and communities. Many non-traditional schools are assigned students who are underperforming academically. The few sent who are performing above average are many times transferred by their parents to other schools. A good number of the students entering non-traditional high schools come in with cognitive deficiencies because of lack of appropriate early stimulation and exposure to life experiences which would help them develop academically.

Conversely, many of these students would have been exposed to emotional, physical and sexual abuse. Some have been exposed to violence in their homes and communities. A number of children have seen persons killed or have had their loved ones murdered. In addition, because of the high poverty level in our nation, many come from homes where they are not given enough to eat and so they come to school hungry. Furthermore, the issue of the neglect of many of our children is becoming widespread. Increasingly, we are seeing not only fathers abandoning their children; more and more mothers are doing so. These children are passed from one relative to another, and once they begin to display any negative behaviour, they are thrown out of the house. These are our Jamaican children. These are the children who come into our schools.

Therefore, when our boys and young men come into school angry and hungry from the homes and communities in which they reside, how are the schools to change their reality? When we try to instill correct values and attitudes in them and they return to homes and communities where the opposite is practiced, how are the schools to reverse the pattern of negative behaviour?

## Non-Traditional Schools Neglected

Are the government-owned non-traditional schools given the resources of enough guidance counsellors, social workers, psychologists to tackle the issues presented by these students? Is there sufficient provision of nutritional feeding programmes to address this stark reality that we face? Are these schools given special educators on its establishment and specialist rooms such as reading labs to address the learning problems with which many of these students enter high school? Are the schools given enough physical, human and teaching resources so that they can assess students' learning, and, recognizing the deficiencies, retain students for more than a year at a grade level if necessary until they have achieved a satisfactory learning standard? Wouldn't that be preferable to sending them through each grade to exit the system barely literate and numerate? Are the schools adequately provided with the financial and physical resources to create an environment conducive to learning where students can feel that their school is a place that is safe and attractive?

These are some of the issues that need to be addressed. But even if solutions are found to the problem of resources in the schools, it will still be the home that is the first point of socialization. Many persons have repeatedly pointed out that we, as a nation, must begin to emphasize the importance of home and family in order to provide a stable nurturing environment for our children. I have written about this over the years. We have spoken about this, but not enough has been done – by either the Government or the private sector – to change the breakdown of the family structure in Jamaica.

Poverty needs to be alleviated, but there are many poor persons who have strong families and do not produce criminals. Let us begin to focus on rebuilding family in Jamaica.

**Published February 2, 2014**

# OF WHAT VALUE THESE EXCESSIVE SUBJECTS?

The article 'Thwaites emphasizes quality over quantity of subjects' in The Gleaner of March 6, 2014 (Francis 2014) highlights some issues in education that I have been concerned about for some time. One of these is the trend in Caribbean secondary schools to have their students sitting more and more subjects at the CXC/CSEC level, seemingly in an attempt to outdo other schools or students to achieve the coveted award of being top student in the Caribbean. This trend needs to be examined. I believe that, first of all, as the examining and awarding body, the CXC needs to determine what's the optimum number of subjects students should excel in to be named top student in the Caribbean. The council should not seem to be responding to the competition where more and more subjects are being taken in order to gain the coveted award.

## Subjects Must Fit into Regular Hours

The number of subjects decided on should take into consideration the number of subjects that can be taught in a regular school's timetable of, on average, five teaching hours per day, for five days for the week. It should not be predicated upon subjects being studied outside of the regular school hours. This might be, but not in all cases, dependent upon parents who can afford to have their children do extra classes to cover these additional subjects. Again, this would be placing the privileged at an unfair advantage over students whose parents cannot afford such 'extras'.

Further to this is the issue of students who are so involved in pursuing only academic subjects, finding little time to be involved in co-curricular activities, whether in school or out of school. As Minister Thwaites pointed out: "What is the meaning of the quantum of subjects that so many have achieved .... Does this make for the rounded, multi-competent Jamaican person who we want, who the economy needs, and who the world craves their services?" Students need to be involved in more than the academics to be truly prepared to face the rigours of post-secondary education and the world of work. A student who is involved, for example, in a team sport learns the value of working with others, of cooperation, of playing for the team and not only for self. These are values that are now esteemed in a world that is moving from organizational structures that are less hierarchical and more flat and broad-based. To learn to work as a part of a team is essential in the education process.

**Performing Arts**

In addition, the field of the performing arts is still largely being developed in secondary schools as a co-curricular activity. Students need time to be able to hone their gift or skill in this area when the school's curriculum does not allow them to do these as subjects during the regular school day. We still seem to be bound by a sense that the fields of the arts, sciences, languages or business are the only areas that are acceptable in the curriculum of our secondary schools. This must change, but until then, we need to allow the extraordinary talent of our Jamaican youth to flourish in the fields of music, drama and dance by allowing those who wish to do so the chance to participate in these as co-curricular activities.

Of equal significance is the importance of students learning the value of sharing by being involved in community outreach projects. This takes time. Time that would be taken up by extra classes to pursue excessive number of subjects that might win the students an award but would not be preparing them as giving, caring citizens.

Dr. Didacus Jules, CXC registrar, made this point in the Caribbean Examiner, Vol. 8 #2, October 2010

'The Caribbean today needs an education system which is an effective vehicle of human empowerment and social transformation. To create this, we must first ask ourselves, 'What must education achieve in the contemporary Caribbean'?" (Jules, Re-thinking Education in the Caribbean 2010)

As a nation and region, we must apply ourselves to this question and put in place a system that will create a nation that will benefit us as a people. Therefore, CXC needs to look again at the criteria that are set for its awards in order to encourage the type of education at the secondary level that will best benefit us as a people and a region.

## Fix GSAT Placement System

I hope to see in the near future that the Ministry of Education will address the nature of the present system of students being allocated to secondary schools, namely, Grade Six Achievement Test (GSAT). It is unnecessary to be burdening our young students with subjects such as science and social studies to be tested at grade six in order to determine their readiness for high school. An extensive system of extra lessons has been developed to ready our students for this exam through rote learning and simply "swotting." The question is whether all this is necessary. Students arrive at high school stressed and burnt out from the pressure that they face preparing for this exam.

On the other hand, teachers in high school complain that the students are not taught to think critically in preparation to do GSAT math and so they have to be re taught when they enter high school. I believe students should be prepared to be competent in mathematics, English, and critical thinking in order to be ready for high school. Let us deliberately look at how we are engaging in the business of education and make the necessary policy changes that will benefit us as a nation and a region.

**Published March 9, 2014**

# MY YEAR AT TARRANT HIGH SCHOOL

**Tarrant High School**

I have spent a wonderful year as interim principal at Tarrant High School. I had been asked at the end of August 2013 to go to the school for a term until a new principal had been selected. That term became a year. What a fulfilling year it has been. I can only report on a few of the initiatives that were undertaken during the year.

The first matter to be addressed was lifting the low morale of the staff. The low morale had resulted in inconsistent attendance and lack of punctuality. Within the first term I observed marked improvement in both of these areas. The number of teachers who were out sick dropped dramatically. Most teachers consistently attended school and would come to school early. We instituted academic staff devotions with me, one morning of the week while the prefects would take charge of the class devotions. During this time, I would lead the teachers in spiritually based reflections on matters such as forgiveness, dealing with anger and handling difficult students. We would pray together. In addition, updates were given as to what was happening in the school and the teachers would be able to share information with their colleagues. The feedback from the teachers is that this has helped considerably to bring reconciliation among some members of staff and to build cohesiveness among the teachers.

**Enough Furniture**

Most of Jamaica came to realize that the Tarrant High school plant needed immediate attention from an article published in The Gleaner about the matter. In spite of mixed reactions, the school was able to receive furniture to place in the classrooms. As a result, the students are no longer fighting over desks and chairs because there is now enough for each student. Teachers no longer have to stand throughout their classes because we received desks and chairs for them to use. I thank Mr. Dave Myrie, principal of Kingston College; Mrs. Carol Alexander, principal of Merl Grove High School; Mrs.

Margaret Campbell of St George's College, Medical Associates of Jamaica, and the Bank of Nova Scotia for assisting us with furniture for the school. I thank the Ministry of Education (MOE) that was able to send us furniture at the beginning of the second term to complete the provision of the school's needs in this area. We are thankful that at the beginning of the school year 2014-2015, we do not have to request furniture since the teacher and students of welding have repaired damaged chairs and desks. We, therefore, have enough for the new school year.

A matter of great concern was the state of the buildings. Maintenance had not been carried out on the plant for quite a few years. We begged paint to begin painting in the Christmas holidays and this is still ongoing. I wish to express thanks to The Paint Shop and Hi-Pro for assisting with donations of paint for this purpose. Sherwin-Williams is now on board to provide us with donations of more paint. The Ministry of Education responded to the urgent need to fix our leaking roofs that were damp and covered with mould. When it rained, students huddled in a corner to try to find a dry area to stay. Teachers taught in classrooms covered in water. Thankfully, the Ministry of Education addressed this matter and the students are now in waterproof rooms.

I was concerned about the poor system of communication from the administration to the school as there was no intercom system in place. I lobbied the board of management to provide an intercom system. With the assistance of the Florida Chapter of the Tarrant Alumni, the board was able to put an intercom in place. What a difference this made to the students' sense of pride in their school and for them to be able to hear announcements each day. I used the intercom to play quiet worship music for half an hour before school began, read them verses from Proverbs both at the beginning and at the end of school, and to pray for the school and the community at the end of the school day. This has had a positive impact on the ethos of both the school and the community. The National Anthem is played at the start of school with all members of the Tarrant High School family standing at attention. The students' comment was that their school "tun big school".[19]

The level of indiscipline among the students of Tarrant High School was a matter of grave concern. It seemed that it was the culture for students to fight as a way to deal with conflicts. The board of management worked with the administration to deal with a number of boys, who were constantly involved in fights. They participated in counselling and interventions without any resulting positive change. Eventually, the boys were expelled from the school and the students began to experience a greater sense of safety. There was a marked decrease in the number of reported fights to the dean of discipline's office after the first term.

**Best Class Competition**

To further motivate students to improve their behaviour, punctuality and keeping the compound clean, I introduced a Best Class Competition in January 2014. Each month, the dean of discipline would calculate from the points earned in these areas which class was the Best Class for each grade level. That class would be given a pizza lunch party, which was sponsored by a friend of Tarrant High School. I thank Virginia Dare for donating the drink mix for the pizza parties. The students began to eagerly engage in the competition and there was further improvement in the general behaviour of the students. The guidance counsellors and the dean of discipline continue to work tirelessly in the re-socialization of the students.

An area that needed to be addressed before I left Tarrant was the curriculum. The school was using the outmoded Junior Secondary school curriculum to which was added the MOE's high school's curriculum requirements, resulting in students of upper school doing 10 to 12 subjects in some instances, while maintaining a poor academic performance. The board agreed for the senior staff to go on a curriculum retreat in the Easter. As a result, the school's curriculum has been brought in line to what is the accepted practice in high schools in Jamaica, while maintaining a focus on the technical/vocational areas. Thanks to all the teachers who came on board and worked to bring about this needed change.

Tarrant High School is moving in an upward direction. Under the guidance of the new principal, Mrs Collette Feurtado-Pryce, formerly vice-principal at Jamaica College, I am confident that Tarrant will become a school of choice for our Jamaican students.

**Published September 7, 2014**

# ACHIEVING VISION 2030 – PIPE DREAM?

Jamaica's Vision 2030 (Planning Institute of Jamaica 2012) projects that by 2030, every child in our country will have the best learning environment. Each student will leave school at the secondary level with at least five CXC subjects including English, mathematics and a foreign language (grades 1-3), and will have a working skill. I believe that although we have made some progress in our education system, we have not yet dealt with some issues that mitigate against our achieving these goals by 2030.

As I move around the country and interact with others in the education system, I hear common themes running throughout. First, many parents do not see or understand the paramount importance that education is to the development of their children. Second, in spite of the Programme of Advancement Through Health and Education (PATH) initiative that the Government has implemented, many parents do not have the money to pay the bus fares for their children to go to school, nor do they have the money to give them to purchase lunch. Third, there are schools that are underpopulated and overstaffed that need to be rationalized.

As a nation, we must find a way to help our people to understand the importance of education to their children's development and success. In order for them to believe this promise, they must see how this can be possible. With the high level of unemployment among the youth who have graduated from high school and even university, there is little to give truth to this claim. Our youth are living in a country where crime and corruption are rampant.

**Static Political System**

The two-party system in Jamaica has failed to move the nation forward. There is a sense of hopelessness that pervades most people, apart from the upper class. The report from the National Youth Values and Attitudes Survey – 2014 (Spaulding 2015) reported that almost a half of the interviewees stated that they would be willing to surrender their citizenship to live in another country, many

citing better opportunities. Many persons were upset at Damion Crawford for saying that he has no problem with Jamaicans migrating to work elsewhere as they can send back remittances and bring back expertise to help the country. (J. Johnson 2015) My question is, are we aware of how widespread unemployment is in this country? Are we aware of how many university graduates are at home not working and being hounded by the Students' Loan Bureau? We need to put our ears to the ground and hear what is going on before we begin to condemn Damion Crawford. If there is a better solution to the unemployment plague, come forward with it. We need to give our young people hope.

I believe that if parents saw that there would be employment for their children after they sacrificed for them to go to school, they would make a greater effort to find the means to send them. But alas, to them, the future looks bleak. May I point out to those who are now saying that we should value education for education sake that this "holds no water" when you are hungry and you cannot pay your bills. As Minister Pickersgill would say, that would just be the view of the "articulate minority".

Another area that needs attention is the placement of students in rural schools that are far from their homes. This practice undermines the intention that our students are to have access to education. Placing a child of a poor rural farmer or an unemployed parent in a school that requires that he or she pays bus fare of $1,000 per week is indicating that the Ministry of Education (MOE) does not understand the realities that are facing poor Jamaicans. If a survey of attendance patterns were done in schools, the MOE will find that many students are not going to school regularly because their parents cannot find the bus fare to give to their children. The irony is that sometimes students are placed at schools that are some 40 miles away, while they pass schools that are 10 miles away from home. This system needs to be fixed. How can children learn if they are not going to school regularly? How can the Government set a goal that each child should leave school with five CXC subjects, then establishes practices to undermine the achievement of that goal?

**Insufficient Resources**

The inclusion of families on PATH does not mean that children go to school each day and are given lunch each day. The amount of money given to the schools to provide lunches for the students on PATH does not cover them having lunch each day. In some schools, students are given lunches twice per week, and in some where it is subsidized, they are given lunches three times per week. For other students, this is their only meal for the day. This programme has helped to a limited extent, but the money given is insufficient.

On the other hand, I want to commend Minister Thwaites for seeking to set some things right in a system that has been fossilized for years. The matter of schools that are operating with a handful of students and almost as many teachers, yet having these students illiterate or innumerate, has been stifling the system. Teachers who do not volunteer to relocate to other schools are allowed to remain in these dying institutions because the minister of education is bound by the Jamaica Teachers' Association (JTA) from rationalizing the system to make sure that both teachers and students are relocated to other schools. Therefore, the move to integrate Charlie Smith High with Trench Town High is a breath of fresh air. It gives hope that at last the JTA will cooperate with the Ministry of Education to ensure that schools that are functioning are viable academically and that the use of the plant is being maximized. No longer should the Government of Jamaica be paying out money to run schools that are under producing academically and under-utilized because of a severe decrease in student population.

**Published February 8, 2015**

# Part 2

# THE STATE OF THE FAMILY
# IN JAMAICA

# MAKE FATHERS' REGISTRATION MANDATORY

A law needs to be passed in Jamaica that the names of the fathers of all children should be placed on birth certificates at birth. Doesn't it take both mother and father to produce a child? Why then is it only the mother's name that is on 80 per cent of the birth certificates of children born in this country? Isn't this practice assisting, reinforcing, enabling the culture of irresponsible and reckless production of children in this nation? Haven't we realized that as a people, we must find ways to hold our parents accountable for irresponsible parenting? I contend that this is one of the first ways to do this.

Now, many in this country might not agree with me. First, there are the men who find the present legal situation convenient and suitable to their irresponsible sexual lifestyle. These are the men who are married and have their legally acknowledged families. They then have other children outside of the marriage with women who are their mistresses or with whom they are having a 'fling'. They produce these children, many times unintentionally, and make it clear that the children are not to have their names because they do not want to be identified as the fathers. They do not want the public to know that they have been unfaithful to their wives or worse yet, that they were not careful while they were having their sexual pleasures. Some of these men support the women and children financially while some cut them off completely and want nothing to do with them.

**Lack of Responsibility**

Second in this group are the men who are not married and they have no intention of having any woman tie them down in a committed relationship. They want to have their freedom and they want to have free sex, consequently, they roam from available woman to woman and they move on. They do not care whether a child is produced after they have had their fill of pleasure. They want no responsibility. They do not want any mothers or children laying claim to their person or money.

Third in this group are the women who, having reached a certain age where they fear that they are no longer marketable in the marriage market, decide that they are going to find a man, have sex with him so that they can have a child. It does not matter that the man has no commitment to them; what is important is to produce a child. Therefore, the man is carefully chosen, for his looks, for his intellect or his pedigree. The man sometimes might be cooperative in this venture, or if not, then he is seduced. One way or another, these women get their desired sperm.

The fourth group are the women who sleep with different men at the same time. They use their bodies as a means of financial support. Thereby, they get money from each of the men with whom they sleep. When a baby is born, she says to each of the men that she needs each of them to support the child. The men do not know this strategy. Each man thinks he is the father. It is quite suitable for her not to have the father named on the birth certificate.

**Common Theme**

There is a common theme that runs through the reasons for all these persons not wanting fathers named on a child's birth certificate. It is selfishness. No one in this group thinks about the impact that such an act will have on the child. A child is named, a mother is named, why isn't the other part of the triangle named – the father?

I have seen the impact of such selfishness and irresponsibility on some of our children. I have heard stories of how psychologically devastating this practice is on the consciousness of many children. They are the ones whose fathers already have their families. Even if they know their father and he supports them, they are not publicly acknowledged. They have their mother's surname or some other name which does not reflect their paternity. They want more than anything to be seen with their fathers publicly, to be proudly acknowledged by the father as he does his other children. These children suffer from a sense of rejection. They become angry and bitter. They sometimes get back at their parents by not performing well in school. They might act up at school so that their parents will have to be called in. All of this behaviour is in an attempt to get attention, even if negative, because the public attention which they should get from their father is not possible. Who is suffering in this situation? The children.

Then there are those who ask their mothers, "Mommy, who is my daddy?" and the mother refuses to tell them. They never see their fathers; they have no relationship with them. These children flounder trying to establish their identity, wanting to understand themselves. They feel like a part of them is missing; they want to understand their DNA, but are unable to. They feel lost. Many become angry and bitter and we hear of some of them ending up in 'The Fatherless Crew'. Even last week, we heard of 15-year-old young men burning and killing in our country. Probably, they are the by-products of this selfish way of producing children.

## Children Suffering

The suffering from this practice of selfishness, of not naming fathers and of not legally acknowledging the paternity of our children, is producing havoc and untold suffering on our country. It is doing damage to us. This practice is producing angry, bitter people who act out their anger in criminality. It is doing damage to the souls and consciousness of our children, even when they become adults. These persons live with a sense of rejection and a need for acceptance from the one person who influenced their genes apart from their mother, yet who refuses to give them what is rightfully theirs: their identity. They long to be acknowledged by their fathers.

I pray that change will take place in this nation, that even as the prophet Malachi says, that the "hearts of the fathers will be turned to the children, and the hearts of the children to their fathers".

**Published July 6, 2008**

# OUR BROKEN CHILDREN

A s a nation, we have reached a depth of degradation that we have never known before. We are sacrificing our children on the altar of violence, vengeance, self-enjoyment, greed, coarseness, crass materialism, slackness and rank immorality.

Men rape babies and innocent, virgin children because they believe it will cure their sexual diseases. Children are murdered to get back at parents who have crossed the drug dealer and the gunman. Mothers send their daughters out to prostitute themselves to get money. A 13-year-old girl-child is allowed by her parents to enter a modelling competition and the organizers select her as the winner to parade her young body in a skimpy bikini before crowds of ogling, lecherous old men. Mothers choose their live-in lovers over their children's safety and well-being. Women bring men into their homes to have sex with them to get money, with their children observing this immoral behaviour. Women move from man to man without regard for the impact this loose sexual behaviour is having on their children. Sometimes, these lovers sexually abuse the daughters of their women, who turn a blind eye to all that is going on because they want the money or the sex that the men give.

**Obscenities**

Our children are taken to lewd dancehall sessions where women gyrate their bodies to sexually stimulate men around them. Parents have children sitting with them watching X-rated movies. Parents use obscenities to their children as frequently as they drink water. When told that these things are wrong and not good for the children, the response you will get is, "A nuh nutten."[20] The practices that promote good child-rearing are seen as old-fashioned and are scorned by many adults in our society. These are habits such as teaching our children good manners, to have a sense of responsibility, and the value of working hard to reach a goal. We need to teach our children to respect other persons, to obey the law, and to love God.

I am tired of hearing that it is because of poverty that things are the way they are. When I was going to school, many children came from poor backgrounds, as I did, but their mothers had pride in themselves. They would make sure that their children went to school with what they needed, at great sacrifice to themselves. They would ensure that their children were going to Sabbath school or Sunday school even if they themselves were not going to church. The children would, in this way, get a spiritual foundation. This is no longer the practice.

**No Time to Rear Children in The Right Way**

Our children are being nurtured on a diet of North American loose, immoral cable-television shows. They are being stuffed with the local dancehall slackness, which is being forced into their systems by the music videos, the sound systems booming on many corners and the dancehall sessions, which increase yearly in our society. Many parents are busy enjoying this lifestyle and have no time or inclination to rear their children in the right way.

A symbol of our condition is how macabre our behaviour at funerals has now become. It is no longer a place of mourning, but a place to profile and show off the latest dancehall hairstyle and fashion. There is little reverence (that's another old-fashioned word) in some of these funerals. Outside of the church, alcoholic beverages flow unchecked, as do the obscenities. We have broken down the standards and taboos in our society and there are no protections left to preserve a civil society. The walls are down and we are now subject to the whims of dons and the drug kingpins. What type of society do we expect to have when our children are being nurtured in this mire of base crassness?

**Children Are Insecure**

We have a society where our children are insecure, not having the knowledge that their parents are there guiding and leading them in the right way. We have teenagers who lack a sense of who they are because their mothers are with so many men that they wonder who their father is. We have young people without spiritual guidance who, in times of stress, inflict wounds on themselves to relieve pain instead of turning to prayer. We have young men without father figures who join gangs to have a sense of belonging and identity. We have young men who put on a posture of coarseness and aggressiveness and spout violence because the role models that they have are the DJs and the dons. We have young girls who think the way to get by in life is to 'wine'[21] and gyrate and do the daggering dance in order to be accepted and to be popular. Added to this is the stimulus provided by the Internet and the exposure that they get by putting their behaviour in cyberspace. There is little sense of what is private and what should be public. Everything is posted on Facebook for the entire world to see, including sex acts, lewd and vulgar behaviour, and unacceptable acts. After all, it is well known in Jamaica that popular media personalities have done this. These are the role models for our children. How can we expect them to do any better? After all, children live what they learn.

We need to heed what God said to the Jews in Jeremiah 6 vs 16: "Stand at the crossroads and look; ask for the ancient paths, ask where the good way is, and walk in it, and you will find rest for your souls." ((NIV) Holy Bible 1984)

**Published October 5, 2008**

# STRONG FAMILIES, STRONG NATION (1)

**Young Jamaican Family**

I am indebted to Sian Williams and Janet Brown for allowing me the use of their Literature Review on Caribbean Child-rearing Practices, an unpublished working paper, for the information used in this article. (Williams and Brown 2006) It highlights some characteristics of child-rearing in Jamaica, that we need to address as a society. Studies on families in poor suburban Jamaica show that although children experience a rich social life and authoritarian discipline, there is little conscious encouragement of play or verbal interaction that they receive from adults. There is a lack of set routines for children, such as bedtime.

The impact of poverty on space in the family yard or home is noted. Adequate space is not available for children to develop identity and social skills. In addition, few children have parents who read to them. There is limited play or reading material in the home and insufficient educational toys such as puzzles and playing blocks. There is a lack of supervision of the children at home where parents are absent or leave early for work. Therefore, the children are often late to school or play truant in these situations.

**Widespread Poverty**

Since the extent of poverty in Jamaica is so widespread, one asks the question, "What can we expect from mothers who are themselves ignorant of what is taught in schools?" If the level of education of our parents is below the level where they can assist their children with school work then the education system needs to be designed to address that reality. We, therefore, need to look at establishing homework times at school as a part of our curriculum. The Government would need to pay teachers enough to facilitate this.

The review finds that the effect of poverty on child-rearing is enduring. It has an impact on the children's development and behaviour, the learning environment and social exposure. Poverty among children is linked to early motherhood, which in turn has a damaging effect on children. The evidence is that the earlier the first pregnancy the greater the risk for the child.

Of particular interest are the findings that show that – children do get a great deal of affection up to about age five but there is little family time spent together such as meal times and this in turn affects verbal interaction and language development. Even when adults are present there is no effort made to get the children to talk to them; and there is limited attempt to praise children and give them positive guidance or direction; instead, the practice is to react to children's misbehaviour with threats and anger.

This description rings true, since I observe that for many teenage mothers the babies are like dolls to play with until they begin to talk back to them, then the frustration is played out in anger and abuse. The child is no longer fun and now becomes a burden to the young mother. The father is usually not a part of the scene.

These beliefs and attitudes influence child-rearing – children are highly valued by many in the society and they should obey their parents, but little value is given for play as being good for children's development; parents depend more on child-rearing practices and beliefs that have been handed down from previous generations than on the advice and guidance of experts.

**Socialisation**

The research recognized the importance for child development of a safe, healthy, caring and stimulating home environment, basic learning resource, and an adult caregiver or someone who is ready to read to the child each day and eventually to listen to the child read to him or her.

The review also looked at the role of fathers in the socialization of their children. In a study done in the Jamaican urban setting it was noted that roughly one-half of fathers live with families, fathers in visiting unions spend about four hours each week with their children and half of the fathers never took their children on an outing. From this and other reports, what emerged was a desperate cry for fathers to get involved in the care and support of their children. The report further shows that the basic expectation of a father is to provide financially and also to be a protector. When a man fails to provide financially he usually sees himself as a failure and absents himself from the family situation. The man does not value the role of assisting in the home as much as being able to provide financially. The woman also tends not to allow the man access to the family if he is not able to provide economically. This practice is damaging to a child's psyche.

**Destabilisers**

The review notes that 'outside' children appear to be more psychologically vulnerable than 'inside' children. Men tend to have children early in their lives to prove their manhood, but these children later tend to act as destabilizers to new families. This child is usually sacrificed by one or both parents to preserve their new families.

The report from a study done in 2001 showed that "80 per cent of children had only a single mother or father figure. The relationship between parents had proven to be quite unstable with more than 40 per cent of biological parents reporting no relationship with each other by the time their child was six years old."

How do we move from this reality to what Maureen Watson and Barry Davidson (Davidson and Watson 2006) describe as healthy families in this country of ours? Healthy families communicate and listen, affirm and support one another, teach respect for others, develop a sense of trust, have a sense of play and humour, exhibit a sense of shared responsibility, teach a sense of right and wrong, have a strong sense of family in which rituals and traditions abound, have a balance of interaction among members, have a shared religious core, respect the privacy of one another, value service to others, foster family table time and conversation, share leisure time and admit to and seek help with problems. To be a strong nation we must find ways to build strong families.

Stronger families, stronger nation.

**Published January 4, 2009**

# STRONG FAMILIES, STRONG NATION (2)

"At least five out of every six births in Jamaica are to unmarried mothers," proclaims the lead article written in The Sunday Gleaner of July 12, 2009. (The Sunday Gleaner 2009) Combine this statistic with the comment in that same article that "Jamaican women seem to have rejected marriage as the path to motherhood", and we realize quite starkly that the concept of the traditional family structure is becoming quite obsolete in Jamaica. This, of course, has implications for the rearing and development of our children.

As I have written before, the state of our nation is linked directly to the state of family life in our country. There is urgent need for our people to understand the necessity of a stable family environment for the nurturing and wholesome upbringing of our children. A stable family structure consists of mother, father and children. The Sunday Gleaner article pointed out that many women were opting to be single mothers. They have divorced parenting from marriage. They simply see men as sperm donors.

**Difficult to Commit**

We need to restore the value of marriage as the base of strong families to our country. Throwing out marriage because some do not work is the proverbial "throwing out the baby with the bath water". Marriage requires commitment; family requires commitment. Commitment is a concept that is becoming increasingly foreign to our society. We opt instead to "feel good." Whatever feels good, we think is the best thing to do. It does not matter if it means taking a life, abandoning a life, destroying the future of a child.

In a Time Magazine article of July 13, 2009, (Flanagan 2009) Caitlin Flanagan addresses these issues in an article entitled, "Why Marriage Matters." She points out that research shows that in the USA in May of this year, 39.7 per cent of mothers are now single women. This she finds to be astonishing. She asks the question, how much does this matter? Her response?

More than words can say. There is no other single force causing as much measurable hardship and human misery in this country as the collapse of marriage. It hurts children, it reduces mothers' financial security, and it has landed with particular devastation on those who can bear it least: the nation's underclass.

Flanagan continues to note that it is not only the poor who are separating parenthood from marriage, but also the well to do. The poor are doing it by uncoupling parenthood from marriage; and the financially secure are doing it by blasting apart their unions if the principals aren't having fun anymore. The growing tendency of the poor to have children before marriage – the vast majority of unmarried women having babies are undereducated and have low incomes – is a catastrophic approach to life.

Flanagan made it clear that the last three presidents of the USA, including Barack Obama, have put emphasis on the urgency of stabilizing family life in their country. The reason being that on every single significant outcome related to short-term well-being and long-term success, children from intact, two-parent families outperform those from single-parent households. Longevity, drug abuse, school performance and dropout rates, teen pregnancy, criminal behaviour and incarceration – if you can measure it, a sociologist has – and in all cases, the kids living with both parents, drastically outperform the others.

The results of the lack of a stable family life are the same in our nation. Many Jamaicans are enamoured by the Obamas. Why? I think one of the reasons is that here is a leading public family that seems to have it together. They are obviously still in love with each other. In Jamaica, few such images exist. Rumours are rife in our nation about the affaires of our public leaders. We need our leaders to set a strong moral example for our people. We need to see strong marriages exemplified for us. We should not be having our public leaders consorting with ladyloves who are pregnant and who are not their wives. This sets a poor example for our people. We need to see before us examples of commitment to marriage and to family.

Caitlin Flanagan continues her article by highlighting that according to research, there are only a few things that set back a child as much as not having a father in the home. She refers to the work of a Princeton sociologist who, as a single mother, assumed that her research would show that if children were born into a single parent household where there is no financial need, that this would offset the negative impact that being in such a family structure would have. To her surprise, she found that children who grew up in a household with one biological parent were worse off than those who grew up with both biological parents, whether they were educated or not.

What I found to be even more poignant is this point: "Children have a primal need to know who they are, to love and be loved by the two people whose physical union brought them here. To lose that connection, that sense of identity, is to experience a wound that no child-support check or fancy school can ever heal."

It means, therefore, that to choose to be a single parent would be a selfish act, which gratifies the nurturing instinct, but does not consider what is best for the child being brought into this world who needs both parents to give them the best chance for success.

The implication of these findings for our nation is that with every five out of six births being to unwed mothers, we are a nation of wounded souls giving birth to wounded souls. Is it any wonder that our students are performing dismally academically, or that our criminals are teenagers? We need to make a radical shift to realize that we must begin to promote good marriage and family life as the basis for a psychologically healthy nation.

**Published August 2, 2009**

# MARRIAGE, HOME, SOCIETY

**Jamaican Married Couple**

What is clear to me, after serving as principal of a secondary school for 11 years, is that students who come from stable home environments, with both mother and father involved in their development, generally do better mentally, academically, socially and emotionally than students who do not have this stable background. This is not to say there aren't students without these advantages who do not do well, but such students do not reflect the normal pattern.

The record of disciplinary infractions over the years reflects that many students who commit serious disciplinary breaches, usually with repeat offences, come from dysfunctional homes. Typically, there is no father figure, or if there is, the child does not see the father as being responsible. What is becoming common, however, is that there are more mothers who are having abusive relationships with their children. This abuse may be physical, verbal or emotional. The child ends up resenting the mother and takes out this anger at school on those around them. In addition, there are many girls who resent their mothers for allowing them to be sexually molested without doing anything about it, or for expecting them to deal with it because they, the mothers, had gone through sexual abuse themselves when they were young. This picture is becoming common, it is frightening. Various kinds of abuses, in turn, result in the children abusing themselves or becoming abusers of others.

**Dangerous Practice of Self-Abuse**

Self-abuse, or 'cutting', is being practiced by teenagers more and more in Jamaica. Children learn this practice from TV shows. They begin to self-abuse and others copy them. The students will tell you that when they take a sharp pen or razor and cut themselves, they find the pain easier to bear than the emotional pain they are experiencing – they feel a sense of release. This is a dangerous practice that parents need to watch out for. Parents with children who are displaying antisocial behaviour need to check their arms or thighs for scar marks which will indicate if they have been carrying out 'cutting'.

More girls than boys tend to get involved in this practice. This is a habit that, if not checked, may lead to the next level: suicide.

According to Dr. Donovan Thomas, (Thomas 2002) research shows that a common underlying factor which leads to teenagers attempting suicide is the breakdown of the relationship between child and mother. When children feel rejected or abandoned by their mother, the results are usually devastating. Equally important is the role of the father in the development of the child's sense of identity, yet we live in a nation where many children are without a relationship with their fathers. I commend the Government for proposing the implementation of the naming of fathers on birth certificates. That, in itself, will not solve the problem of the irresponsible behaviour of some fathers, but it is certainly going in the right direction. A stable family environment is essential to the wholesome development of the child. Research has shown this over and over, yet as a society, we have been downplaying the role of marriage as the basis of a stable home environment. Contrary to commonly held views, I have seen no other workable alternative that has evolved or that has been proposed to form the foundation of the family unit.

Marriage represents a legal commitment, and this is necessary to provide a safe place for the development of the family unit. Statistics show that the single mother oftentimes ends up being poorer than the married woman, and that her children end up being deprived of essential provisions because of this. This reality creates a vicious cycle, which we see being played out over and over again in this society.

In order for our society to be productive, we need to have secure home environments created to rear our children. The accepted norm of man a 'dawg' and has 'gyal in a bungle'[22] has to change. The practice of women moving from one baby father to another for financial gain has to change. It is these cultural norms which are producing children who are insecure, abused, destabilised and marginalised. These children grow up to be adults who have warped personalities, and who, in turn, become involved in irresponsible sexual behaviour which sometimes results in children being born who are then abused. This cycle needs to be broken if our society must become stable. Stable families produce stable societies.

**Greater intervention needed**

I think it is time that corporate entities that spend their funds on activities which are not promoting wholesome lifestyles should begin to look at funding programmes, which the Ministry of Health could produce, that educate our people on positive family life. There are a few being done, but there needs to be greater promotion of such programmes through the audio-visual media. Our people are generally not interested in reading and are keener to listen and watch. Therefore, we must communicate the vital message of responsible family life and values through these means. Our corporate bodies should realize that it makes good financial sense. A society developing individuals with positive values and attitudes will also be shaping better workers and thinkers. This means that the cadre of grounded, emotionally intelligent individuals from which to gain employees will widen.

There is a point which I need to interject. I listened to one of the presenters at the International Conference on Education for CARICOM Countries highlight that research shows that countries where civility is part of the cultural norm are the wealthiest nations. In Jamaica, we are experiencing a paucity of civility. The teaching of civility begins in a stable home environment where good manners will not only be taught, but also caught.

**Published June 5, 2011**

# FATHERS, FAMILY AND MARRIAGE

**A Caring Jamaican Father**

I n the month of June, we celebrate Father's Day. On this day, we seek to acknowledge the fathers who have been playing a positive and significant role in the lives of their children. We need to find ways to encourage our fathers to take their place in their families. Not only that, we need to encourage them to make a lifelong commitment to their partners in marriage. Even though marriage is not always successful, it is certainly better than having a family where getting up and opting out of the relationship is easily done. Even with this encouragement to promote marriage as the basis of the family in our nation, comes the highlighting of the fact that more and more, fathers are being marginalized in the lives of their children through the actions of the mothers.

In Jamaica, the pattern seems to be, in many cases, that women bear a child for one man, that relationship breaks up, and the man goes. The father might want to be involved in the life of his child, but many women will not allow him to if he is not supporting them financially. The father might not be able to support the child financially because he has no source of income. Some mothers do not allow fathers to have any connection with their children because of this. To these women, it does not matter that the father wants to be able to nurture and help to shape the character of his child. The mothers use this alienation of the fathers from their children as a form of punishment, or they do this out of spite.

There are other situations where the mother cannot afford to have the old baby father around, since she has a new baby father whom she cannot offend because he is now the one to whom she is looking for financial support. This scenario may be played out multiple times in one 'family'. This scenario sets the background for the tragedy that happens in the lives of many children who have been alienated from their fathers. It is the children who are the casualties of this war being played out between adults who are not prepared to act responsibly as parents. It is the children who are the casualties of the game that some mothers play with various men "to get a man to support dem".[23]

Dr. Herbert Gayle of Fathers Incorporated speaks to the importance of fathers in raising their children. "We at Fathers Incorporated are convinced that there is a critical third dimension to fathering: nurture. In order for a father to nurture, he has to be active in the lives of his children, and be informed about parenting, since it is mostly social or learnt .... At Fathers Incorporated, while we respect the immense value of mothers, we maintain that both parents are different and critical to a child's development. We believe that a father's nurture is different from a mother's nurture – a mother cannot father, and a father cannot mother." (P. H. Williams 2010)

## More Paternal Custody

Lanny Davidson, chairman of Fathers in Action, stated:

"Too many boys are growing up in female-headed households, and because they don't have a strong father figure, they often go astray." (The Gleaner 2009)

He states that fathers being away from children is "dangerous", adding that one way to stop this is to give custody of boys to their fathers in instances where both parents do not live together.

Households devoid of fathers have been blamed for churning out many of society's delinquents. In the United States, for example, 85 per cent of prison inmates had no fathers at home, according to data from the Texas Department of Corrections. Not only do our boys need their fathers, but so also do the girls.

Dr. Barry Davidson, executive director of Family Life Ministries, addresses the impact of fathering on girls.

"Somewhere between the age of three to six years, the girl goes through a very important stage of development in which she is closely drawn to her father. This phase influences her relationships with men later on. If there is no father in her life, some of the fullness of womanhood will be left out.

"He is her first link with the male world. The emotional strength built up with father will lay the foundation of her friendships with boys. During adolescence, girls who lost their fathers through death or divorce before the age of five years spent more time seeking male companions than in the learning of skills or in recreation," Davidson says.

He continues:

"Girls brought up without a father are less disciplined and have more conflicts. It is well known that girls brought up without a father, or with an unsatisfactory relationship with her father, will not be capable of a mature sexual relationship with a mate. They engage in early sex, the fulfilment they did not find in their fathers. The Bible makes it clear that the ideal pattern for every home and family is built on a godly father. The father ought to be the dominant figure in the family, and his role is vital," Davidson observes. (Bellanfante 2010)

A strong family culture is the basis of a strong society. Statistics show that countries with strong family culture are those that are prospering. Jamaica is known for having a high rate of children being born out of wedlock. This correlates with the breakdown that we are seeing in the family structure and the attendant sociological and economic problems that we are experiencing. We need to make intentional and determined efforts to promote positive family life and values in our nation. In addition, the Church needs to stop being apologetic about promoting marriage as the basis of family and begin an aggressive campaign to promote marriage in our society. After all, it is God who established the family structure and who set up marriage as the basis of that structure.

**Published July 3, 2011**

# THE PRIME MINISTER: A FAMILY MAN

Within the last five years, Jamaica has had three new prime ministers. With each inauguration comes a sense of expectancy and renewed hope among the Jamaican people that the new leader will make a difference in the political culture and the economics of this nation. Portia Simpson Miller had an appeal to the grass roots of the nation and she has the distinct historic position of being Jamaica's first female prime minister. Bruce Golding transitioned from the National Democratic Movement (NDM) to the Jamaica Labour Party and became the party leader. There was hope that with his ascension to the post of premiership, he would bring with him the fresh ideas that he had espoused in the NDM. Now Andrew Holness has succeeded Mr. Golding as the youngest prime minister in Jamaica's history. He is a post- Independence baby, coming to the post with energy, focus and passion. Jamaica hopes that he will be a new type of leader, the one that will be courageous to make bold decisions that will move us forward economically, politically and socially. There is one fresh image that the new prime minister has introduced to the steps of King's House and Jamaica that I will focus on. That is the image of a family man, a man who seems to love his wife and children.

This image of a prime minister, comfortably holding his wife's hands, being affectionate to her in public, showing care for his sons, is unusual in Jamaica. It is an image that we urgently need to see depicted before our eyes. It is an image I hope will prove to be more than a symbol but will also be shown to be real. It seems to be a matter of course to hear various anecdotes and rumours about our leaders' dalliances with women other than their wives. This culture of unfaithfulness has permeated every level of our society. This has resulted in general cynicism about marriage and family in our nation. This culture needs to change. The change needs to begin at the top level of our nation.

A strong family structure results in a strong nation. Persons raised in a stable family structure are likely to be productive citizens. They are usually taught good work ethics, to have ambition, to value life and to exhibit the common courtesies that create a civil society. Many of our people, especially the young, are lacking these values. The schools alone cannot effect the change in the churlish, boorish behaviour that has become a norm in our society. It must begin in the home.

Our people are excellent imitators. They have aped the bleaching of our entertainers, the fashion statement of the popular artistes and the destructive values of the dons and artistes. We need to change this. We, therefore, need a leader who can be an example to our fathers as a family man. We need a leader who is monogamous and who will love his wife. We need a leader who can counteract the negative male image that has been perpetrated by the popular dancehall and don culture.

**Opportunity to Be A Positive Role Model**

With all the hype surrounding the youth of the prime minister, he has the opportunity to create this alternative image. He has the opportunity to be a positive role model for the fathers and young men of our nation. During his inauguration speech, Mr. Holness made reference to the importance of fathers taking care of their children. He appealed for a change in how men looked after their families. I have not heard this included in any such speeches before, and I take this reference to the family to be an indication that our prime minister sees the family and its role in the nation as being of great importance. As the minister of education, he would have been exposed to the condition of our youth in Jamaica. Persons who work in the sector can attest to the fact that many of the students who are focused, well rounded and are academically successful are normally from strong families. Within these families they are supported emotionally, mentally, spiritually and physically. Even when there are financial challenges, once there are the other elements of support, these students are able to be successful.

For us, as a nation, to ignore the reality of the impact of the quality of family life on the development of our young people and indirectly on our workforce is to be hiding our heads in the proverbial sand. The fact that over the years schools have to be employing more and more staff to deal with the psychological trauma that many of our children face, not only in their communities but also in their homes, reflects the increasing disintegration of Jamaican family life. Therefore, the new, young, fresh prince of Jamaica House carries with him this responsibility: to enable the Jamaican people to see a leader who understands the value of a strong family and who will show them by example how such a family operates. I believe this aspect of the new prime minister's life should be highlighted. I hope it will not prove to be a sham, but a reality.

If we do not change the culture of irresponsible parenting that is so common, we are going to be in an even worse state than we are in presently. What the Zambian proverb says is quite true, 'The trees that are growing are tomorrow's forest. (Hodari 2009) What type of forest are we preparing? I congratulate the Honourable Andrew Holness on becoming Jamaica's ninth prime minister and I pray for him the courage of David, the wisdom of Solomon, and the spirit of Moses.

**Published November 6, 2011**

# MAYDAY IN MAY.
# CHILDREN IN DANGER

May is Child's Month. It's a good time to reflect on the condition of many of our children in Jamaica. Repeated reports in the newspapers, talk shows and other media highlight the pockets of good Samaritans around our nation who are reaching out to assist so many children who have little or no financial or emotional support. I am thankful for these caring individuals in our society. There are, however, too many of our children who are suffering abuse – physical, emotional, mental and sexual. The horror stories of sexual abuse being reported in the last month were unbelievable in some instances. The tragedies that have been made of some of our children's lives by fellow Jamaicans are heartbreaking.

These reports speak to a nation that needs to stop and assess our culture and address those aspects of our thinking that have led us to brutalize our children. There are some persons who see 'culture' as a sacrosanct construct. Once something is done in the name of 'culture', it's generally accepted. Our culture includes not only our art, music and literature, but it encompasses our philosophy, values, beliefs and principles. With this definition in mind, it must be clear to us that something is seriously wrong with aspects of our culture. One thing that's definitely wrong is the way we view our children. Many of our children are conceived unintentionally. This, is in spite of widespread birth-control campaigns. These children are mere by-products of sexual passion. They are not planned for, nor prepared for. Many of them are seen as 'accidents'.

These children are born into this world to a mother who sometimes is not even quite sure who the father is. Then there are mothers who are having affairs with married men and who don't want to say who the father of the child is. Furthermore, there are girls who have gotten pregnant by some 'big man' in the community or society and whose mothers have deliberately given them to these men – and there are other variations of this story. In addition, there are the girls who are made pregnant by their mother's boyfriend, stepfather, brother, uncle, cousin. Incest, as is being revealed, is widespread in Jamaica. The scenario changes, but the story remains the same. Many of our children are born into this world but are not wanted.

The most revolting situation is that of so many girls and babies being raped. Sometimes these girls get pregnant. The belief that a man will be cured of sexually transmitted infections if he has sex with a virgin has resulted in much abuse. This is a part of our culture that needs to change. The widespread practice among some men that if they are supporting a family and the little girl enters puberty that they must 'taste first', is disgusting, to say the least. The practice of the dons in communities mandating that a mother must send her pubescent daughter to him first is sickening. All of these practices are part of our culture. We must change our nation.

The UNICEF report on children in Jamaica states the following:

"Children are the most affected by the increasing violence in Jamaica, as it undermines their access to education, their learning abilities, and affects their psychological and social well-being. Sometimes physical and psychological violence is inflicted on children by those entrusted with their care, including parents, guardians and teachers. A 2004 survey among Jamaican parents of six-year-olds found that the majority (46.6 per cent) used physical assault as a disciplinary method with their children. This included spanking, beating, pinching, tying of hands, and shaking.

Migration of parents who seek more lucrative employment abroad has had a negative impact on Jamaican children. Some children are left in the care of strangers, neighbours or even older siblings who are still children. These so-called 'barrel children' are left without parental guidance or adult supervision, yet with access to significant material resources in the form of cash remittances and barrels of clothing and toys sent by absentee parents." (UNICEF 2011)

Many of our children do not know their fathers, or do not have a relationship with their fathers. It is heartening to know that the law now requires that the father's name be entered on a child's birth certificate. Notwithstanding this, there are so many children who are suffering from various psychological problems because of rejection by their fathers or abuse by their fathers. A large number of our children are not being properly socialised. All of this impacts the child, not only socially but also cognitively.

The child entering basic school who is having difficulties learning the alphabet has sometimes not learnt many basic skills through early stimulation. One belief that affects the cognitive development of small children is that of "unnu play too much".[24] Some persons do not realize that it is through play that children learn and develop their psychomotor skills. These children have difficulties coping in school. The Grade One Readiness Inventory will be reflecting the lack of readiness of many of our students for a long time unless we begin to change the destructive aspects of our culture.

This problem of lack of readiness for the various grade levels carries through into high school. We will, therefore, continue to have children going into high school who are illiterate and innumerate. Many of these children have not been taught how to relate to other persons in non-violent ways. They get angry easily and resort to the learnt behaviour of retaliation by violence. Therefore, we end up with a school population of students, many of whom have little love or support at home, some of whom have been poorly socialized, many who have learning challenges, and a great number with a hopeless view of themselves and their future.

I believe that as much as our environment is in trouble, our children and family life are in even greater trouble. An arm of the Government should be set up to address this immediate and terrible danger.

**Published May 6, 2012**

# GOD AND SEX

"Wow," Adam proclaimed, "She is bone of my bones and flesh of my flesh." ((NIV) Holy Bible 1984) Instant attraction, chemistry activated, orchestrated by no other than the Creator, Almighty God. He brought Eve to Adam and they became 'one flesh'. This first act of sexual intercourse was fashioned by God. Sex is His creation, His idea.

In His blueprint for mankind, the Bible, He outlines how His creatures are to use and protect this sacred, potent gift. Because of how powerful sex is, He ordained it to be enjoyed in an exclusive, private relationship between one man and one woman in marriage. (See Genesis 2:21-25 NIV) ((NIV) Holy Bible 1984)

Think about it. This gift can be compared to the rarest jewel that is kept under conditions conducive to its being well preserved and to ensure that its beauty is maintained. It is kept secure under high-level protection. In God's blueprint, marriage is that place of protection and security. It is the safest context for the gift of sex to be enjoyed between one man and one woman. Paul highlights this in the New Testament by saying that we are to:

"Honour marriage, and guard the sacredness of sexual intimacy between wife and husband. God draws a firm line against casual and illicit sex." (Hebrews 13:4 The Message Bible) (E. H. Petersen 2012)

Marriage provides a safe place to develop the intimacy that is important in God's blueprint for sex. Sexual passion is like a fire. It ignites life and energy, it gives warmth, but misused and uncontrolled, it becomes a destructive force.

**Enjoy Sexual Love**

There are some persons who would want us to believe that God does not want us to enjoy sex. They could not have read the erotic Songs of Solomon nor the verses describing married love in the book of Proverbs 5:15-20 (NKJV). (The Holy Bible New King James Version, NKJV n.d.)Verses 18-19 are clear that we are to enjoy sexual love:

"Let your fountain be blessed, and rejoice with the wife of your youth. As a loving deer and a graceful doe, let her breasts satisfy you at all times; and always be enraptured with her love."

God also created marriage as the foundation for the family and, in turn, the structure of family as the foundation for society. Marriage, then, was intended by God to be the bedrock on which society is built. His intention was to create a safe and wholesome environment for bringing children into the world and for rearing them to be wholesome individuals who would, in turn, contribute to a productive nation.

**Abusing Sex**

This plan became distorted when man began to misuse and abuse the gift of sex. All around us we see how the misuse of this gift has caused mankind limitless sorrow. On a personal level, persons suffer the effects through self-esteem issues, promiscuity, sexually transmitted infections, unwanted pregnancy, broken families, rejection, suicide, and personal setbacks. On a societal level, there are unwanted children, fatherless children, public-health crises, "gangsterism," crime and poverty. In Jamaica, the misuse of this powerful gift has brought dire consequences. In spite of the many positives in our country, there are many negatives that originate in the abuse of one of God's most awesome gifts to us. Many of our men have bought into the mindset, instilled in them by our slave masters, that in order to be a 'man', you need to have, not one woman with whom you have children and raise a family, but 'gyal in a bungle'[25].

So many of our men think they are being free by doing this, yet instead, they are simply following the call of their groins, perpetuating the stud mentality that was nurtured in a plantation system that was more concerned about slaves breeding like animals instead of nurturing a stable family. A stable family would have been a threat to the colonial masters. When are our men going to realize this?

**Responsibilities Not Considered**

Our women assist in this practice by allowing themselves to be used as a repository for men's seed. It seems that there is little thought given to the responsibilities that come with having sex. One major responsibility has to do with parenthood. Even in an age when birth-control methods are common, there are still many unwanted children who are born as products of sexual unions that were enjoyed simply for the moment, with little thought of the consequences. Passion without responsibility always produces dangerous results. So, we have 80 per cent of our children born out of wedlock. Many of these children have no relationship with their fathers. It is as if they were produced by simply a sperm donor. The problem is that their mothers, many times, cannot support them financially. Therefore, a cycle of poverty continues and develops in another generation.

Not only do we have perpetuating poverty, but we have children who have a sense of rejection from having no relationship with their fathers, or having fathers who are abusive. Furthermore, in Jamaica, we are hearing of more and more children being abandoned or abused by their mothers. Many of us who work with children know that, oftentimes, those who are brought up in homes with a caring and supportive mother and father usually succeed academically, are socially well adapted and move on to be productive citizens. The converse is also true – that many of the children who grow up to be maladaptive and who exhibit antisocial behaviours come from a background of neglect and abuse.

Therefore, when are we, as a society, going to realize that it is economic sense to promote a healthy family life by beginning to promote the use of sex the way God intended it? We should promote this lifestyle and reap the attendant benefits, instead of enabling a sexual culture that is anathema to good sense.

**Published July 1, 2012**

# PARENT TRAINING – THE WAY FORWARD

The Gleaner hosted a forum with the young men of Jamaica College who seemed to have been clear and forthright in their view that many parents are failing to give the guidance to children that will keep them from getting involved with drug abuse.

Once again, the cry echoes that our family structure in Jamaica needs strengthening. Our parenting skills need to be developed. This message must be carried far and wide in our nation. I am heartened to see the Government putting in place a support programme for parenting in our communities. I hope that the legislative process will not delay the implementation of this much-needed programme. The various social agencies in our nation need to work together to address the eroding family structure and poor parenting skills in our country.

The churches need to engage in parenting training programmes in the communities in which they exist. In many rural communities, the church is sometimes the centre of social activities. Therefore, this provides the opportunity for the church to deliberately create a strategy to help to stem the poor socialization of our children and the lack of early cognitive stimulation. There is the need to address the verbal, physical and emotional abuse that is administered in the name of discipline. This strategy must also seek to educate our people on the value of life and respect for the young. There must be education on the boundaries that need to exist regarding sexual conduct. Men need to see children as vulnerable and dependent on them for protection, and not as an opportunity to fulfil their lustful desires.

**Innocent Impressionables**

Women need to see their young as impressionable and innocent and requiring their care and protection, and not as expendable in their attempt to get money. Too many women feel that because they were abused when they were young, nothing is wrong with their daughters being molested by their baby-fathers, brothers, uncles or grandfathers. We need to change this culture. As a nation, we cannot continue with the view that because parents are failing, therefore, the schools must take up the slack in bringing up our children. This does not work. The children's attachment to their parents is greater than their attachment to their schools. Home is the first place of socialization. This is clearly seen when observing children as young as age seven and eight in classrooms whose behaviour is evidently reflecting what they have seen at home and in their communities. Little girls speak in loud, vulgar tones, imitating the quarrelsome voice that they grow up around. They are ready to fight for the slightest offence. Self-control is lacking. This is also seen in the little boys' behaviour. They seem unable to sit still for even 15 minutes to engage in a learning activity. They shove, push and strike each other as a matter of course. The teachers are unable to get on with the teaching activity because so much time is spent in trying to control the children's behaviour. Combine this with the apparent lack of early cognitive stimulation and you have children who are unable to recognize letters and sounds at the age-appropriate levels.

If this pattern continues, we will not see an improvement in the Grade 1 Level Readiness Inventory or in the Grade 4 Literacy and Numeracy Tests. The home and school must work together if we are to move forward as a nation. The need for the training of our parents is, therefore, an urgent necessity. For this training to have an impact, however, parents need to realize that there are certain attitudes that they must adopt to become effective in bringing up their children.

Parents need to recognize that until their children become self-sufficient, they must put the needs of their children first. Second, in order to bring up children well, we must first be disciplined in order to discipline them fairly and wisely. Third, we must realise that we are rearing our children not only for ourselves and for their future, but that we are building future generations.

**Many Advantages**

If as a nation we can get our parenting practices right, it will help to address a number of societal issues. First, there will be growth in the educational achievements of our students; second, our teachers will be dealing less with serious behavioural problems in the classrooms and instead a better learning environment will be created; third, we will have less crime in our country if we have more of our students being educated and staying in school; fourth, we will increase the cohort of skilled and educated workers for the job market; fifth, our economy will grow because we will attract more investors to our country that will have more skilled and disciplined workers and less crime.

This might seem simplistic to some, but if we look at what has been happening in our nation, we will realize that all of these outcomes are linked to each other. We need to turn our culture around. A strong family leads to a strong nation. Our parenting practices need to change. Adults need to begin to take responsibility for their young offspring and ensure that they bring them up to be adults who are contributing to their families and in turn their nation.

On another note; as a follow-up from last month's article, I am glad to see that the Ministry of Education has followed through with its promise to deal with the persons who were involved in including, without authorization, the controversial pro-homosexuality material in the HFLE curriculum guide. We need to continue to try to protect our children in an age when perversity, abuse and violence are being perpetrated against them.

**Published November 4, 2012**

# EARNING A PARENTING LICENCE

A Happy New Year to all Jamaica. I pray that 2013 will find us being more at peace with ourselves and with each other. We have many difficulties facing us as a nation, but we have overcome before and we will overcome again with the help of God. To begin this New Year, I wish to focus our attention on one of the most important ingredients to creating a stable society: the family. In order to have a stable family, we must have committed parents. As someone has said, we have to earn a license to drive a car but not to be a parent. So many persons become parents because they have sex, not because they want to, or are prepared to be parents. For example, there are so many young mothers who are lost as to how to bring up a child and need guidance. Drs. Barry Davidson and Faith Linton have written a book for Jamaicans that meet this need – Answers to Questions Parents Ask. (Davidson and Linton 2012)

So many books on parenting are set in a North American context, but this book is written for Jamaicans by Jamaicans. Professor Maureen Samms-Vaughan, in the foreword summarizes the focus of the book in the following words:

208

"Faith and Barry have ensured that all aspects of parenting are comprehensively addressed, from the pre-natal stage to the teenage years. Age-old parent-child challenges of time management are included, as well as modern concerns of sexuality and the use of electronic media. The authors tackle areas of parenting which challenge Jamaican cultural and religious beliefs, including single parenting and discipline. On the other hand, there are also references to the Bible, as a typical and integral aspect of the upbringing of Jamaican children." (Davidson and Linton 2012)

The authors in the introduction describe the context that this book addresses.

**Single parenting in the Caribbean**

Single parenting has, for generations, been a major feature of some Caribbean societies. Over the years, we have had good reason to applaud our single parents. The challenges of their lonely task have often served to bring out in them, inner resources of self-sacrifice, perseverance, energy and enterprise, by which they have blessed their children. At the same time, single parenting is not an ideal situation, as many of the most successful single parents would agree. Yet, there are several communities in the Caribbean where a stable, committed union of father and mother, is more the exception than the rule. In too many cases, childbearing and child-rearing are no longer seen as closely connected responsibilities, to be undertaken seriously by two mature parents working together. Young males and females are growing up with the aim and desire to produce a child, but with a rather limited understanding of what it takes to nurture and train up that child.

In spite of the fact that single parenting is the reality that faces us as a Caribbean region, it does not negate the fact that the child that is brought up by both mother and father in a stable home environment is given an advantage in his or her development. The book, while dealing with single parenting, therefore, holds up ideal of both mother and father parenting a child and the effect that this has on the child's development.

The authors address the importance of the father's role in the life of a child even before birth. They make the point that when a father participates in the birth process and is one of the first persons to hold his child, that he is likely to become more involved with the child from the start. They make note that studies have shown that the father's involvement with the child has a positive effect on the child's early development. This is always better for the child. This involvement of the father is important even before the child is born. A pregnant woman who has the full support of her partner is more likely to be contented and relaxed, as well as pleased and excited about the pregnancy with positive benefit to the child. A mother or a father who is absent during the first six years of the child's life loses the opportunity to be the main influence in the child's growth and development, not only physically, but emotionally, intellectually, morally and spiritually as well. They go on to show the impact that the relationship of both father and mother has on the development of the child's intellect and character.

**Real-Life Situations**

Throughout the book, the authors use real-life situations to illustrate the points that they seek to make. This makes reading easy and enjoyable. For example, in dealing with being a successful single parent, they use the story of Rita, who as a single mother, was successful because of the following:

1.  She was well-informed and understood what young children needed in order to develop properly.

2.  She made a serious effort to find persons who could be a father figure to her boys.

3.  She put trust and confidence in God and relied on Him to direct her, and to provide for and meet her personal needs.

The last point that I will make from the book deals with the importance of relationship and firmness. The importance of these two areas is summed up in the following way: Firmness without relationship leads to rebellion; Relationship plus firmness produces a positive response. Our children need to have these two factors included in how we raise them as parents. The tendency to overindulge or to be too harsh and abusive has led to a society with too many undisciplined, rebellious, angry and self-destructive youth.

This book can help us as a society to learn how to parent. Through reading it and following its guidelines, we can begin to improve our parenting practices as a people and, hopefully, be able to pass the test as parents and earn the parenting license. What an impact that would have on our society. We would see the benefits, socially, spiritually, intellectually and economically.

**Published January 6, 2013**

# FAMILY VALUES FALL-OFF, FUELLING SOCIAL ILLS

We are our choices. As a nation, we have had politicians who have chosen various paths for us to follow, some good, some bad. How did we arrive at this place as a nation? What were the choices made that have us now facing dire consequences? When did vulgarity and lewdness become the hallmark of our culture? Who allowed this to happen? Why is it that when Jamaicans are now travelling abroad we are viewed with suspicion? We are now embarrassed by the reputation we have gained.

Why is it that so many Jamaicans who have resided abroad and returned home to retire have to live in fear of their lives? When did it begin to happen that schools and churches are targets of gunmen, thieves and bandits? There are those who blame our condition on the poverty in the country. But are we the only nation that has high levels of poverty? Are the other nations where poverty is as pervasive as violent as ours? Is the level of uncared for, abandoned children the same? The Status of Children Act of 1976 dealt with the unfair impact on children who, through no fault of theirs, were prevented from benefiting from their father's estate. Although this act dealt with this unjust result, it created another problem. Because of this law, marriage was no longer seen as necessary and the result of that decision is glaring. Eighty per cent of our children are born out of wedlock. More children are being abandoned by not only fathers, but mothers as well. This is happening in spite of all the family planning advertisements.

**Re-Establish Cultural Mores**

We must recognize that we have lost our moorings as a people. We need to re-establish our cultural mores, based on our motto, anthem and pledge. These should frame our belief system and our choices. We are a people who believe in God, "Before God and all mankind ..." our pledge says. Our anthem establishes this fact, "Eternal Father, bless our land, guide us with Thy mighty Hand." If we were following God's plan for parenting, we would not be in the situation where we are now, with 80 per cent of our children being born outside of marriage. We would not be in a situation where lack of good parenting has resulted in myriad social problems in our country, the greatest of which is the level of violence that has now been accepted by many youths as the norm. I do not always agree with Daniel Thwaites' views but in his article, 'Nuh bastard nuh de again'[26], (Thwaites 2013) he expresses his concerns about the social impact of The Status of Children Act 1976. I agree with him in this instance. I see the effects first-hand in the schools of our nation. Here are his words:

"My question can be reframed as follows: Can the Jamaican State afford to be completely morally neutral regarding a distinction between wed and unwed mothers? What happens when people get the message that 'it nuh mek nuh difference'[27]? And what happens to a society when the young people do not feel any pressure whatsoever to impose traditional order on their personal lives? When it becomes the cultural norm and habit to expect little discipline in this most crucial and intimate aspect of our lives?

With all the imperfections of marriage, it does have significant advantages as a social institution geared towards protecting society's most vulnerable: children. It also is a stable, reasonably predictable avenue through which society reproduces itself, transmits values, trains future members, etc. It forces men to channel social and material resources to their offspring. When the family disintegrates or is weakened, it is the State that fills the breach. If the father scurries off and refuses to contribute to the child's upkeep, tax dollars must flow through PATH or other social-welfare mechanisms to upkeep and protect the child."

We need to reaffirm who we are as a people and base our decisions at policy, community and personal levels on values and mores framed from the motto, anthem and pledge. Think about the difference that would make to us as a people. We are our choices.

Using the motto, anthem and pledge would deal with the challenge of persons who are policymakers trying to determine the basis on which to make policies for our people. This would also ensure that we do not use our personal experiences to influence our decisions but rather have an objective standard by which we measure our choices. In an age where tolerance of all things seems to be the determining factor in policy-making in the nations of the West, using the motto, anthem and pledge as the standard would provide a framework within which Jamaica could act.

We cannot use the measure that the other nations are doing this or that so we must follow suit as the way to determine our policies. This is the thinking behind so many who conveniently turned blind eyes to the Nazi atrocities of the early 20th century. Many nations pursuing one path does not make that path correct.

In the past, we had some unsuccessful attempts at introducing a values and attitudes campaign. We need to revisit this goal.

**Published January 5, 2014**

# HEAL THE FAMILY AND SAVE THE NATION

**Three Generational Jamaican Family**

One of the observations that impressed me most on our principals' visit to China in May-June was the value that nation placed on family. I observed it in the way I saw families walking together on the streets during a holiday weekend. I saw couples holding hands. I saw it when we were reading a wall in a secondary school where students wrote ambitions they had before dying.

Many of them wanted to visit other countries or vacation sites with their parents. I realize that family is an important facet of the Chinese culture, economic structure and future. This emphasis on the family as the basis of society has helped to make China strong, even if there are other areas of concern. This nation, which has a history of thousands of years, has realized that the family structure must be nurtured and protected if China is to achieve its destiny.

Jamaica is 52 years old as an independent nation. Our history has been shaped by traumatic events such as colonization and slavery. These experiences have fractured the family structure our fore-parents had in Africa. The deliberate attempt by colonizers to destroy the cohesion of the African people who were brought to the West Indies as slaves by demolishing the family bonds has had seemingly irrevocable consequences on our understanding and practice of family life. In Jamaica, we tend to comment on how the Chinese stick with each other as families, while adding, "Black people dem jus bad mind and nuh look out for each other."[28] The juxtaposing of those two descriptions captures in a nutshell what will be the triumph of a nation and the downfall of another.

It is a matter of urgency that we, as Jamaicans, regain what the colonizers have stolen from us. We must place at the centre of every effort to attain the Vision 2030 the healing of the family. It is with this vision in mind that Dr Michael Coombs envisioned and brought to birth the National Association of the Family. Dr Coombs pointed out the following:

"Healthy families are now recognized as key to national development by the UN, WHO, and International Pro-Family Organisations such as the Doha International Family Institute (DIFI) and the World Congress of Families (WCF) through their positive impact on social, health and economic indicators."

To underscore this outlook, Dr Coombs cited a statement from Masud Hoghughi, consultant clinical psychologist – BMJ 1998.

"Parenting is probably the most important public health issue facing our society. It is the single largest variable implicated in child-hood illness and accidents; teenage pregnancy and substance misuse; truancy, school disruption, and underachievement; child abuse; unemployability; juvenile crime; and mental illness. These are serious in themselves, but are even more important as precursors of problems in adulthood and the next generation ...." (Coombs 2014)

As an educator, I am aware that the strength of our family structure in Jamaica is weakening even further. The increase in sexual abuse of our youth, the feeling that each man or woman is looking out for themselves, the fuelling of the sense that self-sacrifice is the way for fools and 'idiat',[29] the perception that what is important is a quick way to 'mek a money'[30], all combine to shape a culture that results in a 'dawg-eat-dawg'[31] nation.

**Healthier Nation**

This is the opposite of a nation that values family, that cares and protects its young, that insists on discipline and education for its growing youth, that requires respect to adults and from adults, and that honours and provides for the elderly. It is this type of nation Dr. Coombs envisages that the National Association of the Family (NAF) will work with other stakeholders, such as the National Parenting Support Commission, to realize.

The vision of the National Association for the Family is:

'A healthy and productive nation built on the pillars of healthy families in the context of Vision 2030'. Its mission is to facilitate transformation to a nation state where social well-being, health, values and attitudes emanate from a sustained foundation of healthy families. The mandate is to advocate for, and support, the development of national legislation and policies that protect and promote the family and all its elements through multi-stakeholder involvement, bearing in mind those already in existence; to advocate for, facilitate and support the strengthening/development and implementation of family life interventions statewide in collaboration with other stakeholders, building on what already exists. (Coombs 2014)

"One of the first initiatives of the organization is to address, along with other stakeholders, the issue of fatherlessness. The absence or non-involvement of fathers in their families has been established by research to have a devastating impact on the social fabric. From early childhood through adolescence to adulthood, children of fatherless homes are at a distinct disadvantage when compared to those parented by both mother and father. With 85 per cent of children born out of wedlock, 50 per cent born to unregistered fathers and more than 50 per cent of households headed by females here in Jamaica, the need to address fatherlessness is irrefutably an urgent one." (Coombs 2014)

To bring focus to this area of concern, the NAF organized marches by fathers in various towns on June 14, the day before

Father's Day. The march in Mandeville was highlighted on national television. This was a symbolic signal that our fathers are intending to take back the next generation by fulfilling their God-given roles and responsibilities. I salute the work of the NAF, the National Parenting Support Commission, and the I Believe Initiative for their focus on restoring the strength of the families to our Jamaican society. In this week where we celebrate our Emancipation and Independence as a nation, we must realize that unless we heal the family, we cannot heal our nation.

**Published August 3, 2014**

# THE IMPACT OF PARENTING ON VISION 2030

According to Vision 2030 Jamaica, our country will develop an education and training system that produces well-rounded and qualified individuals who will be empowered to learn for life, able to function as creative and productive individuals in all spheres of our society, and be competitive in a global context. Our literacy rate for those over 15 years old will exceed 98 per cent. (Planning Institute of Jamaica 2010)

For the goals stated above to be realized in 16 years, we have to address a number of issues that will require the full participation of the society and a multi-agency approach. The Vision 2030 document outlines some of the challenges we face as a nation to achieve this educational outcome. One that is most pressing is the involvement of our youth in crime. Vision 2030 indicates that "youth are the primary victims and perpetrators of crimes, particularly violent crimes. The large proportion of youth in our working-age population presents an opportunity for our country's development. It is, therefore, essential that we build the capacity of this group to ensure that it is integral to development planning and implementation". (Planning Institute of Jamaica 2010)

The other pressing challenge to attaining our education goal in 2030 is the matter of the lack of readiness of our children beginning primary-level education.

"Some parents are ill-equipped for their role as caregivers and to provide a supporting environment for the development of their children. As a result, many children attain primary-school age without the necessary preparation to access the primary-level curriculum; they underperform at higher levels of the school system."

— Vision 2030 (Planning Institute of Jamaica 2010)

I want to focus on the issue of parenting as an essential component to our students being at a place to enable Jamaica to achieve the education goals of Vision 2030. The two challenges referred to: youth involvement in violent crimes and our children's lack of readiness for primary education can be addressed if we begin to seriously implement strategies to deal with training our parents in child-rearing. Even though the Ministry of Education has been putting programmes such as Health and Family Life Education (HFLE) in the schools, it cannot do the work of character development without the support of parents. Teachers will tell you that when children are taught positive attitudes and behaviours at school, many go back into homes and communities where the opposite is practiced, which undermine any achievements made at school. Cultural practices from the home, in many cases, involve using violence to resolve any conflicts or any perceived disrespect. This mindset is counterproductive to academic achievement.

Teachers who work in schools where the majority of the students come from this background have to spend the majority of the class time dealing with discipline. In this situation, not much of the curriculum is taught. In schools where students come from homes where they are taught self-control and peaceful ways to deal with conflict, teaching can produce a greater level of academic achievement. Furthermore, students who are raised in homes with parents who help to stimulate them cognitively from an early age by reading to them, exposing them to books, and other forms of play designed to help them develop their psycho-motor skills come ready for learning at the early childhood level. Compare that to children from homes where they are exposed to violence to resolve conflicts, where they receive verbal and physical abuse for their actions, where they are condemned because "unnu play tu much",[32] where they never see a book nor have anyone read to them, and we realize that how our children are parented has a marked impact on how they achieve in school.

## Home and School

It is when we begin to see a synergy between home and school in terms of the values and standards taught that we will begin to observe more of our children coming to school ready to learn and display less antisocial behaviour. Positive parenting is key to attaining our educational goals for 2030.

We need to realize that many young people who are now parents have had no positive role models from whom to learn. Many such parent the way that they were brought up – involving a lot of verbal and physical abuse. There are too many young people who are parenting themselves and who come to school without the love and support they need in order to achieve. We do have some exceptional cases, but these are so rare that when we find them, they are highlighted on TV.

I know that we have various groups working to develop parenting skills in Jamaica, but I believe that in addition to these activities, the Ministry of Education and the Ministry of Health should work together to ensure that mothers and fathers who access care at prenatal clinics should be required to participate in parenting classes before their child is born. Caregivers should be sent into homes when children are at the preschool stage to further teach parents how to help their children develop positively. This multi-agency approach would improve the readiness of our children for early childhood training and, ultimately, reduce the appetite of youth for violent crime. Only then will there be a greater likelihood of Jamaica attaining the education goals of Vision 2030, even if the timing would be a little off-target.
**Published October 5, 2014**

# FLM: MAKING JAMAICA'S FAMILIES STRONGER

**Original Board of FLM with the Governor General**

The make-up of the Jamaican family has changed since 1962. Inevitably, this has caused a transformation in the Jamaican parenting process. The evolution of the family structure has resulted in parenting being more challenging now than it has ever been (Professor Elsa Leo-Rhynie). (Palmer 2012)

"It is counterproductive to sit and complain that our children lack discipline without first accepting that they are a mirror image of the society." These expressions were taken from an article written in The Sunday Gleaner of December 9, 2012, 'The evolving family', by

Stacy A. Palmer. (Palmer 2012) It was a similar concern that family life in Jamaica had changed, not for the better, that caused eight families to get together in 1982 to support each other in raising their families and later to determine to do something to positively to impact family life in Jamaica. It is from this group that Family Life Ministries (FLM), now widely known across Jamaica, the Caribbean and the diaspora, was born. These persons did not sit and merely complain, as many do, but they resolved to do something, and they did. The couples were: Ivan and Faith Linton, John and Vilma Keane, Hope and Arnold Aiken, Barry and Beverly Davidson, Grace and Charles Royes, Grace and Gordon Russell, Paulette and Brendan Bain, and Angela Ramlal, who later married Calvin Williams, who also joined the ministry.

Contrary to the pattern of broken marriages that is becoming commonplace, all eight couples are still happily married to each other. Their children are all grown, with their own families, and the founding couples are now proud grandparents. Oh, that more of our marriages would be as sound and stable as these. Our country would see a reduction in crime and violence since sound marriages evolve into good parenting and, therefore, wholesome children.

**Inter-Denominational Movement**

It was in 1983 that the team developed a plan to launch an inter-denominational movement to serve the churches and the wider community in Jamaica, and also in the Caribbean when opportunities arose. In 1984, FLM became a registered organization. The board of directors consisted of the eight couples mentioned before. The ministry began to provide speakers to address a wide range of family-life issues not usually dealt with in churches: God's design for marriage; rekindling romance; you and your sexuality; parenting; singleness; family financing, among other matters.

Over the years, FLM has expanded its programmes and activities to include counselling services, workshops and seminars, radio programmes, employee-assistance programmes, research and writing, along with linkages to other groups promoting marriage, family and parenting. The ministry's counselling centre at 1 Cecelio Avenue, Kingston 10, is one of the largest in the Caribbean, seeing more than 5,000 clients per year, with a cadre of more than 30 counsellors who work on contract with FLM. There is also a satellite counselling centre in Portmore at 117 Cecile Avenue. (Family Life Ministries, Jamaica 2014)

Of pivotal importance to the development of FLM is the role that Dr. Barry Davidson has played since 1983 as its chief executive officer, director of counselling, and also its former chairman.

Dr. Davidson has become a well-known voice and face in Jamaica as he represents FLM in addressing the many and varied concerns about family life in Jamaica and the Caribbean. His contributions to academia have been numerous. He was a visiting lecturer at Azuza Pacific College in California, currently lectures at the Caribbean Graduate School of Theology, and is a part-time lecturer in the Department of Sociology and Social Work at the University of the West Indies, Mona. (Family Life Ministries, Jamaica 2014)

**Promoting Healthy Family Life**

Dr. Davidson provided a much-needed resource to premarital counselling in Jamaica when he authored the counselling manual, Before They Say I Do, that is widely used by ministers and counsellors. More recently, he co-authored Answers to Questions Parents Ask, with Dr. Faith Linton; (Davidson and Linton 2012) and previously, a book, also co-authored, with Maureen Watson, Healthy Families – A Caribbean Perspective. (Davidson and Watson 2006) Therefore, Dr. Davidson's induction into the Order of Distinction in the rank of Commander (CD) is justly deserved for the outstanding work that he has done in promoting healthy family life in Jamaica.

Listen to what some clients had to say about how FLM has impacted their lives:

"I sought the help of FLM .... My wife and I separated and I needed help to deal with the separation, to remedy the behavioural issues I have, and finally to help my wife and I to reconcile our differences. I found the staff at FLM to be warm yet professional. The sessions with my counsellor have changed my perspective on life and on my marriage in particular. The advice I received I found to be relevant to my situation and has helped to put my wife and I on a path to reconciliation." (Family Life Ministries 2014)

**Transformation**

"I started attending counselling sessions at FLM courtesy of an employee-assistance programme arrangement by my company. My assigned counsellor has led me through a transformation, offering guidance, asking relevant questions and recommending books for me to read. After approximately seven months of ongoing sessions, I have learned much about myself – my preferences, setting boundaries at work and in my personal life. I am learning to say no to others and no to me. I am stepping out of my emotional comfort zone, testing waters, taking risks and restoring relationships." (Family Life Ministries, Jamaica 2014)

FLM is built on a sound foundation in God. The pioneering work of FLM has served to inspire and persuade individuals and groups to pay more attention to family life. There is now a very strong interest in the development of professional and lay counselling that can be partly attributed to the presence and influence of FLM.

These eight couples did not only complain; they set out to make a positive impact on family life in Jamaica, and indeed they did. Now, more than ever, we need to strengthen the family bonds in our society. The abuse of our children, the violence and crime being committed by our youth tell us that we still have a lot of work to do to restore healthy family life to our land. Join the effort: strong families, strong nation.

**Published November 30, 2014**

# HOPE FOR IMPROVED FAMILY LIFE IN 2015

L ast year was one of difficulties, globally and nationally: The Ebola crisis; the ISIS spread, the disappearance of two airlines in Malaysian airspace; the sinking of the ferry in South Korea. Nationally, the Chik-V virus that has negatively impacted the health of many and complicated existing health issues, in some cases resulting in death; the impact of International Monetary Fund (IMF) on our standard of living, rising prices and dwindling income.

In the midst of all of this seeming doom and gloom, we must hold on to hope. Hope that as a nation, we will reach a new level of understanding of who we are as a people and in spite of being the third most murderous country on earth, we will begin to have a new appreciation of life and the value of life. There are glimmers of hope with the reduction in the murder rate for 2014, the passing of the IMF tests, and hopefully, finding out the truth about the Tivoli killings.

I, however, cannot over-emphasize how much we need to refocus our attention as a nation on building our family life. Mahatma Ghandi is said to have uttered the following: "There is no school equal to a decent home and no teacher equal to a virtuous parent."

The family is the building block of the nation. Where we have crippled and fractured family units, we are going to have an equally fractured society. This is what is happening in Jamaica today. So many academic pundits and opinion leaders are quick to say that we have to accept the fact that Jamaica does not have a nuclear family structure. The point is, the nuclear family is the ideal and we must continue to strive for the ideal. Why? Because the research has shown that children reared in a stable family structure develop into rounded individuals who form healthy relationships and help to build a stable society. The converse is true, children who are not raised in a stable family setting but who have been neglected and abused are more likely to become sociopaths and display anti-social behaviour.

**Nuclear Family**

We, therefore, need to find the ways and means to encourage our nation to go back to seeing the nuclear family as the ideal. I have been quite heartened to see various corporate companies airing advertisements that promote strong family values. These ads include Jamaica Nationals ad about the son seeking to look after his ailing mother and how the family came together to help; the Singer ad; the NCB Omni ad; and the Digicel Christmas ad. This Digicel ad was quite a relief from that other hyped-up pseudo-cosmopolitan ad that had become quite nauseating in its frequency.

As a nation, we need to find ways to generate income. We need to encourage entrepreneurship among the young. The financial agencies need to create innovative ways of helping persons with viable ideas to bring them to fruition. Thereby they will be creating jobs for themselves and others and generate income in the society.

The latest Bamboo initiative is such an example. I look forward to tasting that Bamboo Ketchup. There are too many young people who have left tertiary institutions and are unable to find jobs. This is demotivating for students who are currently in high school and who are being told that they need to earn good grades in the Caribbean Examination Council (CXCs) to get into university. This has no impact on them as they will tell you that they know many graduates who are now indebted to the Students Loan Bureau, but have no source of income to repay the loan.

This leads me to the matter of the society and the government expecting that all students in secondary schools are to gain five or more CSEC subjects at the end of grade eleven. This is the same as saying that we are going to achieve the goals of Vision 2030. This is not going to happen. Certainly, not in the state we are now. When we have students who are coming to high school not being able to read at their grade level, who are mentally disturbed, emotionally troubled, physically and sexually abused, who are undernourished, hungry, are we expecting them to produce those five CSEC subjects at the end of grade eleven? We need to start seriously addressing these issues that originate in the homes and communities before we can expect to fulfill Vision 2030.

The Ministry which is responsible for education should realize that we need to address the problem of poor family life on a short-term, medium-term and a long-term level. In the short-term, we need to put in place a complete and thorough assessment of the students throughout high school. This assessment should include their cognitive, social and emotional levels. This needs to be done throughout all the schools. Currently, some schools do this but the parents have to find the money to pay for the assessments.

**Basic Provisions**

Many parents in Jamaica do not have the resources to give their children lunch money or bus fare much less to pay for this assessment. The schools then need to be provided with the human resources to deal with the outcomes of this assessment. This would include social workers, psychologists and special educators. At present, many teachers are overwhelmed at having to play all these roles for which they are not trained or equipped.

The medium-term intervention is to have aids going into the homes where there are children at the pre-school and early-childhood level to teach and assist parents how to rear their children.

In the long term, the nation must begin to promote positive and strong family life. All partners in the society such as the private sector, the musicians, DJs, the dramatists, the media, health sector, the Church and the education sector must come together to bring about this change.

Here's to positive growth in Jamaica for 2015.

**Published January 4, 2015**

# THE FAMILY, OUR CHILDREN – HELP!

The family is the basic unit of society. Our family structure has suffered repeated blows to its stability: from our fore parents being forced to leave their families in Africa to be chattels of slave masters without control over their own destiny, to being sold to different slave owners without regard for family connections, to our men being used as studs to impregnate women to produce slave children without connection to their fathers, to being freed from slavery without the resources to build a stable economic foundation. The disintegration continued further with our people being chained in the mental slavery of their minds following the patterns embedded in their national psyche with men continuing to operate as studs and women enabling them. The family needs to be rebuilt in our society.

The family provides for the young a place of nurturing, safety and security. It is where parents should guide the young, having had the benefit of learning from experience and exposure to knowledge about the importance of family. Unfortunately, an even further breakdown has occurred in the family structure when, because of economic pressure, many parents, mothers in particular, chose to go abroad to work and leave their children in the charge of a granny or some other relative. The phenomenon of the 'barrel children' in Jamaica is well known and does not need to be rehearsed.

As educators, we are aware that many grannies do not have the health or energy to parent young children. Many of the children are, therefore, left on their own, to bring themselves up. Furthermore, there are a number of our young people who are living by themselves. They might get money from their mothers abroad to pay the bills and buy food, but they are without guidance and training from a responsible adult. When we understand that many of our children are bringing up themselves guided by what they see on TV or the Internet, we understand that the next generation is at threat of being even more wayward than the present.

**Feedback from Educators**

We are hearing more and more feedback from educators lamenting the behaviour of the students in the schools. The younger year groups coming in are even more undisciplined than the older ones. With the onset of puberty and with no guidance as to how to control their newly developed sex urges, a number of these 12- and 13-year-old girls engage in unbridled sexual behaviour with boys in an attempt to be popular, receive love and acceptance, and satisfy raw desire. The matter of the emotional trauma that this type of behaviour will produce for them is not in their minds; the possibility of developing STIs, among other things, is far away from their thinking.

These 'orphan' children living without parents or parental guidance are added to those who are being pimped out by their parents.

The disrespect, lack of self-control, fighting and unbridled sexual behaviour that our students are displaying in many schools in Jamaica are causing high levels of stress for many teachers. The situation is becoming so dire that the Government needs to do a realistic assessment of the situation. Social workers and clinical psychologists need to be allocated to the schools to address these behavioural issues.

Whereas a teacher can address non-submission of homework on time, talking out of turn, and minor infractions in the classroom, schools should have specially trained professionals to whom they can refer children who have serious behavioural issues. The deans of discipline, many times, are not trained to analyze and address these behaviours. The guidance counsellors are overwhelmed and are only trained to deal with these behaviours to a certain level. They, too, need to have social workers that will engage with the students in their homes and communities to address the issues that originate from these sources.

The guidance counsellors are tasked with doing group counselling classes and many times do not have enough time to advise the children on a one-to-one basis. They need to have clinical psychologists to whom they can refer students with serious issues. Our teachers are being required not only to teach but also to parent. This situation has to be addressed. The cultural issues that breed the errant, maladaptive behaviours in our children need to be a focus of our government, civil-society groups and the Church. Our family structure must be rebuilt and strengthened if we are going to progress as a nation.

We have read and heard repeatedly the statistics related to the outcomes of children who grow up without a father; even more those who do not have a stable family support system. We have heard this and it seems as if we expect that in Jamaica our situation will be different and that the outcomes will be different. Look at the students who are doing well in school. Most of them come from stable family backgrounds. Those who are from single-parent homes have mothers who sacrifice for them and ensure that they are properly monitored and that a male figure is in their lives to provide help for them.

We, therefore, need to take the necessary actions to rebuild the family structure in our nation. We need to put in place required parenting sessions for mothers and fathers who go to the prenatal clinics for care. We need to expand the practice of sending home assistants into homes to teach parents how to nurture the little ones. It is not now an optional matter; it is mandatory if we are to save our nation.

**Published June 7, 2015**

# PREPARING FOR END OF LIFE

I recently read a column by Ellen Goodman published in **The New York Times** titled 'How to talk about dying'. (Goodman 2015) It caught my attention because this is a matter that I think many of us who have been born in what is called the baby-boomer generation need to begin thinking about.

As one person commenting on the article said: "No one likes to think about their mortality until we are forced to face it. It is an unfortunate truth about the human condition that even though everyone will die, eventually no one wants to talk about it." (Goodman 2015)

We live with death all around us in Jamaica since we are a country with a high murder rate. Therefore, the extent of our lives is uncertain. When you couple that stark reality with the pervasiveness of cancer, which seems to be taking the lives of many persons in their 40s-60s, you realize that we need to face the strong possibility that we may die before we reach the much-heralded 'three score years and ten'. Yet many of us refuse to talk about the matter.

First of all, there are some people who are so afraid of the issue of preparing for death that they refuse to think about buying life insurance, which would provide some support for their families after their death or that would cover the cost of a funeral.

There are some of us who superstitiously believe that if we wrote a will, something would happen to shorten our lives. We, therefore, continue in this belief and leave our loved ones to face the confusion that comes in the aftermath of our passing because we have not written a will. The State, then, has the responsibility of dealing with the estate of the departed one. This is usually a long, painful process, with families left bereft not only emotionally but also, in some cases, financially.

Second, there is another group of persons, Christians, who believe in supernatural healing, who, when they are ill, do not speak to their loved ones about preparing for death because they feel that to do so would expose a lack of faith. In taking this approach, some persons have deprived their ill loved ones of the benefit of spending their last days reflecting with their family, preparing for the future without them, speaking words of comfort to the dying one, and preparing for their passing.

## Church Help

As a church community, we need to help persons prepare for death. After all, as Christians, we believe, as Paul the Apostle said, that we *"would prefer to be away from the body and at home with the Lord"* (2 Cor. 5:8). ((NIV) Holy Bible 1984) Death, for us as Christians, is the gateway into the presence of Jesus Christ. We believe that we will be resurrected into a new body that will be able to do marvellous things. Why should we then fear death? Instead, we should be comfortable in making preparations for our home going.

There are some suggestions that Ellen Goodman makes on preparing for the end of life, along with pointers from what is called the Starter Conversation Kit that I would like to share with you. First of all, Ms. Goodman made the following point: "The difference between a good death and a hard death often seemed to hinge essentially on whether someone's wishes were expressed and respected. Whether they'd had a conversation about how they wanted to live toward the end." (Goodman 2015)

Some of these pointers are:

1.  Think about what you want for end-of-life care.
2.  How involved do you want your loved ones to be in making decisions about your medical care?
3.  Who do you want to be involved with your care?
4.  Who should speak for you - children, siblings, doctors?
5.  Are there any disagreements or family tension that you are concerned about?
6.  Where do you want or not want to receive care (home, nursing facility, hospital?)
7.  What kinds of aggressive treatment would you want (or not want)? (Resuscitation if your heart stops, breathing machine, feeding tube)
8.  What affairs do you need to get in order or talk to your loved ones about? (Personal relationships, property, finances)

(Source: **http://theconversationproject.org/wp-content/ uploads/2013/01/TCP-Starter**...)

Let us, therefore, think about the heritage that we are leaving for our families and our loved ones. Let us do what is necessary to make the aftermath of our death less stressful than it would be when we do not prepare.

I want to honour the home going of a stalwart of Jamaica and the church in Jamaica, Patrick Smith. Patrick lost his battle to cancer in the last month. His life has impacted so many persons who knew him. He was a Christian who lived his life to please God and to help others. Patrick was a family man who cared deeply for his family.

I honour Patrick's wife, Heather, who stood by her husband steadfastly and lovingly as he battled cancer. Patrick was a man of integrity and compassion who strove for excellence in all his endeavours. Of even greater importance to Patrick than his secular life was his involvement in the Christian community as a deacon in his church, working with the youth and heading various ministries.

I know that he is in a better place.

**Published July 5, 2015**

**Part 3**

# SOCIETAL VALUES

# AN ABSENCE OF RESTRAINT

**Jamaica Carnival**

As a society, we have placed ourselves on a slippery slope which will end in mayhem and anarchy. The lack of restraint in many areas of our nation's life is a cause for great concern. This lack of restraint is far-reaching in its impact.

There is insidious and widespread corruption in the public sector; bribery and chicanery have become a way of life. The police who are supposed to be the guardians of law and order are themselves working to destroy law and order. Our politicians are pointed at by many, as being participants in the corruption, whether by active involvement or by silent acquiescence. The Church is being fingered as exploiting those who come to them for solace – the children and the women, in particular. Churches are being vandalized with impunity. In the schools, parents and children see teachers as available targets of violence and abuse. The schoolroom where our young are educated is torn apart and robbed by thieves and criminals. What is cast as our culture are forms of music and drama that cater to our base instincts. We glorify the DJs who extol gun violence and portray our women as "beef" with which they engorge their sexual appetites. These DJs set the pace for the behaviour of our young people; they determine their mannerisms – which are usually crude and vulgar. They establish the dress code – which is excessive in 'bling' and scarce in decency.

**Atmosphere of Excess**

We have removed inhibitions and taboos, thinking that freedom is what we should aim for in all spheres of life. Yet, in every society, there has to be law and order and there has to be boundaries within which a decent and civilized society operates. It seems that as a nation, our sexual cravings and our appetite for bloodshed have been given full rein. Even the young are being reared in this atmosphere of excess. As we look around us, we see three-year-olds "wining" and "grinding" as they imitate the sexual and erotic motions of the adults. This is described as 'dancing' and adults stand by and cheer them on.

We extol erotic dancing to the point where it was put on display at the opening ceremony of the Cricket World Cup. The dancers' bottoms gyrating in the audience's faces was the major part of the anatomy that was projected in Sean Paul's performance. We have endorsed this type of behavior to such an extent that we displayed it to over one billion persons on international television as a part of our culture. Parents are exposing their young to X-rated movies and pornographic magazines; mothers are using their sons as sexual partners; and, children in school are acting out what they are being exposed to in the society.

As a society, we have lost respect for life. Children are exposed to murder and bloodshed on a daily basis. They have become desensitized as a result of a surfeit of gore and killings.

In the classrooms, guns and knives are becoming commonplace. Children tell you that they need to defend themselves. Why? Because they are being killed for their cell phones. Babies are being murdered without reason. Old people are raped and murdered at an alarming rate. There is hardly a day when the newscast does not broadcast murder and bloodshed in our nation.

What type of people are we? We are a people who have cast off restraint – in which case, we cannot escape the consequences.

I note the decrease in the number of tourists arriving for this winter season. The reason given is the CARICOM visa requirement. Yet I believe that as our name as a nation falls into disrepute, we will find fewer persons willing to risk their lives by coming here. In addition, as Jamaicans, it is becoming more and more difficult to gain easy entrance into other nations, since we are seen as a murderous and undisciplined people. Immigration barriers are being created in various countries to stop our easy access to them. Investors are chosing to go to other countries, because they do not have to contend with the high security costs that come with operating in Jamaica. They do not have to deal with the rampant indiscipline which characterizes our society. We, as a people, need to take stock of where we are headed. We need to look at what has brought us to this point and halt the dangerous slide that we are on into mayhem.

## Setting Examples

The leaders of our society cannot continue as if it is business as usual, otherwise they will find themselves with an ungovernable nation. The infighting among the politicians needs to stop. Both sides need to work together on solutions for this nation.

Public and private-sector leaders need to set examples as to how they operate the affairs of the nation. The irresponsible behaviour which is exhibited in Parliament and at public functions must stop. They need to realize that they model for many of our people what is appropriate behaviour. When they use words recklessly to malign each other, they are spurring on the people to do the same. They must appreciate that our people no longer argue over differences, instead, they kill over differences. Our people do not know that many of these politicians party together after they berate each other publicly. The change must begin from the top-from our leader, otherwise we will be left standing on our own in an increasingly globalized world. Shakespeare's words in King Lear seem applicable to us: "Wisdom and goodness to the vile seem vile; filths savour but themselves." (Shakespeare 1993)

Soon, we will be by ourselves in our mayhem and anarchy.

**Published May 6, 2007s**

# INNOCENCE LOST

A volley of shots rang out on Tuesday, June 26, 2007, shattering the calm atmosphere at Ardenne High School at 10 Ardenne Road. Sitting in my office in a meeting, I was in disbelief that this was happening until I saw students running and heard shouts and screams. Running outside, I was greeted with a scene of pandemonium. Students were running helter-skelter across the compound, some crying and some looking dazed. The confusion began again as another shot rang out from within the school – in the staff room. Students, adults were running from the staffroom to the front of the school. Chaos raged. I called the police at Half-Way Tree to get help.

On the ground, a man of unsound mind is babbling, "I am Cinderella with a long, brown hair, there is my golden sister"; a man disheveled, without shoes, shirt unbuttoned, with blood splattered on his hand and feet. Students gather around him, no one is helping him because the police say no one should. Everyone is speaking in groups. Past students from overseas who are back home in Jamaica for Ardenne's Homecoming Week are in shock, their faces registering disbelief. Past students are on their cell phones, calling overseas, sending back the details of what, unbelievably, has transpired before their eyes. While all of this transpires no one from the security forces came to take the wounded man to the hospital.

The police arrives  from the Half-Way-Tree Police Station. Children are crowding, teachers whispering, past students commiserating and Board Members are gathering. The talk is, "The man needs to get some help." The police comes; the police hesitates; they need gloves, they have no gloves. We get them gloves. One policeman gets to work and gets the man up. The mad man does not want to be touched. The mad man is naked from the waist down. He had taken off his pants, pulled them down, turns over back to front, front to back, genitals out for all the world to see. The students, whose cell phones are banned in school, are taking pictures of the scene. Mad man, police, students, teachers, alumnae watch each other. Eventually, one policeman gets some assistance from another policeman and puts the mad man into the car.  They said the police car could not be tainted by blood therefore they had to put newspaper on the seats so that the man could be put in the car. The man is moved, but we are still shaken. Innocence is lost.

Reports fly around: The little girl, the little girl in the van at the gate has been hit. Two policemen had taken her out of the van, with her mouth all bloodied and had taken her to the hospital. Call the little girl's school. Which school? It is the Covenant Christian Academy Prep. School. The school is called. The school calls the mother. The mother screams.

## Sense of Security Ravaged

The innocence, the sense of security has been ravaged and demolished. Why? Because of a lack of thought and care. The good intentions of a policeman to assist the passerby being stoned by the madman had turned into chaos and mayhem. Bodily harm, emotional and mental trauma had been inflicted on the young, the innocent and the unsuspecting.

Never again can we regain the age of innocence; we have lost it as a school. We have become a part of the angst and pain experienced by the soul of Jamaica. The soul of this nation cries out in anguish, and we no longer can operate as if there are any enclaves of safety. All are being pulled into this twisting, agonizing cry of a country burdened and shamed by the innocent blood that has been shed with bodies that have been maimed and twisted and mothers' anguished cries bawling out for their sons and daughters gone too soon. Gone too soon by the hands of gunmen who are boys with undeveloped minds, toting guns with seared consciences and blighted spirits. Blood is being spilled by lawmen stressed and fearful who ignore procedures because stress erases judgment and care. These are lawmen, who too need to be seen as human beings with cares and needs, whose lives are threatened by death at every turn. They crack too.

The powers that be were shaken. They expressed concern and assurance that sure and thorough investigations would be done. Reports were taken, questions asked and checks were done.

Get it right. No mistakes are to be made here. Convince the teachers that not all policemen are careless and trigger-happy. Make

251

them believe that they can rely on us. Damage control is necessary. Watch those unbelieving eyes as the police explain that they are our friend, that they will deal with the situation justly and fairly. Only the outcome will tell.

## No Immunity

The news media are all around. There is a story here. This one will sell the newspaper. There are many good things, wonderful things that happen at this school, but that gets little media attention. This does, though. This sell. The features of a good story lie here: police, mad man, gunshots, blood, schoolyard, children, teachers, staff room. All the elements of a good story packaged together. But teachers, students, learning, achieving, sacrificing, overcoming – too nice, too clean. No story lies there.

Alas, in this our 80th year of existence, we have entered into a new phase – a phase that highlights that there is no safety in location. It does not matter that we are situated across from Jamaica House where the Prime Minister's office is located – there is no immunity. There is no immunity in the rural areas; there is no immunity in the town. There is no safety downtown; there is no safety uptown. We are all a part of the great world woe and grief that have engulfed us as the savage beast of crime and violence ravages us all.

Yet, as a school, we know one thing: We will continue to strive for excellence and godliness and in this school; we will continue. Deo Duce Quaere Optima – With God as Guide, Seek the Best.
**Published July 1, 2007**

# A MATTER OF SELF-CONTROL

It seems that in Jamaica self-control has become our most despised and best forgotten cousin. We have embraced as our closest siblings, vulgarity, indiscipline, self-indulgence and a lack of restraint.

We are reaping the results of this attitude in every area of our society. It is seen in the level of corruption in the public sector, the lack of respect for law and order and how the police enforce the law. It is seen in the way people drive on the roads, in the breakdown of family life, and in rampant, unrestrained sexual behaviour. It is seen in the lack of discipline in the schools, the lack of respect people display for each other and the expression of unrestrained anger. It is seen in the rising incidence of domestic violence. It is seen in the high murder rate. It is seen in the high level of child abuse. It is seen in the music and fashion of the dancehall culture. It is seen in the abuse of the environment.

## Approach Backfired

We have sown to the wind and we are now reaping the whirlwind. For all those persons who thought that it was modern and liberal to throw away restraint in our conduct, they should now clearly see that such an approach has backfired. The corruption which has now become a characteristic of public life has tainted our nation. Since last year, Jamaica has fallen by 23 places among the countries on the International Perception Index which ranks corruption in 180 countries. Of the seven English-speaking Caribbean countries, we rank sixth. This should be a wake-up call to us as a nation. We cannot hope to get assistance from the international community with this type of reputation. We need courageous leadership in order to clean up the sty of corruption that exists within this nation.

The impact of our lack of restraint is also seen in our children. My heart weeps when I read the stories written about our children in The Gleaner: those who are left on their own so that their parents can go out to wear "bling"[33] and "spread out" [34] at "Passa Passa"; those who are subject to gunmen hiding in their homes and can do nothing about it; those, both boys and girls, who have been raped by adults. Our children are suffering; our children are being scarred. We are sowing seeds now for the destruction of our country beyond anything we have seen.

There is an urgent need for our family life to be addressed. Families form the basis of society. This should be the structure within which morals and values are taught. Self-control should begin to be practiced in this context. Our family structure, however, is now fragmented because of our unrestrained sexual behaviour. There is an urgent need for persons who want to have sex to understand that this means that they are potential parents and be prepared for parenting. The Government needs to mandate parenting classes for girls and baby fathers (who need to be identified) at the early stage of pregnancy. This should be continued at every level of the child's development. This is not a matter of interfering in persons' lives; this is a matter of the survival of our nation.

Sex was created by God for the context of marriage. Our using sex outside of its right context has resulted in untold suffering to our people. Sex is for marriage, marriage is for adults, and, therefore, children should not be given the okay to be having sex. The fact that we have lowered the age of consent to 16 shows that as a nation, we are far from understanding the social and moral impact of unrestrained sexual behaviour. The Time magazine of May 10, 2004 published an article, 'What makes teens tick', (Wallis and Kristina 2004) which discussed the most recent findings on the study of the brain, using MRI, which shows that the brain develops from the back to the front. The area at the back which matures earliest controls the development of the senses, vision, hearing etc. The last area to mature is the forebrain, which controls functions such as planning, setting priorities, organizing thoughts, suppressing impulses and weighing the consequences of one's actions. To summarize – the area of the brain which makes humans more responsible is not finished maturing in the teenage years. As a matter of fact, the article suggest that this area becomes mature at age twenty-five.

**Self-Respect**

As Jamaicans, we need to practice what Abraham Heschel says in The Insecurity of Freedom: Essays on Human Existence:

"Self-respect is the root of discipline: The sense of dignity grows with the ability to say 'no' to oneself." (Heschel 1967)

It is necessary for the family structure to be functioning as a place of nurturing and guidance for our young, because our children need that context within which to mature. Let us rebuild the family in Jamaica. Let parents be not only biological producers of children but be nurturers and role models as well. Only then will our society move from this place of despair. If we lose our families, what have we gained? I salute the work of organizations such as Mother in Crisis and the Fletchers Land Parenting Association which are seeking to help parents guide and nurture our children. Let us all join in that fight to reclaim the Jamaican family.

Finally, let us pray that God will grant the leadership of this country the courage, wisdom and foresight they need to direct our nation in its rebuilding process.

**Published December 2, 2007**

# THE CENTRE CANNOT HOLD

T he world as we know it is changing. The assumptions on which many of us based our sense of security have been shattered. Our faith in world systems has been destroyed by the events of the past few months. This man-made centre cannot hold.

Many of us have been brought up to believe that if we made enough money and invested wisely, saved in the bank and acquired assets, that would make us financially secure. We put our trust and our faith in this world system, believing that it would provide security and prosperity for us all our lives, if we did as it said. Clearly, the financial crisis that began in the United States and which has spread to the rest of the world, gives clear indication that this system is not fool-proof. Even though our Government would want us to believe that Jamaica will not be very affected by this fall-out in the financial sector in the US, we know otherwise.

Jamaica depends on the remittances which come from Jamaicans overseas and this, most certainly, will be affected by the number of persons who have been and will be losing jobs in the USA. The impact on tourism will be enormous. We have not yet begun to see the full impact of the global financial crisis. If we cannot depend on our wealth to provide security, what then can we depend on?

## Developing Other Wealth

We need to look at developing wealth in our relationships: relationship with God and relationships with people. That is where the real wealth resides. When we develop a strong relationship with God, it gives us a sense of security that is not based on physical realities, but on spiritual realities. These realities are not determined by our physical circumstances, but by an intimate relationship with God. The possibility of having a sense of His presence with us is not mumbo jumbo, as some would think, nor is it a figment of our imagination. The proof of its reality is seen in the impact a relationship with God has on the lives of those who practice living with a sense of His presence daily. The changes in the physical realm do not destroy their peace. It, rather, strengthens their determination to know God even more. We need to shift our centre to something that remains unshaken no matter what our circumstances are.

## Relationships

The other area we need to give priority to, in order to develop a sense of wellness and security, is our relationships with our family and friends. In our society, money has become the driving force for many persons' actions. If they have money, they plan to get more, and if they do not have money, they plan how to get it. This desire absorbs the minds of many people. In the drive to acquire money, many persons forego building relationships, because it takes too much time. We see this principle operating in the breakdown of family relationships in this country. It does not matter what socio-economic level the individual is at, whether upper or lower class.

Some members of the professional class are driven by a need to be the best at their jobs, to climb the social ladder, to be seen on page two of the newspaper. They leave their children to be brought up by helpers, yet later wonder how they are not able to relate to their teenagers when they try to influence their behaviour. They have lost the opportunity of investing in their children's development by choosing upward mobility instead of time to pour values and standards into their children's lives at an early age. They find out that the relationship with their children has been badly damaged because they did not spend time with them while they were young. Then there are those who feel that if they give their children the material things that they want, that it will make up for the lack of time that they spend with them. These parents are usually in shock when their children begin exhibiting destructive behaviour. Having alienated their children, they find themselves growing old without the emotional support that they need from a close family structure. Money, it is clear, cannot buy close family relationships. Then, there are those persons who go abroad to work for the mighty US dollar. They produce the barrel children. The phenomenon of these barrel children has become well known in Jamaica. These mothers might come back to Jamaica when the children are grown, to find out that they are strangers and that these children feel no emotional bond with them. Money cannot build relationships.

## Network of Close Friends

Apart from our families, we need to build strong relationships with a network of close friends. It takes time to build relationships. Whether we maintain relationships that we have built from our school years, from attending our social clubs or churches, we must spend time to build them and invest in them. Many persons who do not have strong family ties but who have close friendships find that in times of distress and ill health, they can depend on these friends to assist them. Money cannot provide a good friend who will be there to go through the bad times with you. Many times, the 'friends' whom we gain because of our material things leave us when the times get bad. True friends are those who give of themselves to others even when it is inconvenient for them.

Strong family ties and lasting friendships are centres that are worth forming. Together with a strong relationship with God, these aspects of life are what will hold when the man-made structures crumble around us.

As the wise man Solomon says, "A friend loves at all times, and a brother is born for adversity." (Solomon n.d.)

**Published November 2, 2008**

# TRANSPORTATION CENTRE: BLESSING OR CURSE?

**The Transportation Centre**

The Half-Way Tree Transportation Centre was opened one year ago to enable more timely and efficient delivery of the public-transportation service in the Kingston Metropolitan Area. Whereas this might have occurred, the Transport Centre has provided, inadvertently, a place where students congregate and socialize and a setting which highlights the anti-social conduct which has become characteristic of some of our young people.

261

In a meeting held at the Transport Centre with the stakeholders involved in the operation of the centre and representatives from various schools, the number of fights and other anti-social behaviours, which take place among the students, were discussed with a view to finding solutions to the problem. Clearly, the Transportation Centre does not cause this behaviour; it simply brings together the students whose socialization does not model for them patterns of how to deal with conflicts and disagreements in a peaceful manner. This has become a serious cause for concern.

We were told that almost every day there was a fight, not only between boys, but also between girls who are fighting over a boy or a man. We were shown pictures of myriads of weapons taken from students by the police who monitor the centre. We understood how serious the situation was when the managers pointed out that during the school holidays, the centre was a peaceful, pleasant place, but when school was in session, the atmosphere became tense and a hub of conflict because of the behaviour of some students.

**Sad Commentary**

In an effort to ensure that during this time of the Boys and Girls' Championships conflicts did not escalate further, the authorities put a ban on schools taking their flags into the centre. This, in the past, had encouraged, not friendly rivalry, but outright fights. This is a sad commentary on the state of our youth. We need, as a society, to look at how we can help to change this behaviour. At the meeting, various suggestions were put forward. Some of these suggestions were long to medium-term solutions, others were short-term. These short-term measures require that schools, parents and other mature individuals to volunteer to help at the critical periods – in the mornings between 6:30 a.m.-8:30 a.m. – to monitor the students at the centre. The Jamaica Constabulary Force needs also to assign police personnel for this period to support the security guards who are stationed there.

## A Bigger Issue

This problem speaks to a bigger issue in our society, however, namely, our young people are not seeing conflicts being resolved peacefully by the adults in their homes and communities. What they see is that any disagreement or conflict is often viewed as disrespect, and disrespect in Jamaica has become, for many, a reason to use violence to gain respect. Not to use violence means that 'yuh saaf'[35]; not to use violence means 'yuh a idiaat'[36]. In Jamaica, this has become the greatest insult.

We need to begin in all of our socialization settings, to teach our young people how to settle their differences peacefully. When I was told by the management that there was an incident where, apparently, a young man had a conflict with a security guard at the centre and in response, his parents drove him into the Transport Centre to attack the security guard with a screwdriver, I understood better how serious a situation we were in. When I heard another story of a mother whose daughter was being teased and harassed by girls from her school and who, when contacted for advice as to what to do, told her daughter "Tek yuh scissors and just stab one a dem inna dem eye"[37], which the child did, we understand that we are in an extremely serious situation.

It is not only the children who need to be socialized properly, but also the parents.

## Set an Example

Do we want our children to respect the laws of the land and to respect those around them? Then, as parents and adults, we need to stop breaking the law – breaking the stop lights, bribing officers of the law, using obscenities as a matter of course, cussing and attacking someone who 'diss'[38] us. We need instead to show our youth that we obey the law because it creates a peaceful and civil society. Socializing our youth cannot only be seen as the responsibility of the school, as many persons of authority in society are now saying. Whereas in the school we teach students one set of values, when they return to many homes and communities they are taught the opposite. Those who are able to stand up against what is accepted in the communities are those who have strong home support. They have parents or guardians who teach and exhibit to them strong positive morals and values and who seek to monitor them within the community.

More of our artistes need to take responsibility to help to impart positive social and moral values to our youth by creating songs that reflect this. More of our police need to be role models to the youth in their communities and not to be seen as corrupt oppressors. Our police need to monitor our students in public spaces, but they need to do so while at the same time showing respect to the youth and allowing them to have their dignity. Indeed, it takes a village to raise a child. We make up that village. As adults, we are the ones who need to claim responsibility for what is happening to our youth and seek to make the change.
**Published April 5, 2009**

# LESSONS FROM THE '70S

**Coronation Market**

Rice wars, flour wars, empty supermarket shelves, scarcity of goods, five flights a day to Miami, mass migration, emptied houses and captured houses.

This picture describes Jamaica in the period of the 1970s. We have lessons to learn from this time. Those among us who were not yet born need to learn from those of us who were here. These times with which we are faced are similar yet different. In the 1970s, the USA became the land of hope and promise for many Jamaicans.

Stories are told of many Jamaicans who left their good jobs here to go abroad to serve at a gas station; some who left their comfortable homes to live in substandard housing in order to escape the fear they had of living in Jamaica. This time, escaping Jamaica will not find us leaving our fears behind, because it is no longer an isolated situation belonging to Jamaica – it is worldwide. In the 1970s, the fear for many was that Jamaica was being transformed into a communist nation. Now our fear is global recession. Therefore, it makes no sense to run elsewhere to escape this fear; instead, we have some lessons to learn from that period on how to survive this recession.

**Feeding Ourselves**

We need to find a way to feed ourselves. We need to teach our children how to grow their own food. Backyard gardening needs to become a way of life for those of us who have backyards. Those of us without backyards need to do container gardening.

In our schools, we used to have a number of students doing agricultural science up to the CXC-CSEC level, but then the interest in the subject declined. Over the last few years, however, students' interest in the subject has been revived. Students are transferring the knowledge learnt about gardening at school to their homes. More of our schools need to engage our students in the rudiments of knowing how to grow their own food.

In addition, we need to find ways to share the excess that we reap with others. We can do this by organizing in our communities, or at work or at church, to determine who will be growing what at each growing period and do exchanges with each other, consequently, nothing goes to waste.

**Accessing Reasonably Priced Dry Goods**

With regard to accessing reasonably priced dry goods, we need to find the wholesalers who are offering good prices for their products. We could again, in our groups, buy these goods wholesale and divide them among ourselves. Instead of buying high-priced meats at the supermarkets, we need to find a source, possibly the market, or else a butcher where we can get meats at a price more reasonable than is offered in the supermarkets. Even if we have to travel to a rural area to get the produce, it would be worthwhile. This could be done even once a month, and again the group would cover the cost of the transportation. This would work out, even with the cost of gas, to be cheaper than buying in the supermarkets. In addition, we need to eat less meat and add more vegetables to our diets. In any regard, it is a healthier option.

With the price of petrol being hiked by the new tax, persons need to again use the strength of community to assist each other. We need to look at carpooling. If your neighbour's children go to the same school as yours, or if you work in the same area, arrange that you share the job of transportation. Half of the week you drive, the other half the neighbour drives. In the '70s, the gas guzzlers on the roads became a thing of the past. Those of us who are now purchasing vehicles need to look at the mileage that the vehicles offer per litre of gas as a criterion for buying them.

Furthermore, we need to learn to be satisfied with less and we need to 'tun our han mek fashion'[39]. In an effort to conserve, we need to seriously look at recycling. Containers bought with one item can be reused to store other dry goods, etc. With regards to our clothing, we would save money if we remove worn collars and sew them back on the reverse side instead of discarding the item of clothing. There are many other such ways that we can cut back on expenditure. The Jamaica Public Service gives tips to the country as to how to conserve on the use of electricity. Let us implement these in our daily lives.

**A Sense of Community**

What I am saying is that in these difficult times we need to develop a sense of community. We need to learn to depend on each other and support each other. A community can be geographical, an organization or your workplace. If you are one of the fortunate ones who are not affected negatively by this global meltdown, then you can help others in your community who are less fortunate. Those of us who were here in the 1970s, and who survived in spite of the economic difficulties that the country experienced, need to share with others how we did this.

As the well-known song says, "No man is an island, no man stands alone, each man's joy is joy to me, each man's grief is my own. We need one another, so I will defend, each man as my brother, each man as my friend."

**Published May 3, 2009**

# DEBUNKING THE CONDOM MYTH

" inch, Pull, roll." To listen to the popular advertisements being aired, you would have the impression that if only our people would use condoms when having sexual intercourse, then all our problems in that area would be solved. The message is faulty and needs serious amendment.

Tyrone Reid, staff reporter of The Gleaner, reported in an article published on May 7, that the Ministry of Education was seeking to put in place a system under which public schools would not provide their students with condoms on campus, but specific members of the schools' faculty and student body would be equipped to tell at-risk students exactly where they could get contraceptives without fear of being judged. (Reid 2009)

## New Approach Misleading

This announcement was enthusiastically greeted by the Jamaica Youth Advocacy Network (JYAN), as reported in an article published in The Gleaner on May 13, 2009. The group sees the ministry's move as an "important developmental step that requires a partner-ship between youth, parents, school administrators and teachers, health professionals and other service providers for us to ensure quality of life and productivity among young people so they can con-tribute to national development". (The Gleaner 2009)

This new approach being considered by the Ministry of Education is undergirded by the belief that if our young people simply protected themselves while having sex, it would allow them to have a good quality of life and to be productive, according to the JYAN.

This is a myth. Condoms cannot protect the youth from being infected by the human papilloma virus (HPV), which causes cervical cancer. This cancer presents itself in Jamaicans at a high rate. The information outlined here is presented by the NJ Physicians Advisory Group. HPV is responsible for 99.7 per cent of all cervical cancer and is seen in oral, anal, genital and penile cancers. Some strains of the virus cause genital warts. Always using condoms may cut the chances of getting HPV only up to half, because it is spread by skin-to-skin contact in the entire genital region.

Condoms do not protect against herpes. Genital herpes is viral and causes painful genital blisters. It can be spread from skin-to-skin contact for which condoms give little protection. Both oral herpes and genital herpes can be transmitted through oral-genital con-tact. Condoms are not foolproof against pregnancy. The failure rate among committed couples in the first year of use is 15 per cent; how-ever, the failure rate for young, unmarried, minority women ranges between 36.3 per cent and 44.5 per cent. Condoms do not protect against the emotional and mental impact of a sexually promiscuous lifestyle. Sexually active teens are two to three times more likely to be depressed than teens who are not sexually active.

More than the need to "pinch, pull, roll," is the need for us to teach our young people how to value themselves and to value others. We need to be conveying to them that true love waits. We need to let them know that delayed gratification is a character quality that will have a positive impact, not solely sexual, but also emotionally and economically.

## Condoms Not the Answer

Condoms are not the answer to the high level of sexual abuse in Jamaica. Dr. Carolyn Pinnock of the Bustamante Hospital for Children pointed out that 33 per cent of girls in the Caribbean are sexually abused before they reach the age of 15. She noted that to address the issue of children being sexually abused in Jamaica, certain issues need to be addressed, one being that paedophilia (love of child sex) was socially accepted, as not many persons had an issue with an older man sleeping with a 14-year-old girl. Condom use cannot heal the emotional and psychological damage that has been done to the women and girls of this nation because of this practice.

We need to begin to teach our children that God created sex as a beautiful gift between man and woman in the context of marriage. We need to teach our children that sex is a private matter between couples who are committed to each other. It is for the pleasure, not of a viewing audience, but of the couple, engaged with each other. Instead, what do we have? What have we been doing? We have been perverting the sexual experience more and more

271

for commercial gain. "Daggering" makes money; lewdness makes money. "Give de people what dem want."[40] What has been the outcome? Our children are overexposed to sexual lewdness that they no longer know the value of intimacy as a necessary component of the sexual act. It is no longer regarded as necessary.

**Protection for The Mind**

Condoms do not protect the minds of our young from a twisted, perverted view of sex. We have come to such a state that some young boys coming into the high schools have now begun to target their female teachers as sexual objects. Are we then to supply them with condoms? As a society, we must realize that relative morality is not the answer. We must set standards of morality, which we teach to our young people. It cannot be that because violence and lewdness sell, that we encourage them. We must stop allowing simply our dancehall artistes to be the ones talking about sex in their perverted way. We must raise up counter voices with positive messages about the value of intimacy and delayed gratification. We need to have leaders in our society who show the value of family by the family life they live. We need our leaders to be role models to the society of fidelity and love of family.

Our message has to be more than "pinch, pull, roll." It has to become, "Value self, value others; self-control and true love waits." This message, Ministry of Education, is what needs to be heard loud and clear.

**Published June 17, 2009**

# CHANGE NEGATIVE CULTURAL NORMS

**Dancing the Maypole**

"Y ou can't keep clipping off the leaves of the tree .... The tree will only make more leaves because it is planted in soil that is favourable. You need to look at the hidden causes to the problems – the root."

I agree with Dr. Doreen Brady-West's assessment of our Government's approach to the social ills that beset our country. Dr

Brady-West is a consultant haematologist and clinical oncologist at the University of the West Indies who is part of the Coalition for the Defense of Life. We are concerned about women and girls having unwanted babies, therefore, we provide abortion. We are concerned about children indulging in early sexual activity, consequently we say, give them condoms. Isn't something missing from this approach? We are dealing with the leaves and ignoring the root of the problem. As a nation, we need to change some of our cultural norms.

**Accepted Cultural Practices**

Some of our accepted cultural practices help to give rise to our irresponsible and even tragic sexual behaviour. We need to change the belief that to be a man, you "mus have gal in a bungle"[41]. We need to wipe out the thinking that if you are female and at age 15 you have not had a child, then you are a 'mule'. We need to eliminate from our cultural consciousness the idea that to cure sexually transmitted disease, all you need to do is to have sex with a virgin. Instead, we need to value our children that our first priority would be to keep them safe from early sexual initiation. This includes the initiation provided by persons, such as the dons in the communities, who feel that they must be the first ones to taste the fruit of the nubile young virgins. In addition, there are the fathers and stepfathers who feel that they have spent money on their daughters, therefore, they deserve to have sexual relations with them as payment.

These ideas are among the beliefs that are helping to destroy the healthy psyche of our people. Many might say that this thinking pattern is an offshoot of our slave history. If this is true, then we need to actively work to change this pattern. To do otherwise is to behave like the adult who has had an abusive childhood and who resents his parents for the suffering that they have caused him but who, on becoming a parent, turns around and abuses his child. As a people, the majority of whom are descendants of slaves, we need deliberately and intentionally to break away from these negative cultural effects of our past. We must begin a public-education campaign to deal with these issues.

In the same way that money can be found for the "pinch, leave an inch and roll" condom campaign, then money should be sourced to effect a broad and intensive public-education campaign concerning how we should be thinking about our children, and to establish healthy sexual beliefs. This is an urgent matter.

Dr. Glenda Simms in her article 'Child sexual abuse and under-development' in The Sunday Gleaner of June 28, commenting on research conducted by the Ministry of Health, noted: "At all levels of the society, we must understand that young children having sex in the first place, and by extension, having multiple sex partners, is a threat to the foundation of development in any society." She further pointed out: "The time has come for the entire Jamaican society to confront the high and enduring levels of damage caused to children and women by sexual abuse." (Simms 2009) This view is further supported by a group of principals who were invited to a meeting by the Ministry of Education where we were presented with a document on the creation of child-friendly schools. A number of principals pointed out that even when there was a child-friendly environment in the schools, there was the bigger problem of a child-destructive community.

Our societal norms need to be changed. This is the root of many of the problems that relate to our children's early sexualisation and overexposure to adult sexual behaviour. The Church and other civil organizations must help to raise voices which counteract this negative pattern in our communities. The church needs to speak to sexual issues in an honest manner. Not only does the general society need to hold up sex as a beautiful creation of God to be enjoyed by male and female in the context of marriage, but even more so the Church. The Church needs to address sex as God created it. There needs to be multi-generational conversations within the Church about sexual values and mores. The older persons need to share their life stories with the younger ones so that they can learn from them. This includes sharing about the wrong and painful choices that some persons made.

**Bible is not Prudish**

The Bible is not prudish in discussing sex, and neither should the Church be. The book of The Songs of Solomon is a wonderful poetic creation reflecting the joy of a man in the body of his young wife. The stories of Joseph and David are replete with incidents of sexual encounters, which we see replicated in modern society. Let us begin to be less embarrassed in the Church about discussing sex and begin to lead the way in the conversation that needs to be heard by our people. The Church could also sponsor a sex-education programme that could be aired on radio and television. This would be more effective than the written media, since we are quite aware that our people are "reading averse".

On another, though similar note, I was quite encouraged to hear the Prime Minister announce that the law is to be changed to require that the names of fathers be placed on birth certificates. This is a step in the right direction in pointing our nation towards taking responsibility for our children.

**Published July 5, 2009**

# THE PASSIONATE PURSUIT OF PURITY

P assion and purity are two words that do not work together in our current Jamaican mentality. Yet, there are young people in this nation who are all excited by their drive for passion and purity. If I were to say this to some of our radio-programme hosts they would say that I was being unrealistic and idealistic. They do not think that such a thing is possible in this day and age. Yet, it is.

For the last two years, hundreds of young people across Jamaica have been gathering for conferences across this nation to celebrate their passion and purity. This movement was started by Donnette and Andrew Norman, trained guidance counsellors. It was first started at the Wolmer's Trust Schools and has spread to other schools, such as Jamaica College and Manchester High School, where conferences have been hosted. This year the conference will be at Ardenne High School.

According to a magazine printed by the movement, 'Passion and Purity' is a non-profit initiative currently geared towards youth and children. The movement, with its motto 'Finding Your Passion

– Embracing Your Purity', is a re-socialising tool aimed at restoring youth to the ideals of being passionate about their ambitions and embracing their purity and childhood innocence. They will be encouraged to find their passion, that is, locating the "object of their enthusiasm" and pursuing it with vigour. Purity in thought, motive, actions and sexuality is also another major aspect of the mandate as these days, youth are being devoured by sexual immorality. The solution must be long-lasting and positive. Boys and girls will be taught the positives of abstinence and how to be proud of their God-given purity. (Passion and Purity 2009)

I have interacted with some of these young people. I want to tell you about Daniel Thomas, who was the deputy head boy of Ardenne High School for 2008-2009. Daniel is now at the University of the West Indies. Daniel is smart, athletic, handsome, charismatic, a leader, and a passionate Christian young man. Daniel was one of the top basketballers on the school's senior team, which came second in the island. Daniel's younger brother, Josef, is of the same mould and is still at Ardenne.

## Corporate Worship

It was inspiring to watch Daniel go on the stage at corporate worship with the upper school in the auditorium and say to the students who were restless, "Shhh. Let's welcome the Holy Spirit," and watch and listen as the near 1,000 students suddenly became quiet, respectful and reverential. He then proceeds to lead them in worshipful songs, pointing them to Jesus Christ. His voice is melodious and you sense the depth of relationship which he has with his Lord. I see Daniel walk around the compound and he is able to correct students and challenge them and they respond to him in a positive manner. To see Daniel at a basketball match where the team is at a crucial point, being led by a few points by the opposing team and he calls the team together to pray, then to watch him go out and score baskets in a dazzling display is truly something to behold. This young man is a top student academically and he is passionate for God, and bold in his declaration of purity.

There are many similar youths in Jamaica. The passion and purity movement is providing a forum for many of them to come together to declare that passion for life, passion for God, and passion for purity is 'It'.

The movement has outlined some healthy habits of a passionate and pure youth:
I am committed to seek and obey God's plan for my life.

I strive for excellence and do my best at school.

I follow the examples of positive people and seek to emulate positive role models.

I remain pure in thoughts and actions.

I am a reader: today a reader, tomorrow a leader.

I avoid pornographic material and anything than can misdirect my passions.

I treat members of the opposite sex with respect and see them as more than an object of sex.

I choose positive entertainment, music, friends and literature.

I am obedient to those in authority.

I choose to forgive those who hurt me, thus freeing myself of the poisonous effect of unforgiving emotions.

Regretfully, it seems that some of our adults who have not made right choices in their lives when faced with the possibility that our youth can make right choices about relationships, about their sexual lifestyle, about their spirituality, find this to be an impossibility. We sometimes seem ready to accept that our youth cannot display self-control, because we are not able to display self-control. We instead seek to enable their negative behaviours in a 'safe' way because this is all what we are capable of.

**Sexual-Lifestyle Problems**

I am, therefore, quite heartened to see that instead of the singular message that condoms is the answer to our sexual-lifestyle problems, that abstinence is now being actively promoted. As the leaders in Jamaica, we need to hold up high standards for our youth to achieve. We need to let them know that it is possible. As adults, let us share with them from our mistakes and help to point them to a better path. A life of passion and purity is possible as Daniel, in one of his meditations to God, reflects: "I release myself to you, for impossibility is non-existent in your hand and after feeling your touch, it disappears, though still seen by many. I release myself to the plans you have for me, because life is only worth living where it is intended to, in the middle of your hand."

**Published September 6, 2009**

# WHAT OF THE
# TRANSPORTATION CENTRE?

I t seems sometimes that for every step we take forward, we take two backwards. I remember the problems being experienced with students hanging out at the bus stops in Half-Way Tree, some at the Mother's bus stop on Hagley Park Road, others at Molynes Road, and still others on Eastwood Park Road.

The behaviour displayed by many of the students was unacceptable, and there were complaints that something needed to be done to better supervise them at these locations after school. The Government constructed an impressive structure in the middle of Half-Way Tree to house the transportation centre. The buses were now better supervised in terms of scheduling. Students and other commuters had a covered area within which to wait for the buses. There were bathroom facilities provided, and even a shopping area. This situation seems ideal. It is what is done in many developed nations.

## One Problem Solved, New One Arises

The Gleaner of January 15, 2008, (Vickerman 2008) gave this report: "It is the city's newest landmark and can be seen from several miles away. The new Half-Way Tree Transport Centre was officially opened on the weekend and the sense of pride of those in attendance was as thick as the massive columns supporting the building. The comments they made demonstrated that, for the most part, people believed that the development of the transport centre was a step in the right direction. 'It pretty, yuh nuh. A long time this should a deh ya,' and 'a first-class building dem ya,'[42] were a couple comments overheard. Alas, this solution has resulted in a problem which signifies the spiritual and social condition of our youth. Students are using the transportation centre as a hang-out spot. Students from various schools congregate not only to get the buses, but to meet friends and foe, to settle disputes, often violently, to 'make out', and even to terrorize adults.

There seems to be a culture of antisocial behaviour which now characterize many of the students who are using the transportation centre. Civility and decency have declined to such an extent that a police officer who works at the centre has expressed disgust at the situation and conveys that he now hates going to work because of the behaviour of some of the students. Increasingly, I hear or read stories, about students stabbing each other, girls fighting each other over boys, students beating up security guards, parents coming in to aid children in taking revenge on other students, boys and girls openly fondling each other and engaging in sexual activity. And the list goes on. Has the transportation centre provided a solution or facilitated the birth of a monster?

Now, this past week, a student from St Andrew College was stabbed to death by a number of other students in the vicinity of the transportation centre. Last year, principals of schools whose students use the facility were called to a meeting by its management to discuss what then was a developing problem, and to find ways to stem the increasing antisocial behaviour. Present at this meeting were representatives from various sectors of the society, including the police. Principals were asked to get parents and teachers to come to the centre and assist in supervising the students at the rush periods in the mornings and afternoons. This plan was not successful because many parents have their jobs to go to, and those who don't, are aware that this task would be a very difficult and dangerous one for which they were ill-equipped. Teachers are already challenged in dealing with these students in school and found it a problem to consistently be available to supervise students with whom they have no relationship. This arrangement met with little success. The police are at the transportation centre, but not in enough numbers. In addition, the officers change shifts at the extremely critical time of 3 p.m., which is the peak period for many students to be at the centre.

## What Then Is the Solution?

There has to be proactive and reactive action. To be proactive, we must work to change the violent and sexually permissive mindset of our people. We need to begin to model to our youth positive lifestyles. I have been seeing some advertisements on the television promoting strong family structures, abstinence from loose sexual behaviour, and positive images of fathers. We need to have more of this.

In addition, we must encourage and promote healthy parenting and family patterns. In such structures, parents are responsible for their children and put their children's well-being first. The schools, churches, and other social organizations would then provide the support for the basic family structure. It cannot be that the schools are expected to turn around the maladaptive behaviours of our youth. That solution is ineffective and cannot work.

Strong societies are based on strong families. If we continue to accept that getting money and pleasure is the highest achievement, we will not be able to stem this slide into mayhem. In addition, the police and the Ministry of National Security need to train and put in place enough officers to cover the transportation centre and its surrounding areas. It cannot be an excuse that because of the change of shifts the areas are not covered. It might mean a staggering of the shifts so that police personnel are always present.

If the present system is not working, there must be an alternative that meets the present challenges.

**Published November 7, 2010**

# MEMORIES OF 'OLE-TIME' CHRISTMAS

C ommercialized Christmas is a term that became familiar to me as an adult. Growing up in Chapelton, Clarendon, I had no such consciousness. My memories of Christmas bring back feelings of warmth, joy, excitement, sharing and the celebration of the birth of Jesus Christ. Christmas time in my childhood was centred on church, friends and Grand Market. Chapelton is a small town in central Jamaica. It came to life on market days on Friday and Saturday. Life in the town became even more exciting at Christmas, with Grand Market on Christmas Eve.

Christmas was when my siblings and I looked forward to getting pretty new clothes to go the big Christmas programme at church on Christmas night. We looked forward to acting in the Christmas play and to performing songs and poems which the whole community would come out to watch. We got excited at the Grand Market money that Daddy would give us to buy our toys. Those would be the only toys we would get for the year. We were allowed to stay out late to go to Grand Market. We would walk into the town centre about a half a mile away from our home and would get home about midnight and stand out on the roadside to chat with our friends.

**House Preparation**

Then there was the preparation of the house. We had to make sure it was spic and span and mama would change the curtains and put on the lovely bedspreads. My sisters and I would decorate the pine tree in front of our house. In those days, we had no extension cord and would plug out the polisher cord to be used as the extension to light up the Christmas tree. Christmas morning was a special thrill. Daddy, who was the pastor of the church, would wake us up to go to early morning Christmas service at 5:00 am. We would have the service and the whole congregation would gather with bottle torches, singing carols along the way, quite lustily and in good harmony, up the hill from Ivy Store following the roadway up to the hospital to sing for the patients. It was a ritual which we enjoyed and have never forgotten. It was a treat for the community every year. The carolling would begin the last week before Christmas and was done by the young people every morning at 5:00 am.

Our parents had no money to buy us presents and we never felt a lack. We had been given Grand Market money and although it was not much, we could buy our dollies and 'fee-fees', 'clappers' and other noisemakers. In addition, we were quite excited in looking forward to the one present that we knew we would get every year from Sister Lucy, who lived across the road from us and who was the church organist. Every morning after Christmas breakfast, we would see Sister Lucy coming over with a small present for each of us children. That was exciting for us, getting those gifts wrapped in pretty paper. It was the only time that we got wrapped gifts. We have never forgotten that. We felt very blessed.

After Christmas morning breakfast with the family, we would be free to play with our dollies before we had to help mama prepare the Christmas dinner. Dinner was not as leisurely as breakfast, since Daddy had to get ready to go to one or two of the 10 other churches that he pastored across Clarendon to do their Christmas programme and to get back to Chapelton for our 'programme' in the night. Along with sumptuous food at Christmas, we had a special treat which were the crates of 'soda' drinks that Daddy would buy at Christmas. We could drink soda to our hearts' content. Then the highlight of Christmas day was participating in the 'programme' at church and dressing up in our pretty new clothes to go to the play. The church would be packed and people would be on the outside looking in. We would finally be putting on the play after weeks of 'practice'. The play was always based on the story of the birth of Jesus.

## A Different Time

These days, Christmas is different. Carols are hardly sung. The ones that are sung have little to do with the birth of Jesus Christ. Children hear more about Santa Claus than about Jesus. Parents focus more on buying fancy gifts for children than about taking them to church to hear again the story of the birth of Jesus.

Clarendon has become so crime-ridden that people are scared to be on the roads when it is dark for fear of criminals. Carol singing in communities is becoming a thing of the past. Grand Market in Chapelton is not what it used to be. Everyone now gravitates to May Pen. Yet, in spite of the crime that May Pen is becoming known for, people still go out to shop. The resilience of our people gives us hope – hope that we can reclaim the positive values of the past.

I am glad that I was a child in the days when Christmas was still Christ-centred, when it was possible to be free to roam the streets and sing carols early in the mornings. Let us return to the simplicity of a Christ-centered Christmas, finding meaning in our relationships with God and each other.

**Published December 26, 2010**

# RETURN CIVILITY TO OUR NATION

**Spanish Town Bride, St. Ann**

I have been increasingly struck by how uncivil a society Jamaica has become. This has come home to me in a stark way after visiting various secondary schools over the past weeks. The behaviour of many of the children is what we see adults display on the roads and in public places and, unfortunately, what we even observe even in Parliament. The generally accepted conduct in schools seems to be: children shouting across the compound to each other; children speaking to each other on top of their voices, even when close by; anger being displayed at the slightest provocation; teachers endeavouring to be heard by these students, shouting at them over the noise. In the classrooms, teachers spend at least 50 per cent of class time seeking to quiet groups of students who are intent on expressing to each other, at loud volumes, whatever thoughts come to their minds. There is little learning that can take place in such an environment.

**Acceptable Crassness?**

It seems that we have accepted that loudness, crassness and vulgarity are part of our national character. It appears that we have agreed that, as Jamaicans, we are not only to be known for our prowess in track and field, our creativity in music and our penchant for double entendre, but we must also be characterized by our loudness and vulgarity in every sphere. This lack of appreciation for what is considered well-mannered conduct was epitomized in the inauguration of the new Prime Minister. There, during the ceremony, were noisy supporters of the Jamaica Labour Party with their vuvuzelas and clangers which spoilt the formality of the occasion. The entire time, no one reminded these supporters that such behaviour was not suitable for the setting. Tolerating this behaviour simply reinforced to our nation that this type of conduct at a formal, official function had now become acceptable.

All around us we see adults behaving uncivilly, children in turn are imitating what they are hearing and seeing. We are a society made up of a large number of persons who tend to believe that rudeness is our right. For some persons, it means that we are indeed independent and strong; it means that no one can oppress us. For others, it means that we have thrown off our colonial shackles. This general uncivil conduct needs to change. The many positive characteristics that we have as a people are being tarnished by the perception that, as Jamaicans, we are 'rude and out o' order'.

**Learning From The Japanese**

It has become an unpleasant experience to go into some public places and observe the loud and coarse conduct of our people. The English writer, Mary Wortley Montagu, notes: "Civility costs nothing, and buys everything." (Montagu Wortley 2010) In a world where nations are becoming increasingly interdependent, it is necessary for us to realize that we will not attract tourists and investors to our shores with our uncivil conduct, adding to the other problems we already have as a nation. Conducting business or seeking to relax among people whose behaviour is boorish is stressful and unpleasant experience. Therefore, persons will choose to do their business elsewhere and spend their vacation time in a more welcoming atmosphere. We need to realize, as Monatagu says, that "civility ... buys everything".

How many of us remember how the Japanese responded after the terrible earthquake that they experienced? Persons had lost their homes, their loved ones, and had to be sleeping in shelters. There were scarce resources being distributed, and these Japanese stood up patiently waiting in lines to receive their meagre allowance of food. No one was shoving or screaming at each other. How many of us remember the stories of money being found in one community and being turned over to the authorities that it could be returned to its rightful owners? Such levels of consideration and kindness had the world looking on the Japanese with admiration and envy. We in Jamaica would do well to practice even a small percentage of such graciousness. Can you imagine the difference it would make to our nation? We need to bring back civility to our culture.

**Re-teaching Respect in Society**

We need to start again to teach courtesy and good manners in our homes, schools and churches. We must teach our people to show respect to older persons, to those in authority and to each other generally. We need to reintroduce habits which we grew up with as children, such as when you enter a room you greet the persons there. As Miss Lou says, "Howdy an tenky bruck no square.⁴³" We need to teach our children the common courtesies such as 'thank you', 'you are welcome', 'excuse me' and other such mannerly behaviour. In our schools, students and teachers need to understand that shouting and screaming belong on the playing field when matches are under way; that behaviour does not belong in the classroom or on the corridors, and certainly not at corporate gatherings.

When we, as adults, remain quiet when our children behave in this way, whether because of fear or because we can't be bothered, we are simply reinforcing the negative conduct. This behaviour takes on a life of its own and it gets completely out of control. We then find ourselves overwhelmed by this crudeness and vulgarity and we then begin to wonder how we got to this place.

I appreciate our resilience as a people. We have strength and determination. Our resilience is shown in our humour. Who can forget Lovindeer's 'Wild Gilbert' after Hurricane Gilbert devastated Jamaica in 1988? That song characterized the ability of Jamaicans to take the worst situation and get humour out of it. We need to add to that the ability to be kind and courteous to each other, even in the most trying situations.

**Published December 4, 2011**

# JAMAICA NEEDS A MORAL IMPERATIVE

"Something there is that doesn't love a wall, That wants it down."

– 'Mending Wall' by Robert Frost (Frost 1914)

oundations, boundaries, values and morals are being destroyed by an egregious philosophy which would have us believe that freedom from restraint is the highest good. As a nation, we have bought into this mindset, and so the old boundaries that determined civil, courteous, good and decent behaviour have been destroyed. Without boundaries, anything is allowed. Freedom without the attendant responsibility has become the hallmark of our culture. Violence is used as the method of choice to deal with conflict. Human life has lost its value. Obscenity and vulgarity reign unchecked in the dancehall culture. Women are objectified as sexual targets. Some women accept this and make it their badge of honour. Men feel that their manhood is tied up with having sex with as many females as possible. Children are simply offshoots of sexual affairs. Girls serve the purpose of quenching a man's sexual thirst. It does not matter if it is a daughter, niece, stepdaughter, underage girl or a baby.

We have lost all semblance of decency and conscience. We are a society that deems sexual depravity as 'ah nuh nutt'n'[44]. Having allowed e perversity to make its inroads into our country, we have now begun to prey upon ourselves. Our babies, our women, whether old or young, our young boys are no longer safe, because we have allowed predators to walk free as a result of our warped justice system and a mindset that has begun to accept a distorted morality; good has become evil, and evil has become good.

The rape of five women and girls, including an eight-year-old, in the parish of St James has sparked a pushback against this mindset of 'ah nuh nutt'n'. As a nation, we must realize that 'a supp'm, a big supp'm'.[45]

We cannot continue to drag young girls who are victims of rape through a court system that is outdated and can only depend on witnesses in order to determine guilt. We traumatize them by having them relive their experience then merely to have the jury free the perpetrator.

I agree with Betty-Ann Blaine that DNA testing should become mandatory for persons accused of rape. (The Gleaner 2011)I applaud the justice minister for seeking to put in place the Sex Offenders' Registry. It is long overdue.

The extent of our lack of restraint is seen with the police records showing increasing numbers of women being accused of sexual abuse. The typical view of women as the nurturers is fast being eroded. They, too, are now being infected with the evil that comes from the breaking down of moral boundaries. Many of us know deep within our hearts what is right. We know that children should be brought into a family with parents who love them. They ideally should have a mother and a father who are there to prepare them for life. We know that having many children for multiple fathers creates poverty, problems with self-esteem, psychological and cognitive deprivation.

**Change the Mindset**

There are men who father many children and cannot afford to support them in a time of economic hardship, even if they intended to do so. These children become alienated and angry. They sometimes become violent, joining gangs such as the Fatherless Crew. The girls continue in the cycle of poverty, many times being sent by their mothers to have sex with men for money. These women move from one man to another, pretending to want to have out their lot. This mindset has to change. It is developed from a slave mentality that has bound us and which is now being reinforced by a dancehall culture with its sexual objectification of the female body.

We need to re-establish the family as the central unit of the society. We need to develop parents who take seriously their responsibility to be role models and a guide for their children. We need to re-establish the value of life, the gift of children, and our women as nurturers.

When our boundaries are down, many prey upon us. This clearly was the intent of the persons who were behind the recent revision of the curriculum guide for the health and family life education programme in schools. Why is it that the parents had to be the ones to point out to the public that something was wrong with the content of the guide? Guidance counsellors and teachers from all over Jamaica were brought together to be trained in this revised programme by the Ministry of Education.

**Training Session**

As part of this training, guidance counsellors and teachers were taken through some of the activities. One such, I understand, required the participants to relax and take hold of their private parts and make a song about it. This was in an attempt to get them to be comfortable with themselves so they, in turn, would go and teach the seventh- and eighth-graders to be at ease with their sexuality, whether it be same sex, other sex, or both sex. Why didn't the public hear an outcry from these participants about the nature of the training?

I applaud the Minister of Education, Ronald Thwaites, for pulling the texts from the schools and for understanding that what was being done was not to educate our students about homosexuality but to condition them to a homosexual way of thinking. (Reid 2012) I am looking to see who will be held responsible for this insidious, deceptive strategy.

**Published October 7, 2012**

# TOWARDS A GENTLER, MORE CIVIL SOCIETY

**White River, St. Ann**

P arliamentarians being abusive in their behaviour; principals fighting teachers; coaches being restrained on the field; passengers becoming violent on buses when fares are demanded; weapons being drawn because of arguments; students knifing each other because of disagreements - we have lost civility, good manners and courtesy as the hallmark of our culture. There was a gentler time, a more peaceful time, when it was common for persons to be passing each other on the streets and greet one another with "good morning" or "have a good day". When you accidentally did something, the accompanying words would be, "I am sorry." The response most times would have been, "It is okay." Now we pass each other with hostile stares and glares. Anger and resentment permeate the air. If perchance you bump into someone, the response is anger, a threat of violence or violence itself. In former days, obscenities were used to express upset and outrage. Now upset and outrage is expressed all the time, and so obscenity is the language of choice.

**Violent Culture Multiplies**

We see this indiscriminate use of obscenity evidenced in the classroom, with children using obscenities in the same way as they would use Jamaican Creole. Children have learnt this in their homes and communities. Not only do we see the free use of obscenity, but we also see children using violence as the means to deal with any perceived problem, such as a student sitting on their chair. The first action is not to ask for the chair but to immediately push the other child and the chair to the ground. This is usually accompanied, in many instances, with cussing and swearing. Imagine an atmosphere like this replicated many times over in our classrooms. Imagine that a teacher comes into a class with more than 40 seven- or eight-year-old students behaving in this manner.

In too many of our classrooms, too little effective teaching can take place because the teacher has to spend most of the time controlling students' behaviour. These students have been social-ized in their homes and communities in such a way that they find it difficult to sit and concentrate for more than a few minutes at a time. They have been socialized to shout out if they want someone's atten-tion, to curse if annoyed, and to hit, if irritated. This behaviour from a significant number of students in an overcrowded classroom of eight-year-olds makes teaching and learning especially difficult.

Schools alone cannot re-socialize our children. Teaching of good manners and civil behaviour must begin in our homes. But here is the challenge: Civility has broken down so much in our society that many of our parents do not have a concept of what good manners are. There are so few examples held up to them in our nation that they have lost the concept of civility.

**Frontrunners Must Do Better**

How then do we restore civility to our society? How do we become a gentler space? It must begin at the top, in how the business of pol-itics and Parliament is conducted. It must be spread through how media practitioners conduct themselves. It must be reflected in the lyrics that the music industry disseminates. It must be reinforced in how the police deal with our people. It must be practiced in the busi-ness places, in our shops, and markets.

Good customer service, which entails civility, is so rare in our country that we comment on it extensively whenever we experi-ence it. We do have a few advertisements now that promote posi-tive behaviour. I encourage the corporate bodies to get involved in sponsoring a campaign to promote civility. The Minister of Youth and Culture should see this as a priority so that we can retrain our people's minds. I encourage the music fraternity to seek to create songs that speak to this type of behaviour. We have artists who do murals on walls around the country, especially in our cities; let us move to have them paint scenes that depict courtesy and good manners. I believe we can do this if we have the will and determination to do so.

In the 1970s, Jamaica pushed the message of self-reliance and black consciousness; in the 2000s, slackness permeates our air waves and consciousness. Let us use the same tools that were used to create the mindset in those days to now promote a positive, gentler ethos, a more courteous environment. brighter future for all. Let us try to promote decency in our relationships with each other. Let us seek to cultivate good manners and respect for each other. Let us treat our elderly with honour, instead of disdain. Let us promote consideration for the disabled and disadvantaged, instead of ridicule. If this happens, it will be easier for learning to take place in the classrooms. Our children will begin to produce better educational outcomes, which in turn will help us to produce more skilled and well-socialized workers. Investors will be more drawn to this country with a people who are prepared with good work ethics and good interpersonal relationship skills.

Some might think that this is a simplistic view of the situation, but the best solutions are usually simple, staring us in the face. They are interconnected. The foundation, the family, has to be fixed. The schools have to become hallmarks of learning. Our society has to become a place of positive social interaction. All of this begins with training in consideration, thoughtfulness, courtesy and good manners at home. Let's retrain our society to be a gentler, more civil space.

As we enter the season when we celebrate the coming of Jesus Christ into the world, I pray that our country will experience a respite from crime and violence and that we can celebrate with our loved ones and family the birth of Our Saviour, Jesus Christ, in peace and with joy. Happy Christmas.

**Published December 2, 2012**

# TIME FOR AN ABOUT-TURN

The following is feedback from an online interview of Yvonne Coke, conducted by Esther Tyson. Coke has committed herself to a 60-day fast.

After witnessing a man being murdered in Spanish Town across the street from my job at Things Jamaican in the mid-'70s and hearing a murderer confess how sweet it felt to see the blood of a victim run down the street, it left me sick knowing that I lived in a country where human life had no value in the quest for political gain. In 1980, I left Jamaica because I became very afraid for my family and myself when the murders escalated. I was haunted to return to Jamaica, however, and my family and I came back fully in 1987. By 1988, I again became aware of the bloodletting which had not abated.

We kept shaking off the violence as someone else's problem. Then it hit home, in September 2012, as Janice Smith, a member of my church, was killed – her throat slashed by home invaders. My 60th birthday was coming up in January and I started thinking about how to celebrate it. In November, while in Pennsylvania to visit my eldest daughter, I learnt that one of our dearest employees at Hands

Across Jamaica For Righteousness, Diann Beech, was missing. I began to scour the newspaper and saw the report about the body of a woman found in the Bog Walk gorge, wrapped in tarpaulin. The Lord said: "That's her." It did turn out to be her.

## Materially Poor

Diann Beech was a materially poor woman but a giant in prayer before God. A valuable asset to Hands who understood Jamaica's purpose and worked to teach children what it truly meant to be a Jamaican citizen 'under God'. She did not deserve to be raped, gagged, bound and strangled to death, as no one else deserves. But that was the violent way in which our country had chosen to repay her service to her fellow citizens. It was then that the Lord said to me: "I want you to give me one day for each year of your life over the 60 years in a fast of silence to end the violence in your nation and you will see what I will do." Sixty days. I thought I must have been going crazy. Well, this was such a persistent request which came day after day and moment after moment that I felt that if there was even a possibility that a miracle could come of such a fast, I had nothing to lose, live or die. Then He quoted from Revelation 12: "They overcame by the blood of the Lamb and the word of their testimony and they loved not their lives unto the death." I agreed. He chose the place, the mode, the time and the base scripture of Isaiah 58 for the fast.

The Lord chose the monument to the murdered children on Church Street, Kingston to be the place for the public expression of the fast. My experiences at the monument have ranged from deep sadness and pain to seeing redemption as people come to the monument with their pain and we are able to lead them to forgiveness and repentance before God. One young man who confessed to being a gunman and a deportee gave his life to Jesus Christ as he was confronted by the evil of the life he was living compared to the life God intended for him as a Jamaican guided by the national pledge. Another came with the burden of hopelessness because he lived amidst constant fighting and quarrelling and all of his relatives had done jail time or were incarcerated. He also turned over his life to God as he did not want to continue the generational trend. He is now happy, employed and supporting his child. He almost daily reports on his new success. A father and mother told us of how the police had (in their words) "murdered" their son in cold blood as he cooked dumplings and they could get no justice. He walked around with the child's picture and documents as he watched his wife suffer cancer from the worry about her son's death. We prayed for him and gave him what words of comfort we could, but the wounds were deep, yet he encouraged us by telling us that the work of Hands in his community in 2008 had brought lasting peace.

**Deafening Silence**

Every day I see a willingness to take responsibility for our own part in reducing our nation to a murderous, lawless island when God has given us so much to inspire others. People are comforted by knowing of the sacrifice of the fast. The silence is crying aloud about the sins of the nation, as we have turned our backs on the keeping of our national pledge. They understand. People come, and as we offer to pray for them, we explain the path to which our nation had committed itself in the motto, anthem and pledge and the way we have strayed from that path which has led us to destruction and poverty. They are humbled by that knowledge and indicate a willingness to change and to cease to blame others.

Father Sherlock said it best in what he said he heard God say in 1996 as I interviewed him for his biography: "I believe I can hear God, looking at this nation on the march and as Commander of this nation, issuing His commands. The first one clearly is 'Stop.' We must halt.' The second command is 'Right about-turn.' We must turn away from the road we are travelling. And the third command is 'March.' March in a new direction, a direction of love and of concern for others, of peace and of brotherhood and of sisterhood – a call to us as a nation to realise that we have lost our providential way and we have no right to proceed on the road which we are travelling."

So, I say from the bottom of my heart what God said, what God wants: "Stop. You are on the wrong road, right about-turn, and march. March away from the destination which will mean ruin and an abuse of Independence which will result in the destruction of our nation."

**Published March 3, 2013**

# STRENGTHENING JAMAICA'S SOCIAL FABRIC

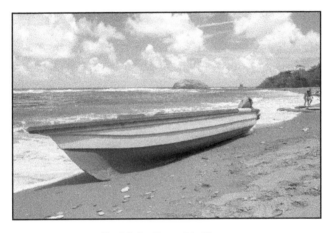

Robin's Bay, St. Mary

Dennis Chung, Chief Executive Officer of the Private Sector Organization of Jamaica, (PSOJ) wrote an article titled 'Social behaviour - the missing link for Jamaica's development' on Friday, April 25, 2014. I endorse the perspective that he shared.

In his article, he makes the following point: *The reasons proper social behaviour is so important to development should be obvious to all, but suffice to say that whether you are in an organisation or in a country setting, no meaningful development can happen without an adherence to rules/structure and the respect of the rights of a citizen in the country, whether they are guilty of a crime or not. It is on these principles of rules, acceptable social behaviour, and respect for the rights of all that modern societies are based. And without these at the base of our development, we cannot consider ourselves a modern society, but rather one with barbaric norms.* (Chung 2014)

T he lack of adherence by many of our people to accepted social behaviour is aiding the fast erosion of a stable Jamaican society. There is, instead, a mentality that reflects the thinking that 'man haffi live',[46] so that makes any action acceptable as long as you can get money from it.

**Free-For-All**

Therefore, on the roads, taxi men and bus drivers drive recklessly by breaking the road code and becoming abusive to those who object to their behaviour. To disagree with this manner of road use is seen as 'baxing bred outa me mout'.[47] The need to 'mek a money'[48] is the standard by which all behaviour must be judged, so there should be no objection to harassing tourists to purchase unwanted items because 'man haffi mek a money'.[49] This mentality speaks to a need for immediate gratification without considering the long-term effects of the action.

The work ethic that you should give your employer full commitment and perform your job with excellence in return for your salary is replaced by a practice of chicanery, where you seek to do the least amount of work for the most money. Many people think it is acceptable to take the company's stationery and other materials without permission. They do not see this as stealing, which it is. This has become a pervasive practice.

In schools, where teachers are allowed a number of days per year as casual leave, some teachers believe that they must ensure that they take these days, even when they do not need to, because it is due to them. They do not think about the students who will suffer for not having their classes taught and who will not have their syllabus completed by the end of the school year.

The respect for rules and authority, which is significant in holding the social fabric of a country together, is barely acknowledged by many people. Instead, our culture has become one of silence when wrong is committed. The lack of respect for laws and rules has given rise to an 'informer-fi-dead'[50] culture. Furthermore, the belief that some policemen are joined to some criminal elements and that it is not safe to make reports to them helps to strengthen this mentality.

**Informer-Fi-Dead Culture**

The story was carried in another newspaper of a lady who, because she made reports to the police of illegal activities, has been harassed and abused by both police and citizens. This strengthens this thinking. This informer-fi-dead culture has been celebrated by our DJs. It has been lionized in dancehall culture. This belief has had a far-reaching impact on dealing with the widespread crime and violence. If we do not change that mentality to one of each citizen taking responsibility to uphold law and order, we are on our way to becoming a failed state. As Dennis Chung says, one with "barbaric norms".

## Impact on Our Culture

What is even more alarming is to the see the children in school who have now been born and bred amid this lack of respect for law and order and common decency. This is how they have been socialized in their homes and communities. This informer-fi-dead attitude and fighting because of any perceived 'diss'[51] is now impacting the culture of our schools. Yet the Jamaican society expects that schools are to achieve a miracle and convert these students, so socialized, into law-abiding, model citizens. It is not a workable solution.

As a people, we must understand that when we tear down the standards of common decency, respect for each other and respect for law and order, we are aiding in digging the grave for our nation. We have economic problems. We have problems with our justice system, and we have added to that the problem of social dysfunction.

We need to develop again the aborted Values and Attitudes Programme that former Prime Minister P.J. Patterson had tried to implement. Only this time, we need to ensure that it is supported and widespread. It means that the corporate entities that are supporting artistes that continue to send out messages that assist in creating negative and violent sensibilities in our people need to instead invest their resources in artistes who are willing to create positive, moral and uplifting lyrics. This will help to change the culture. It means that the media must join in advertising messages that will positively impact our thinking. We need to advertise messages about matters such as courtesy, good manners, helping others, and being kind.

If we do not realize that we are in a crisis and do not seek to aggressively change the thinking and behaviour of our people, it will destroy all the great plans for investors to come to Jamaica and help in our economic recovery. Our culture must return to one where good manners, courtesy, and respect for law and order are what are feted in our music and art forms, and not crassness, vulgarity and Anancyism[52].

**Published May 4, 2014**

# DOUBLE STANDARD, MINISTER?

The issue of what is appropriate content for young children is once again a matter of concern in Jamaica. In May 2013, a friend of mine who was then a member of the board of directors of the National Gallery of Jamaica (NGJ) brought to my attention images containing anal sex and lesbian sexual encounters that were part of the NGJ's Biennial Exhibition 2012. This exhibition ran for three months and ended in March 2013.

Why did he bring these to my attention? Because he was concerned that the board insisted on zero censorship as its policy and was refusing to place appropriate signs in the appropriate places to warn school groups that would normally bring children to the gallery, and other patrons, who might not want to see such images, that they were being displayed in a particular area.

I was later sent a copy of the letter that my friend had sent to the board of directors, dated February 17, 2013. I later learnt that the needed signs to inform patrons of the content of this exhibit were only put in the appropriate places a mere three weeks before the end of this three-month exhibit.

I was asked not to write about this matter last year since the board member was seeking to address the matter internally. He also told me that he had to consider resigning, since most board members did not support his view of the material being shown and how it was being shown and because of their insistence on maintaining a zero-censorship policy.

He resigned from the board two months ago in consideration of the fact that, not being satisfied with the board's position on zero censorship, he had sent a letter to the Minister of Youth and Culture, under whose ministerial portfolio the NGJ falls, but has received no response. He had been informed that the Minister endorses the NGJ's position of zero tolerance.

How can a National Gallery that is sponsored by government funds be displaying images of anal sex when this is illegal in Jamaica? Further, how can our children be deliberately exposed to such visual material in the name of art while we are justifiably objecting to their being taught about anal sex in an education manual in children's homes?

**Art for Public Consumption**

Even more so, why has the Broadcasting Commission been given a mandate by the Government of Jamaica to regulate music and videos that promote violence and inappropriate sexual content, yet the National Gallery of Jamaica, which is open to the public, is displaying images of sexual intercourse that is illegal in Jamaica?

Why has the Minister of Youth and Culture objected to the inappropriate training manual in the children's homes, yet she has been silent on this display of pornographic material at the NGJ? How is it that the board of that institution has said it is insisting on zero censorship and that the Minister endorses this policy?

Are we saying that art stands above the laws of Jamaica? If so, on what grounds? Is there yet another outside partner who is twisting the arms of NGJ to adopt such a policy? Is the powerful arm of money at work here as it is with the firing of Professor Bain and the sudden and strange retirement of the most productive police commissioner that this country has seen in years? Are we once again being colonized? Are we no longer a sovereign nation? Are our rights being sold out without our knowing?

I believe that the Minister of Youth and Culture needs to address this matter. We must be consistent in our policies. What is inappropriate in the children's homes cannot be appropriate in the NGJ. This is part of a statement issued by the NGJ on June 26, 2014 in response to the matter being made public:

"In the case of the 2012 Biennial, cautionary signage was prominently posted and viewers informed of the content of the exhibition before entering the Gallery. The statement also offered assistance from the Gallery's Education Department for guidance, where needed or desired. Several additional cautionary signs were also added near the artworks under discussion.

The images that have now been circulated to the media have been altered and are not accurate representations of the artworks that were on display during the 2012 National Biennial. The images now circulated are, in effect, enlargements of small images that were in a collage and two other pieces of the 126 individual pieces in the exhibition."

## Nationwide Interview

In an interview with Cliff Hughes on Nationwide on Tuesday, July 1, 2014, the board member made it clear that signs were not placed in suitable locations until three weeks before the end of the exhibition. (Jamaica 2014) Furthermore, I viewed a video about the 2012 Biennial Exhibition on the NGJ's website. In this video, the head of the NGJ is speaking about the exhibition with some of the pieces on display in the background. In one of the pieces, which was a collage, I could see one of the images that was offensive quite clearly. Yet the board, in its statement, has accused the former member of circulating enlargements of small images.

All this discussion of appropriate signs and enlarged images is secondary to the issue that the NGJ, with its policy of zero censorship, has mounted an exhibit with displays that contain images of an act that is illegal in Jamaica. Over to you, Minister Hanna. We look on in earnest to see how this seeming double standard will be dealt with.

We must seek to protect our young in every way possible. They are being over-sexualized, sexually abused, overexposed to violence, and violently abused. They hear it, see it, experience it. The result - their sensibilities are being warped. We are sowing to the wind and we will reap the whirlwind.

**Published July 6, 2014**

# THINGS FALL APART

"Things fall apart, the centre cannot hold; /Mere anarchy is loosed upon the world, / the blood-dimmed tide is loosed, and everywhere/The ceremony of innocence is drowned."

— William Butler Yeats (Yeats 2011)

These lines aptly describe the violence and abuse being meted out to Jamaica's children and the loss of innocence for many. For years, I have been saying that if we do not deal with the rapid erosion of the moral fabric of Jamaica, we would be reaping a whirlwind of destruction. We are now experiencing the whirlwind. I remember saying in the 1990s when there were so many reports about children in the USA being abducted that at least in Jamaica, we look out for our children. This has rapidly changed. Now we are afraid to have our children play out in the yard without adult supervision, feel fear when we see children walking on the streets alone, and no longer fear for only our girls, but also for our boys.

The recent incidents of two 14-year-old girls being impregnated by adult men who later murdered them indicate how far we have fallen as a nation. Following on that is the report of the 11-year-old girl in Clarendon who was raped by two men and the lack of response by the police when the matter was initially reported. This approach by the police is the result of a systemic lack of regard to the sexual and physical abuse of our children. We have heard repeatedly that when rape or sexual abuse cases reach the courtrooms, there is hardly any offender who is given the punishment that he deserves by the jurors because the attitude is, "A nuh nutt'n, a likkle sex."[53] In addition, when some of our girls, who have been abused by family members – father, stepfather, brother, cousin, try to let their mothers or grandmothers know, they are verbally and physically abused and told they are lying. This is particularly so when the accused supports the mother financially.

There are many stories of girls being abandoned by their mothers because the mother's baby father, who sexually molested the daughter, says that the girl is lying. Some mothers do not even go as far as to question the man, but immediately becomes defensive in fear of losing the 'bread and butter', and even kicks out her daughter. Then there are those mothers who, when confronted with the situation by a teacher or guidance counsellor, says, "A nuh nutt'n. Me go tru it, she nuh can go tru it too? It never kill me."[54] Even more reprehensible are those who actually pimp their daughters to men who can give them money and support their families.

**Fear**

Many of our children are so intimidated by the power structures in our society that they never speak out about the abuse that they are experiencing because of fear of reprisal, of being accused of lying, of being abandoned by their families, church or school. Too many times when persons in authority in the Church are involved in sexual abuse, the victims and their families are made to feel like outcasts. So, 'insult is added to injury' when the abuser is defended and protected and the abused suffers rejection and cursing. There are too many instances where because of the sexual abuse our girls suffer at the hands of men, they begin to turn to other girls or women for emotional and sexual intimacy.

I am thankful that the Child Care and Protection Act has been put in place and more persons are being sensitized to the rights of the child. There is still, however, a lot more that needs to be done legally to ensure that our young girls are protected from predator parents and men who want to use them to fulfil their warped financial and sexual needs. A recent report from the police speaks to the practice of teenage boys robbing people in downtown Kingston. Investigations have revealed that parents are sending these boys out to rob and bring the proceeds home. Laws need to be enacted and enforced to punish the parents who are using their children in this way. Furthermore, I am tired of hearing of these men who are impregnating young girls and cannot be identified because the families and the girls protect them. There must be ways that investigation can be done to find out this information and bring the men and the parents to justice.

**Byword**

Jamaica's name is fast becoming a byword internationally because of our high levels of crime, violence, corruption and our economic woes. This latest phenomenon of big men murdering underage girls whom they have impregnated has brought us to an even lower level of disrepute. We must begin to restore the moral fabric of our nation so that we will display the right values and attitudes that will uplift us as a people.

We need to realize that money is not the greatest good. The example of that message being touted in Jamaica is seen in Digicel using Michael O'Hara in a marketing stunt at Champs. The rampant buying of students by well-endowed schools is another such example. If corporate Jamaica and principals are chasing winning at any cost what can we expect the young to do? We need to use our music, dance, and media to teach our people consistently to honour God first, their families, nation and themselves above money. If we continue to make it excusable for people to be lawless on the roads, in daily transactions, on the buses, in government business because to obey the law means "Yuh a bax bread out a me mout,"[55] then we are sowing further to our own destruction by holding up money as the highest good. If so, "dawg nyam we suppa".[56]

We need to remember that righteousness exalts a nation, but sin is a reproach to any people.

**Published April 5, 2015**

**Part 4**

# THE IMPACT OF DANCEHALL ON THE JAMAICAN CULTURE

# "SLACKNESS AND MORE SLACKNESS"

B ob Marley's, **One Love** is heralded as the song of the 20th century. Jamaicans are jubilant about this. We boast of the impact of such songs as Redemption Song in encouraging the anti-apartheid movement in South Africa. Millions across the world identify with the message in Bob Marley's songs. We agree that music has tremendous power and effect. Isn't this evident in how Jamaica has become known worldwide because of Bob Marley's music? How is it then that the same voices that acknowledge the powerful effect of Marley's music now seek to deny the effect of dancehall artistes such as Vybz Kartel's lyrics on the minds and subsequent behaviour of those who listen to them?

Dancehall has moved from the space that reggae occupies, in its promotion of social and political consciousness, to the elevation and advancement of slackness. This affects our youth in a negative fashion. Dancehall is not only the music, but it is a culture which impacts dress, fashion and body language; it influences attitude. Dancehall dress leaves little of the women's bodies to the imagination. It is this mindset that is now affecting many of our young people in school. They are following the dancehall culture of 'bad-manism',[57] 'hottie girls',[58] 'nuff girls',[59] 'nuff skin'[60] and body parts exposed, 'nuff slackness',[61] public wining and grinding,[62] 'bling and more bling'[63], and everything else that the culture promotes.

**Parents Also Indulging**

There are parents who are indulging in the dancehall lifestyle and who, therefore, cannot guide their children to lead moral, self-disciplined lives. The children and the parents are now both indulging in dancehall slackness. We see the effects of this in our schools. We see it when little children are taken to "Passa Passa"[64] and adults delight in watching them "wining and grinding" their undeveloped hips in imitation of adult slackness. Before these children can begin to know what innocence is, they have lost it. Their innocence has been aborted. This exposure to unbridled slackness from an early age has ensured that we produce a generation whose morality has been warped from the beginning. They will now believe that this slack and loose behaviour is the norm.

**Women as Sex Objects**

We add slackness to slackness when the songs played on the sound systems and the images portrayed in the music videos all promote women as sex machines. That these women represent themselves merely as objects of sex is made clear by how they dress and by the sex-simulating gyrations they indulge in, which are termed 'dancing', with bottoms bouncing and going around like gigs and pelvic thrusts emphasizing their genital areas. With such a constant diet being fed to the senses of the young, how can their conscious-ness develop in an innocent, childlike way? Add to these stimuli, the images of 'upstanding' Jamaicans "wining and grinding" on the roads during carnival; women sandwiched by men from behind and before; women and men of all shapes and sizes, some totally unknown to each other, wearing the barest of coverings, indulging in unrestrained sexual conduct on the streets with the media promoting and cov-ering it, with hordes of police (including high-ranking police officers) guiding the train. What are we saying to our young? We are saying that slackness is acceptable, that sexual behaviour is not a private matter; that sex can be practiced publicly with society's approval.

Why, then, are we shocked when our schoolchildren display this same type of behaviour on the streets, at the transportation hubs, on the buses, on the school grounds? Why are we shocked when they want their sex acts to be video-taped and published? "Children live what they learn." They have simply taken a step further than what they have been taught by the 'big people', the adults, around them. We are simply reaping what we have sown.

This is what some young teenagers say about the impact of dancehall on their behaviour:

"It makes me break out of my little shell. I am an innocent girl and dancehall music breaks that barrier."

"It makes you feel all gangsterish and cool. And the music teaches you how to dress."

"The lyrics are influential. They tell you to walk roun', smoke weed and buss gun[65]. Many people, children in particular, look up to some of the artistes who feature these lyrics in their songs and they actually do some of these things because they feel that if their favourite artiste is doing it and they are 'hip' and admired, then why not do it too. Hence, dancehall music is influential, not only to me, but to the wider society."

"I have stopped listening to dancehall music now and that's good because it had such a negative influence on me. At one point, I found myself acting in the way that the songs portray a 'hot girl' should be."

## Eroding Society's Moral Fibre

It doesn't matter that the academicians say that dancehall is reflecting what is happening in the society – Jamaicans know and teachers can testify to the fact that this culture is helping to erode the moral fibre of this society. If we do not begin to accept that this is happening and do something to halt it, we are going to be seeing more of the slackness, badmanism[66], disrespect, lack of self-control and general lawlessness being played out in our schools. We are teaching our young the wrong things and, therefore, they are displaying the wrong, 'anti-social' conduct which they have learnt from society. What hypocrites we have become. We need to begin to send clear signals to our young people about what is right and what is wrong. Our media, our music, our theatre, our government, our private sector, our churches, our schools, must decide what type of

Jamaica we want to have and if what dancehall promotes is it, then let dancehall reign.

"Righteousness exalts a nation but sin is a reproach to any people," says the Bible. (NIV) Holy Bible 1984)

**Published April 06, 2008**

# 'RAMPIN' SHOP' – MUSICAL POISON

As a principal of a school of over 1,930 students with approximately 1,000 being boys, I am faced daily with the fact that as a nation, we are rearing our children on garbage in terms of the values that as a society we are passing on to them. There are some parents who try to counter the effects of this filth that permeates our society, but it is becoming increasingly difficult when the Government will not censor the filth that portrays itself as entertainment in the audio and visual media.

The belief that music and videos that promote unbridled sexual expression, violence, the debasement of women and disrespect for authority is acceptable, is further reinforced by entertainers and academics who, on talk shows and interview programmes on the television, speak about the right of the people to express themselves in the dancehall space. I have a feeling that in the same way that Vybz Kartel does not allow his children to listen to his slackness, that many of these academics do not expose their children to this type of entertainment, which they glibly promote as being acceptable. I cry shame on them, because I am seeing the damage that their endorsement and promotion of such filth is doing to our children.

## X-Rated Lyrics

My outrage has been fuelled by the knowledge that one of Vybz Kartel's songs, Rampin'' Shop, was being voted on FAME FM in its #1 vote for favourite song for the week recently. I will describe this song to you in as decent terms as I conjure, which is extremely difficult. The song is done by Vbyz Kartel and Spice. It is done as if two lovers were having violent sex and describing in graphic, vulgar, obscene language, how it should be done. The introduction begins by Vybz Kartel introducing himself as, "ah di teacha",[67] with Spice replying, "And ah spice".[68] They then go on to condemn same-sex relationships, and while launching into what can only be described as something which takes place in triple x-rated pornographic movies. Who is responsible?

We must work together to stop enriching people like Vybz Kartel who create filth and are then paid when they release it on the public. The corporate giants in this nation who are promoting such filth need to come into the schools and see what is happening to the minds of the young. Vybz Kartel needs to have his children listen to his songs and analyze them and give him their feedback. Government ministers, such as the Minister of Education and the Prime Minister, need to sit and listen to some of these songs and understand the devastating impact they are having on the psyche of the Jamaican children.

**Students' Views**

I will now share with you some of the views of some students on this song. Students from seventh, eighth, ninth, 10th and 13th grade gave 115 written responses. All but two of these students describe the song as being disgusting, inappropriate for air play and having a negative impact on their psyche.

In Tenth grade – "The song Rampin" Shop by Vybz Kartel and Spice can be heard everywhere. While walking on the road it is playing in the cars of motorists passing by. The schoolchildren play it every time on their phones. They play it with the expletives, unedited, having no respect for the other passengers on the bus. It is played on the television, radio and the Internet. A song of this manner should not be available to the underage public. It is poisoning the minds of children and should be banned."

"This song is a total disgrace to Jamaica. I hear it every night when they have dances down the road from my house. Vybz Kartel went all out for this song. It is very slack and when I hear it I feel very uncomfortable about my body because of those hard-core lyrics. Spice is no better. She is a disgrace as a woman and she is no help in how men view us as women. Sex was created by God for marriage. It is special. Kartel makes it seem like a video game."

"The edited version does not make sense because even with the edited parts out you can know what is there."

"I think I'm becoming addicted to it because it's basically every-where I go. I know what the lyrics are saying is wrong but it's hard to resist something that's constantly around you."

Thirteenth grade – "Honestly, that song is lewd and disgusting as, not only is it degrading women, but it also reflects the direction in which this country is going. I see children as young as four years old singing that song from beginning to end. That is basically giving the step by step process of how to take part in sex activity."

Ninth grade – "I think that Spice is not setting a good example for her child and a lot of people look up to her. For her to sing a song like Rampin'' Shop shows she has no self-respect and none for her fans. As a mother, she should not be behaving in such a manner."

Eighth grade – "One night I was singing it loud as if I wanted to do what Spice and Vybz Kartel was doing."

Seventh grade – "In my opinion, Rampin'' Shop has a very negative effect on our youths. We have to listen to these sexual lyrics not because we want to, but because it is polluting our communities."

"I have been disturbed by this song. The morals are very unsuitable for young children, teens or even young adults. They have put together the "sketel" and "badman"[69] of dancehall and the product? Immorality. I know that Jamaican teens love it because it is very easy to catch on to, but how does this help our young people?"

All I have left to say is this. Until the decent, well-thinking citizens of this nation begin to be outraged and put a stop to this airing of filth, then we have condemned ourselves as a nation doomed for destruction. We are destroying the psyche of our children – our future.

**Published February 1, 2009**

# LET'S TAKE BACK OUR SOCIETY

I am encouraged to see that well-thinking Jamaicans are expressing outrage over the exposure of our children to the lewd and violent lyrics that is destroying their innocence. I congratulate the Broadcasting Commission for banning these lyrics from being played on the airwaves. As a nation, we need now to work together to clean up what is aired on the buses and taxis. In addition, music that is for adults should be played in restricted areas, away from the ears of children.

The Minister of Education, in addressing the press conference at Jamaica House to launch Peace and Love in Society's Peace Day 2009, at Jamaica House, informed us that the powers that be would be engaging the franchise holders of the buses to educate the bus drivers on the type of music that is suitable to be aired, as well as songs that are not suitable. In addition, the Minister of National Security has said that the police would be enforcing the ban on lewd and violent lyrics on the buses. All well-thinking citizens need to play their part in making sure that the guidelines laid down by the Broadcasting Commission are followed, as well as insist that these unacceptable lyrics are not aired in public passenger vehicles.

## X-Rated Productions

The behaviour of many of our young people, especially those from dysfunctional homes, is largely directed by the music that they listen to and the videos that they see. The children gravitate towards the buses in which they can hear the X-rated songs and watch the X-rated videos. If you go to Half-Way Tree, you would realize that many students are not going to the Transportation Centre to take the JUTC buses; rather, they are by Mandela Park and the Mother's bus stop to take the franchise buses that will offer them this diet of violence and slackness. These buses need to be monitored.

Marcia Forbes, coming out of research that she did for her doctoral thesis, wrote an article, Language and Lyrics- the rampin' debate. In it she noted,

'Our teenagers know the lyrics of Rampin Shop. They would be in tune with Kartel'sexual joy of being squeezed like handcuff and Spice's encouragement to him to "ramp nuff till me belly cramp up."[70] (Forbes 2009)

Not only do they imitate sexual behaviour, but both boys and girls adopt the attitude and violent behaviour which these lyrics reflect. One of our popular reggae artistes, speaking at a forum at Jamaica House on this aspect of our music, stated that in Jamaica, the artistes have the manual for behaviour. Further to this, the Prime Minister made the point that no one could counter the fact that music has great power in Jamaica.

**Right Values and Attitudes**

These statements ring true, since as Jamaicans, we can see that the music has helped to transform our culture to one where to be disrespected is the greatest offence. The music gives the right to anyone who is disrespected to use violence in retaliation. It is our music that has helped to develop among us the culture that to speak out against wrong means that you are an 'informer' and that 'informer fi dead'.[71]

If we are to become a nation where violence is no longer our hallmark, the music must change. The music, with its power and influence, can be used to help our children to learn appropriate values and attitudes. The music can help children who will not learn at school to begin to take their schoolwork seriously. More of our artistes need to use their creativity and sense of rhythm to accomplish this. We know this from hearing about mothers who, instead of teaching children their 'ABCs', are having their little three-year-olds sing all the 'daggerin'[72] songs and are teaching them the dances. Can you imagine what could be done if the music were used to teach positive messages about life and to teach them how to read?

I want to encourage the powers that be to do something about the violation of the rights of decent well-thinking citizens who live in the inner cities and who have to be subjected to the diet of music filled with lewdness and violence. I agree with Ian Boyne on this matter. Why do we assume that decent people who go to church and who want to bring up their children in a right and godly way don't live in the inner cities?

336

I read the letter in last Tuesday's Gleaner written by one such citizen who made it clear that he wanted to be able to live in peace, to raise his children free from this violation and to have his elderly father be able to sleep and rest, free from lewdness and violence. (Dawkins 2009) In addition, I will quote from a letter sent to me by another citizen who lives in a community where children are being violated by adults using the music to stir their base behaviour.

"In my community, every Wednesday night they have daggerin' in the middle of the road. Anyway after 10 o'clock, they play all dirty song. They had a mattress. They made the girls from nine years old to 15 years old, put dem one one on the matress, then the music man started to play. Then he say, 'Little gal, you go on the matress'.

"He call the man dem by dem name. Say get on top. Then he began work. He say words like this, 'We inna the rampin room, so a just sex'. 'Wine gal, sen it in ... hold her down, give it to her, doan mek she get way'. Bad word, bad word. It sick my stomach. When you hear eight-year-old child say the song make she want sex, it getting out of hand."

"Everywhere you went di man dem dying for Wednesday night to come to go dagger di pickney dem. I wish if di police dem could lock off it all the times. Too much ting happening now. We want back Jamaica from the nasty song, from rape, from gunman, from all who doing this to our country, to our nation, to our people. Enough is enough now man."

**Published March 1, 2009**

# MORE THREATS AGAINST OUR YOUTHS

W hen will it stop? Other threats to our youths are surfacing, adding to what can be deemed to be an already volatile culture where danger seems to lurk around the corner.

In this new school year, the attacks against students walking to get transportation in the Half-Way Tree area have increased. Students are being held up walking along Hope Road and in Mandela Park in Half-Way Tree. As a result, there is increased fear among students and parents because of this spate of incidents. Parents are therefore being forced to spend more money paying bus fares or getting other means of transportation directly from school to home, because they fear for their children's lives or well-being when they are walking on the streets. This is putting additional strain on parents who are already burdened with the increases in the cost of living and especially the cost of textbooks. The effect of this added fear is the sense of threat that hangs over our students and parents. This increased fear and tension will result in psychological problems and physical ailments. Already, there is a sense that as a people we are on edge with fear and worry.

As if this were not bad enough there is yet another threat which has surfaced in the entertainment sector. This is the now bitter feud between the Gaza/Gully factions. Gaza refers to the Portmore area where Vybz Kartel resides, while Gully refers to the area of Kingston where Mavado lives. Gaza is linked also to the Portmore Empire of which Vybz Kartel is president, while Gully is linked to Alliance of which Mavado is president. Now, Jamaicans have become accustomed to these feuds and clashes between rival dancehall artistes. This feud, however, is getting totally out of hand.

## Embracing Violent Feud

Stories are circulating of persons being physically abused because they reside in an area of one or the other of the groups and dare to play the music of the rival artiste. Other stories concern drivers going through a community playing the songs of the rival artiste in their vehicles and being stopped and physically abused. Then there are the selectors who suffer physical retaliation from the hands of opposing sides because they do not play the music of the chosen artiste. These are but a few examples of what is taking place in our society as a result of musical choices made by supposedly free citizens of our country.

This conflict has descended to a lower level than those clashes of the past, such as those between Bounty Killer and Beenie Man. The students in schools are embracing this violent feud. Many unthinkingly identify with one side or the other and take on the spirit of the feud. Now, we recall how assiduously the security forces have been trying to stem the violence at the transportation centres where these students gather. The society does not need another source of divide to add to what is already a very tribalistic culture. I agree with Bounty Killer that these artistes need to speak out at a public forum against this destructive mindset that has evolved from what is supposed to be a lyrical clash. The media need to give as much coverage to this event when it occurs as it does to the violence which results from the clash of Gaza and Gully.

In The Gleaner editorial of Wednesday, September 23, the following comments, which summarises the current state of this conflict, were made:

"There is something different, however, about the Gaza-Gully-Kartel-Mavado phenomenon. It has embraced a violent intolerance. Increasingly, knives, guns and other forms of physical violence are being brought into play. So far, no one has been reported killed in any of these episodes of violence but the possibility is grave." (Editorial 2009)

**Usain Bolt's Endorsement**

Given the increasing gravity of this situation, I was concerned to see our esteemed world record breaker Usain Bolt endorsing one of these sides on national television. Even if Usain meant no harm, his gesture and endorsement will simply add to the already heightened conflict between the Gaza/Gully groups. Usain's management team needs to help him understand the level of influence that he exerts in this nation. He needs to quickly appreciate that what he says and does has indelible impact on the minds of many of our young people who uncritically follow his every move from 'To the worl' to 'Gaza'. He must be careful to realize that his is a 'world' status and cannot be tribalised to merely a 'Gaza' status. His is one of the voices that could serve to quell the senseless abuse being associated with this Gully-Gaza feud. In this divided nation, we need voices to encourage peace not conflict.

On a more positive note, I want to commend Dr. Mary Campbell, assistant chief education officer in charge of the core curriculum in the Ministry of Education, for hosting the first Ministry of Education's expo for the principals of the primary and secondary levels. This two-day expo was a huge success. Principals were addressed by various officers of the Ministry of Education and treated to materials for their schools, ranging from mathematics to the performing arts. This expo is a step in the right direction, as for the first time there is a sense that the ministry is integrally involved in ensuring that needed materials necessary for the efficient delivery of the curriculum is directly placed in the hands of the schools' principals. Most of these materials, including books and charts, were free of cost to the schools. This move, along with the book-rental system, will help to level the playing field among the different schools. I encourage the officers of the ministry to think outside the box in addressing the crucial education needs of our students, given the increasing limited resources with which we are working.

**Published October 4, 2009**

# MONEY AND MORALS

I listened to a very revealing discussion hosted by Cliff Hughes on his programme, Impact, aired on TVJ on October 22. The discussion surrounded the current topic of the contribution that our dancehall music is making to the violent behaviour being displayed by many of our youth. The participants in the discussion were Cliff Hughes, moderator, Skatta Burrell, Queen Ifrica, Foota Hype, Mystic, Mr Vegas and Robert Livingston. (Burrell, et al. 2009)

Throughout the discussion, all the participants, apart from Queen Ifrica, maintained that dancehall was benefiting the society because it provided employment to the various persons involved in the industry. This benefit was what was paramount in the discussion. When asked if they did not see a relation between the violent lyrics and the violent behaviour of youth, most of those present denied this impact. These artistes proceeded to say that it was the responsibility of parents to monitor their children and determine what influence they come under. I was amazed at the hypocrisy of this response and I was glad to see that Queen Ifrica added a voice of clear conscience to the discussion. She was the voice that tried to get the group to see that there was a connection in what message the music was sending and what was happening in the society.

## Free to Write

The other artistes in the group pushed the idea that they should be free to write, promote, play and sing what they chose because it would be bought. Creative license is clearly determined by the financial reward that it brings. How can parents who have to allow their children out in the public, to take our public transportation, walk on the streets, interact with other youngsters at school, be the only agents responsible for the socialization of the youth of our nation? Parents play an important role but they cannot be the only ones whose responsibility it is to shape the behaviour of the nation's young. All the stakeholders in the society must play a part, especially those who have the greatest powers of influence on our young.

This is Jamaica. In Jamaica, one of the greatest influences on our youth is our music. It is disingenuous for us to argue otherwise. Therefore, when artistes try to pass off the responsibility that they have to shape our nation's youth to be only that of the parents, it is dishonest, to say the least. The discussion also addressed the matter of the morals involved in this position that the artistes have taken in promoting violent lyrics because it sells. The following comment was made by Mr. Vegas concerning this point, "How yu mus talk bout morals wen yu hungry?"[73]

## Immoral Behaviour

This begs the question. Is need the excuse for immoral behaviour? Do we excuse the thief who breaks into a store and steals goods to sell because he needs to feed his family? Do we excuse the man who breaks into another man's house to steal and when confronted, kills the owner because he does not have a job? Do we excuse the woman who sends her daughter to sleep with a man to get money because she needs to feed her family?

Are we saying that morality should not set boundaries for our conduct? If as a society we do not establish standards of what is right and wrong behaviour; if we do not acknowledge and accept that such considerations are important in how we relate to each other, then we will continue on the downward spiral into baseness and anarchy.

I was heartened to see on All Angles, hosted by Dionne Jackson Miller on Wednesday, October 28, that the participants included an academic from the University of the West Indies who acknowledged that the current clash between Gaza and Gully was having a negative impact on our youth. She agreed that music has an incredibly strong influence on the behaviour of our young people. (UWI 2009) This position was new coming from the University of the West Indies, since other academicians from that institution who publicly discuss the dancehall phenomenon in our society usually take a position of defence as it relates to the genre's negative impact on our youth.

## Favourite Dancehall Artistes

A guidance counsellor from Holy Trinity High School, who was also a participant on that programme, pointed out that many of our youth, as our examination results show, are not able to comprehend at an advanced level. They, however, know the lyrics of all their favourite dancehall artistes. The music, therefore, he says, becomes the manual for these young people's behaviour. This is what many teachers and educators realize, and if our artistes are honest, they themselves will accept this. I am asking our artistes to use this awesome power that they have over our youth to influence their attitudes and behaviour in a positive way. Begin to write and promote music that will motivate our youth to work to develop their minds, to get a skill and to do well in school. Begin to write about our social issues in a way that proposes positive solutions, not death, violence, blood and gore. Begin to encourage our young people to resolve conflicts peacefully, without the knife and the gun.

If we continue as a nation to believe that we must excuse negative behaviour and attitudes because "man affi eat a food",[74] then we are going to see more and more lawlessness in our society. Former Prime Minister, P.J. Patterson, spoke about a values and attitudes campaign which never got off the ground. I think the Government and the private sector need to make a serious attempt at promoting such a campaign.

The present prime minister made the point some months ago that even if we got all the money needed to address our financial problems, without a sense of morality, we will not succeed as a nation. It is now or never.

**Published November 1, 2009**

**Part 5**

# THE CHURCH IN THE JAMAICAN SOCIETY

# THE CHURCH IN THE NATION

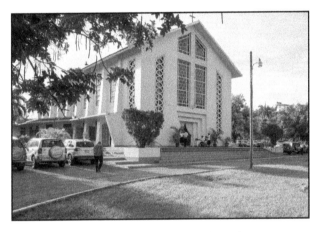

**A Church in Kingston, Jamaica**

T he Church in Jamaica is the most powerful non-governmental organization in this nation. There are more churches per square mile in this country than in any other. As a nation, we are in a state of crisis: economically, socially, morally and spiritually. The high levels of crime and violence have affected every aspect of our society. If we are to survive as a people, the Church needs to take a more proactive approach in affecting what is happening in the nation.

349

The work of the Church in education is well known as are its efforts in assisting the elderly. There is, however, the need for the Church to have a greater effect on decreasing the level of crime and violence in this nation. There are churches in every ghetto and garrison community. There are women, in particular, who are benefiting from the spoils of dons and gunmen who are members of churches. These women, mothers and wives of dons and gunmen cannot be allowed to feel comfortable partaking from the spoils of their sons and mates while they are sitting comfortably in church. Pastors and leaders of these churches have a responsibility to influence what is taking place in these areas through relating what the Bible teaches about ill-gotten gain to their congregation.

**Complacent**

Other members of the Church must be careful that they, too, do not become complacent about crime because they are indirectly benefiting from it. The reality is that if the ill-gotten gain coming into the Church's coffers is addressed, the financial state of that Church will be negatively affected. We must never forget Jesus' action in dealing with ill-gotten gain in the temple, he overthrew the money tables and whipped them out of there. The spiritual effectiveness of the Church is being seriously affected by the blind eye that some church leaders turn to the link to crime that some of their members have. There is the element of fear that underpins all of this. Some leaders might ignore a situation of which they are aware because they are afraid to deal with it because they fear for their lives. In the article that I wrote last month, I pointed out that this 'Goliath' of crime and violence in this nation need to have some 'Davids' to slay it. Our church leaders must become 'Davids' in this situation for change to take place. In Colombia, the high level of crime was brought down because there were men and women who were willing to put their lives on the line in order to make this happen. People did lose their lives, but crime was brought under control.

Another barrier to some churches seeking to be involved with what is happening in the nation is the view that in the last days things will get worse. This teaching holds that the Church is to expect this and therefore its role is to separate itself from the world and wait for Jesus' return. This view goes against the role of the Church being salt to purify the society as Jesus taught and being a light to penetrate the darkness around us. The Church must see itself as an agent of change in this society.

**Crucial Role**

In the history of our nation, the Church played a crucial role to bring about change during the time of slavery. Our history is replete with evidence of the Baptists and the Moravians teaching slaves to read and write so that they could be equipped with the knowledge that they needed to fight against the oppression of slavery. Sam Sharpe and Paul Bogle were leaders in the Church who fought against the oppression of the colonial masters in order to right the wrongs done to poor black people. Here we are again in a crisis with our nation under serious threat because of crime and violence. We need the Church at every level to think right and do right in every community within which it operates to assist in defeating crime.

In addition, although there are some church leaders who are seeking to make their voices heard in relation to the state of the nation, there are others who seem intent on maintaining the status quo. This is not a time for our church leaders to seek comfort and acceptance from the powers that be. For example, the Church needs to actively lobby the Government on the various legal changes that must take place in order for our laws to have teeth to affect the crime kings in this nation. The laws that govern the Government confiscating the assets of those involved in crime must be widened and strengthened in this nation.

Furthermore, the Church must not only be concerned about horse racing on Sundays, but must also be concerned about the poor being taxed to become poorer while the rich escapes the tax net and gets richer.

## The Church Must Be Actively Concerned About Justice

The Church must make sure that it resurrects its prophetic role in this land. It must seek to point out what is wrong and direct to what is right. It cannot afford to become bedfellows with politicians and others who have a vested interested in maintaining things as they are. If the Church finds itself in this position, it means that it has compromised its prophetic voice. There are outstanding examples of leaders such as Martin Luther King Jr and Desmond Tutu, men of the Church who dared to stand up against what was accepted as the norm in their society and to make a difference. Our country is in a state where many Church leaders will be confronted with spiritual and moral decisions to make to determine whether they will ignore the ill-gotten gains and injustice facing them or they will decide to make a stand like David for what is right in the face of Goliath-like evil.

**Published January 3, 2010**

# THE CHURCH IN SOCIETY

In recent weeks, there has been much criticism concerning the role and work of the Church in Jamaica. This has come in response to church-related groups speaking out against the advocacy for a repeal of the anti-buggery law.

Critics of the Church have stated that Christians are still operating in the 15th century. They think that the Church needs to be relevant to this century. Some go as far as to say that we would be better off without the Church functioning in the Jamaican society in the way that it currently does.

First of all, I wish to point out a well-known truth. The Church is not perfect. This is a result of it being made up of human beings. These are human beings who are followers of Jesus Christ, but who are still in the process of becoming like Him. Having acknowledged this, however, I want us to examine the Church's contribution to Jamaica. Let's look at our history. Wasn't the Church involved in educating some of our forefathers when they were slaves? Wasn't it members of the Church, such as Sam Sharpe, who were involved in advocating for the end of slavery? What about the development of education in Jamaica?

Apart from the trust schools, weren't most of the schools which are now highly regarded as providing the best education at the secondary level started and owned by churches? What about the myriad preparatory and basic schools that are church-owned that provide education at the early-childhood level? What other single group or entity, apart from the Government, has historically done as much to develop educational facilities and programmes in Jamaica as the Church? If the Church were now to pull out of providing education to our society, what effect would that have on our development?

**Service to The Poor**

Let us reflect on the churches, or their members, who are involved in giving service to the poor and the needy. The Bible instructs followers of Jesus Christ that when you give to others, you should not publicize it. This limits the public relations thrust from the Church that would allow the general society to know about all the help that the Church provides to the poor and the needy.

There are, however, some church-based organizations that are well known in Jamaica. These include Father Ho Lung and the Missionaries of the Poor, Father Ramkissoon and the Mustard Seed Communities, Ferdinand Mahfood and Food for the Poor, and the late Father Hugh Sherlock and Boys' Town.

Most churches have, as part of their programmes, provision for assistance to the poor among its members and also from surrounding communities. There are a number of children's homes and homes for the elderly that are built and run by churches. There are so many other initiatives that it would not be possible to enumerate them in this limited space. Let us imagine taking out of Jamaica all of the efforts that the Church has put in to alleviate poverty in our nation. What would it look like?

We need to acknowledge the pastoral counselling that is provided to many Jamaicans. I know that we have stories of abuse of this responsibility. Such pastors bring the important role of counselling into disrepute. In spite of this, the contribution that genuine leaders of churches make to the spiritual and emotional well-being of their congregants cannot be devalued.

Many persons who are church members develop work ethic and values based on the teachings of the Bible, which encourages us to not be "men pleasers" but to do your work with excellence in order to please God. Genuine Christians make the most dedicated workers.

Along with pastoral counselling, the Church is involved in mediation in disputes in families and communities. Given the current Jamaican culture which sees being 'dissed' as a cause for violence against persons, and which is the root of many conflicts, the role of the Church in defusing conflict through mediation cannot be downplayed.

Furthermore, the Church is being accused of not being concerned about the abuse and violence being perpetrated by criminals in the society. Yet, I look at the work done by advocates such as pastors in Spanish Town who have made concerted efforts to galvanize church members in public outcries against crime in the Old

Capital. I think of the initiatives undertaken by Pastor Henley Morgan in Trench Town.

## Other Crime-Fighting Initiatives

There are other initiatives in crime alleviation that are being spearheaded by the Church. We have had repeated accounts of criminals turning their lives around by committing their lives to Jesus Christ. There are prison ministries in some churches that seek to reach out to those who are incarcerated to help them to change their criminal mindset.

These are simply a few areas in which the Church has functioned in society to assist in education, poverty alleviation and conflict management. An even greater area of impact that the Church has had in our society, however, is in the foundation of Jamaica as an independent nation.

Our motto, anthem and pledge are all developed by Jamaicans who were involved in the Church and who gave of themselves to establish a strong foundation based on a Judaeo-Christian world view. Therefore, our anthem is a prayer to our 'Eternal Father'; our pledge begins with 'Before God' and refers to 'under God'. In spite of the problems we are experiencing as a nation, we still have a sense that we are accountable to God.

Are those who are attacking the role of the Church in society proposing that we change the foundational principles of our nation, change our core values that are so integrally tied up with an acknowledgement of our commitment to God? To do so would undermine the work of such fathers of the nation such as Father Hugh Sherlock.

So, what type of Jamaica would we have without the presence and influence of the Church? Each Jamaican needs to think about that for himself or herself.

Jesus Christ said that the Church is to be salt in the earth. I agree that the Church needs to improve its savour, but I believe if that if the salt is removed from our society, we will end up with an even greater stench and putrefaction.

**Published July 7, 2013**

# THE CHURCH IN THE STREETS

A man who was overwhelmed, distraught and contemplating murdering his girlfriend and committing suicide, as she had abandoned him for another, after she had taken all he had provided, including the house, was counselled by a Street Pastor one night. Other Street Pastors followed him up by checking up on him. Subsequently, when the man saw the Street Pastor who had first counselled him on a later patrol, he called him over to express his gratitude, as he was doing much better and was at a much-improved place. Praise God.

This is the report of Richard Delisser, co-chairman of Street Pastors, Jamaica.

The church has taken to the streets of Kingston, in the night, in an unprecedented move that has galvanized Christians from across various denominations to move the Church out of its buildings to where the people are.

## What Is Street Pastors, Jamaica?

Street Pastors, Jamaica (SPJ) was officially launched on Friday, January 31, 2014 at the Webster Memorial United Church. There were approximately 200 guests in attendance from numerous churches and organizations from across Kingston and Jamaica. The Rev. Les Isaac, OBE, CEO of Ascension Trust and pioneer of Street Pastors UK, was the guest speaker. Special greetings were brought by National Security Minister Peter Bunting. The initiative is part of the operations of Operations Save Jamaica in partnership with Ascension Trust.

## Quiet for too long

The Church has for a long time been regarded as a far too dis-engaged, sleeping giant with the potential for significant positive intervention through united effort. Concerned leaders from several denominations have now come together in a broad-based effort to engender a 'take-care-to-the-street' intervention. Street Pastors represents that effort. Street Pastors are church leaders/ministers or members with a concern for society, in particular for young people who feel excluded or marginalized. Street Pastors are willing to engage people regardless of where they are, both in terms of mindset and location. The first phase of this outreach is in the Half-Way Tree (HWT) area of the parish of St. Andrew.

The first Street Pastors HWT patrol was held on Friday, February 7, 2014 from 8 p.m. to midnight. Street Pastors patrol teams have been out every Friday night since then with an average contingent of 12-15 Street Pastors in three teams and four Prayer Pastors at the base (Covenant City Church, Cecelio Avenue). Street Pastors patrol on foot and cover areas around the York Plaza, Clock Tower, HWT Transportation Centre, Mandela Park, Pavilion Mall, Burger King, the greater plaza areas, and environs. The general response of the public to Street Pastors has been overwhelmingly positive. Almost all who have encountered Street Pastors (SPs) on patrol have been welcoming and approving of the Church coming out into the streets to the people. In particular, they express strong encour-agement when they discover that Street Pastors is not the effort of any single church or denomination but, rather, a united effort of the wider church. Many have verbalized their desire for the team to keep coming back.

I know that some readers might be thinking that this outreach won't be sustained. I believe that it will not only be sustained, but that it will develop and grow. The example of Street Pastors (UK) demonstrates that, as Les Isaacs, founder of that initiative, came to Jamaica and observed the work of pastors united on the streets of Trench Town. He took what he saw back to UK and began Street Pastors (UK). There are currently some 11,000 trained volunteers in approximately 250 teams around the United Kingdom.

The Street Pastors Initiative was pioneered in London in January 2003 as part of the Ascension Trust, and has seen some remark-able results, including reduction in crime in areas where teams have been working. Street Pastors, Jamaica (SPJ) wants to see teams trained and sent out right across Jamaica. Where there are at least four churches from various denominations coming together in an area, Street Pastors will come in to train and activate the team in their community.

I believe that the potential for the Church to be out on the streets of Jamaica impacting the lives of our people and reclaiming our communities is unprecedented. Jesus Christ says that the world will know that we are His disciples by our love. This initiative puts feet to the church to carry out that mandate to show love to our people of Jamaica. The vision of SPJ is to activate the local Christian community to take ownership for the wider community, by demonstrating the love and compassion of Christ in ways that are proactive and practical and primarily on the 'street corners'. One expected outcome of this outreach will be the uniting of various churches in their communities. The need is urgent for the Church to put aside its differences to overcome the scourge of crime and violence in our beloved Jamaica. This initiative brings that opportunity. Here is another story from the work already being done by SPs.

In the first week, we prayed with a young man who gave his life to the Lord. In subsequent weeks, we have heard and seen that this young man is now radically changed. He is preaching in Half-Way Tree and praying for persons daily. His ministry and testimony have had a powerful impact on other young men who hang out in the area, such that a group of about 10 young men has approached Street Pastors for instruction in the Bible.

Street Pastors go through training before they are sent out on the streets. For this pilot phase, 48 Street Pastor volunteers from 11 churches participated in intensive training from January 27 to

February 6, 2014. All the volunteers are presently serving in the Half-Way Tree community. In welcoming the local proposal for Street Pastors, Minister of Security, Peter Bunting said, "I need a thousand points of light." Street Pastors promises to be examples of these "thousand points of light".

**Published April 6, 2014**

**Part 6**

# THE ABORTION DEBATE
# IN JAMAICA

# THE 'AFTERWARDS' OF ABORTION

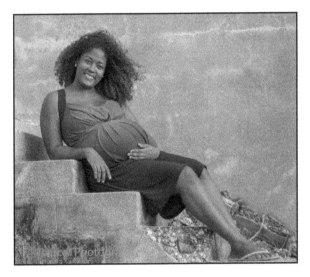

**Ruthie –Joyful Mother**

A mid the debate that is raging concerning the rights of the child as against the rights of the mother and on whether life begins at conception or after 12 weeks, I want to introduce a story – the story of women who have faced the choice of abortion and what they went through afterwards.

*Ah Suh Me See It, Ah Suh Me Say It*

I remember being on the University of the West Indies (UWI) Mona campus in the 1970s and a friend of mine became pregnant in her second year. Her boyfriend, a medical student, wanted nothing to do with a pregnant girlfriend. She was advised to abort it by her boyfriend and her boyfriend's parents, who had no intention of having their son disrupt his medical career by this ill-timed baby. She, on her side, had a father who advised her to abort the baby and a mother who was not around for her. She was in the United States. She, a normally bubbly, vivacious sophisticate became a confused, desolate girl. She was not sure she wanted to do the abortion. Why? She had already had one. She already gone to the psychiatrist for treatment for the post-traumatic distress she was experiencing from doing the first abortion. She could not face the thought of doing another abortion. After going through much struggle, she decided to keep her baby. She left campus, had her baby and returned later to complete her degree. There are many such stories out there, many cases of women who are undergoing serious psychological problems such as suicidal thoughts.

In another case, a friend, who was pregnant with her second child, found out in her first trimester that she had been exposed to German measles. Her doctor told her that this would affect the normal development of her child and strongly advised her to have an abortion. It was a difficult and traumatic time for my friend. She and her husband were Christians and abortion was something that they felt was wrong. Here she was, personally confronted with this situation. Her husband disagreed with the advice of the doctor but she was in a state of conflict and distress. She feared the future. After

368

much struggle and prayer and soul-searching, she decided to have her baby. He is now a handsome grown man who has completed his tertiary education and is living a normal fulfilled life.

## Documented Cases

There are many documented cases such as the one from which the following quotation is taken: "Abortion wrecked my life. Emotionally, I was a different person before and after it. It left a path of destruction in my life. My family, my first marriage, my image of myself – all a total wreck. Nothing will ever be the same." The Post-Abortion Review 1(3), Fall 1993. (Elliot Institute 1993) The story continues with Christina Milford from Montego Bay:

"I chose to have and raise my children, against all odds. Yes, we were shrouded with shame, despised, stigmatised, and experienced rejection ... but I overcame, and today, I am a proud mother of two sons and their wives, and grandma of two wonderful grandchildren. I too was pressured to abort my children, and came pretty close to doing so with the first. At 12 weeks' gestation, the doctor whom I consulted, warned me against abortion and about the risk I ran of either killing myself, or becoming sterile for life. Thank God, doctor, you counselled a frightened, angry, teenage girl, presenting options that have left me proud to be a mother during these my years of generativity. My children are both successful citizens – my first now pursuing his doctorate as an engineer and a Christian, my second, a well-respected Christian businessman.

Christina continues, "Recently, I participated in an Abortion Recovery retreat where several women for the first time, felt free to express the grief they had held for years relative to the abortions they could not take back. We had a shared sorrow. Mine was the grief connected to all that went with raising children regarded as second-class citizens in society. Theirs, the grief associated with destroying their children in abortions – done to appease society's double standards (and maintain the status of being a 'good girl'). I feel their pain as a woman who was almost there."

**Teens Pressured**

Says Christina, "Our teens today are no different from those in my days – except that they are pressured on every side to be sexually involved, with a promise of being fine, as long as they 'use condom every time'. Surprised by an unplanned pregnancy, rejection of the baby's father, and the looming threat of family and society's response, a teenager tries for a quick fix – abortion. But, she will never forget. Her hurt and loss in the child that dies will be real. She will not have permission to grieve, not from herself, not from anyone else, and no-one will console her. She will bear her pain and guilt alone, and the fear of breast cancer will plague her when she knows of its connection with abortion. Abortion is traumatic to a woman, resulting not only in the death of her child(ren), but a lifetime of prolonged sorrow. I have been privileged to share in a healing experience firsthand. Healing is available after an abortion. If healing is necessary, abortion cannot be good for women. Let us present some better choices to our youth ... not only of life or death. Let us believe in them and their ability to make informed decisions about their sexual and reproductive health. Let us give them the facts, the truth, and better options."

Christina Milford is the founder and director of Pregnancy Resource Centre of Jamaica in Montego Bay.

The pressing call for abortion is due to society's desire for a free sexual lifestyle. This breeds the need to destroy an unwanted baby, the outcome of sex, limb by limb. Let's look back and destroy the root cause, not the offshoot of the problem.

**Published March 2, 2008**

# IS ABORTION THE ANSWER?

I commend Eve for Life for launching the 'Nuh Guh Deh'[75] campaign dealing with adults having sex with children. At the launch, stories were told of what some of the girls that Eve for Life has helped have gone through. (The Sunday Gleaner 2013) I read some of these stories online.

What is horrific about these tragic stories is that I have heard similar ones repeatedly. This practice of girls being plagued by the sexual perversion of men needs to stop. It is a cultural norm that is harming our society. The nation keeps focusing mainly on teaching children how to use birth control, yet we need to address a wider cultural issue if we are to improve the lives of our children. We need to change the thinking among Jamaicans that says, 'Ah nuh nutt'n, a little sex.'[76]

**Shame on You**

Women who were sexually abused as girls need to start talking about it and explaining how the experience has affected them.

Mothers and grand-mothers need to stop using their girls as cash earners, allowing men to use them sexually so they can get money and other material benefits from them. Shame on you. Mothers and grandmothers need to protect their 'girl chile'[77] from perverted men who believe they can cure disease by having sex with a virgin. Men who have sex with young girls need to be arrested, charged and sent to jail. They need to be made examples to others who have the same mindset.

What is being done about the young girls who are under 16 who are having babies? Victoria Jubilee Hospital is filled with them. What does the Ministry of Health do in these situations? Isn't there a law that says that girls under 16 cannot give consent to have sex? So why aren't we prosecuting those who made these 'girl baby-mothers' pregnant? Once again, we always seek to cut off the branches off the trees instead of digging out the root.

Dr. Sandra Knight, head of family planning in Jamaica, is proposing that we legalize abortion. (Jamaica Observer 2014) I guess when the big men impregnate the little girls, they will now be able to get rid of the evidence legally and easily. Well, well, we add to all the problems we are having, including a high murder rate, more murder. Dr. Knight does not want the discussion to involve either religion or politics. Here again we keep trying to disconnect our bodies from our souls and spirits. What we do in our bodies affect our minds and spirits. The untold number of women who suffer from depression as a result of abortion tells this story. Dr. Knight admits that she is following the practice of the countries in which she was trained. In those countries, abortion is legal; therefore, it follows, in her line of reasoning, that it needs to be legalized here. The assumption gives us an insight into her thought pattern.

Can we seriously begin to deal with our root issues of how we value family, our women and our children? Can we deal with how our men see themselves? Can we begin a campaign to change how we value sex? Can we target the men, especially, who feel that they have the right to exploit girls? Can we teach mothers to protect and believe their 'girl chile' when they tell them that they are being abused? Can we teach them what signs to look out for that will give them some indication that their child is being abused?

**Shocking Frequency**

My heart is burdened because the sexual abuse of our girls is too rampant and it seems that the emotional wounds are not being taken seriously. Too many girls have had their lives warped and thrown off track because of this malady in our society. If a survey were taken of guidance counsellors and teachers in the schools concerning how many stories they have heard about girls being sexually abused by men, Jamaicans would probably be shocked by the result. Apart from young girls who are still children themselves having babies, there are sexually transmitted infections, including HIV, that these girls contract. The trauma that many of them live through has some turning sexually to other girls.

Added to this are the older women who prey on these girls who are vulnerable because of abuse from men and are therefore responsive to their attention. These women provide material and emotional support for these girls before sexual favours are procured. Would legalizing abortion deal with these societal issues? Would this deal with the sense of low self-esteem that these girls feel? Would it take away from them the mistrust and anger that they feel towards men generally? Would it relieve the feelings of vulnerability and shame? Let us face what we have before us and deal with it. We are too ready to follow what our North American and European cultural masters are imposing on us. We need to look at what we need to improve our situation.

Can we begin to use our art forms and the media to change the mindset of our people? Can we engage our musicians in creating songs that address these issues? I am so glad to see that we have some advertisements on TV that show healthy family life and young people choosing to make right choices about themselves and their sexual practices. Can we do more of that?

Could we look further than accepting that we have a poor family structure, a skewed view of sex and sexual relations, and look to how we can educate our people on what healthy families and sex lives look like? I do not think that this is impossible, but the policymakers must first have a change in their thinking in order to see Jamaica's future in another way; they must begin to believe that it is possible to change cultural patterns and norms.

We need leaders who believe that our country can be different from what our North American cultural masters are feeding us.

**Published November 2, 2014**

# EXPANDING THE CULTURE OF DEATH IN JAMAICA

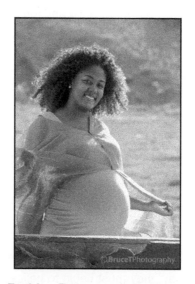

**Ruthie –Expectantly Pregnant**

T he Minister of Youth and Culture, Lisa Hanna, wants Jamaica to legalize abortion as a way to stem the number of women who are poor and are having unwanted children whom they cannot support. (RJR News 2013) Ms. Hanna wants the conversation to begin about changing the laws on abortion in our nation but has expressed her view that this conversation needs to be devoid of emotion and reference to biblical scripture.

This position, if explored, would reveal a thought pattern that does not value the strong spiritual culture that exists in Jamaica. If we delve into this position, we would realize that whereas the honourable Prime Minister is calling on parents to send their children to Sunday (or Sabbath) school in order for them to get the spiritual and moral foundation that many seem to lack, Ms. Hanna would want the opposite to happen. She would want for these young people not to be influenced by the teachings of the Bible. Some policymakers seem to have an insidious agenda to soften the opposition that Jamaicans have to practices such as abortion that are commonly accepted in North America and Europe. Policymakers such as Ms. Hanna seem to assume that if they can undermine the respect that Jamaicans have for the Bible, a number of laws and policies based on Judeo-Christian ethics can be changed. Such a shift in policy would make our populace's commonly held beliefs more acceptable to powerful North America-based donors. Once this agenda is fulfilled, we would have solved our poverty problems by opening the doors to grants that are currently unavailable to Jamaica. On the surface, this appears to be a win-win situation.

## Think Long Term

The problem is: Not every decision that looks expedient in the short term is the best choice to make for the long term. Jamaica has many problems, one of which is the high murder rate. We have added, in recent times, the killing of our children, especially girls who are having sexual relationships with older men and being murdered when things go sour. We know because of poverty, many parents are pimping their daughters for economic gain. Is the solution to this, abortion? Do we solve one problem by creating another?

There is a pervasive sense of lawlessness in our nation that has led many of our citizens to feel that they have the right to do anything as long it can help them to 'earn a bread' and 'mek dem feel good'. When we add the killing of innocent babies in the womb to the high level of innocent blood that has already been shed in this nation, we are creating an even greater evil. Indeed, we are embedding a culture of death in our nation. If Ms. Hanna's wish is fulfilled, I shudder to imagine how many more girls may be raped and abused by perverted men who reason that now they can have the girls abort any unwanted babies they conceive. These men do not use condoms because they want to go 'bareback' when having sex. In addition, they give these girls HIV and other STIs, not only babies. Would abortion help that?

**Treating Symptoms**

In this country, we keep treating the symptoms of our problems and not the root cause. We need a cultural paradigm shift in which our girls and women learn to respect themselves and their bodies, and men learn to control their penises. With the increased ability to see babies in utero through sonogram technology, more and more persons are coming to the realization that the baby feels and responds to the pain caused from abortion. This is why there is an increasing number of reports asserting that millennials (i.e., persons born between 1980 and 2000) are less in favour of abortion than the previous generation. One must also ask why countries such as Russia are now legally restricting general access to abortions. When death is seen as an answer to unwanted pregnancy, where the personhood of the baby is seen as expendable and where life is not valued, we are embedding a culture of death. We will start our descent down the slippery slope of moral relativism when Bible-based morality is taken out of the picture.

The next logical step will be legalizing euthanasia as a way out of pain because each person should have the right to determine what to do with his or her body. In fact, this logic has played out in many European countries. Where will it end?

Ms. Hanna cannot expect that Jamaica will have a conversation about abortion without reference to the scripture. In spite of so many things that are going wrong in our nation, respect for the Bible is one area where we have a light and hope. We have seen repeatedly that the lives of persons have been transformed through teachings of the Bible, which many of us believe to be the Word of God. We have seen hardened criminals change through that Bible. Ms. Hanna, even though many Jamaicans do not follow the Bible as they should, they still respect what it says. You are seeking to change a national culture that has been embedded in us for years. It is the Bible that gave strength to our national heroes: Sam Sharpe, Paul Bogle and George William Gordon. Our anthem is a prayer to the God of the Bible. Ms. Hanna, what do you propose to use to replace the Bible in the minds of the Jamaican people?

**Published May 3, 2015**

**Part 7**

# THE LGBT AGENDA IN JAMAICA

# FAMILIES: SAME OR BOTH SEXES?

The Gleaner on Wednesday, October 31, carried as its front-page headline, "Same-sex lessons". (Reid 2007)The article informed the public that a textbook, CSEC Home Economics and Beyond (Management), by Rita Dyer and Norma Maynard, is a recommended text on the CXC-CSEC syllabus for the subject, home management. The article carried an excerpt from the text which discusses the matter of family structures. The controversial clause states:

"Today, there is much discussion about what constitutes a family. There seems to be a broadening of the traditional definitions of a family structure. When two women or two men live together in relationship as lesbians or gays, they may be considered as a family. They may adopt children or have them through artificial insemination."

Although Ardenne High School does not teach home management, I feel that as a school based on Christian principles and founded by the Church of God in Jamaica, I have a responsibility to respond to this view of families, which is being pushed in the official curriculum supplied by CXC (Caribbean Examination Council).

The views that I express reflect the thinking of the Church of God in Jamaica and the chairman of the board of management of the school.

## Promoting the Homosexual Agenda

We are aware that the homosexual agenda is being promoted throughout the Western nations of the world by homosexual activists. We are aware that it is now the norm that on television programmes originating out of the United States of America, and made accessible in Jamaica through the cable network system, movies are projecting the homosexual way of life as an alternative, acceptable lifestyle. We are aware that the agenda being pushed is that to be heterosexual and to object to the homosexual lifestyle is backward, politically incorrect and narrow-minded. We are aware that the homosexual lobby groups try to punish those who oppose their agenda through various means. In spite of all of this, we must maintain, that as a nation whose world view is based on Judeo-Christian principles, that homosexual unions are not acceptable. As a nation, we have upheld heterosexual unions to be the correct sexual union. Are we then going to hold up as an alternative to our students, unions which are not accepted as correct in our nation? Further, the homosexual lifestyle is immoral based on the teaching of the Holy Scriptures. Yet, these unions exist and, therefore, we need to discuss them with our students, but in the context that these are aberrations of nature in the same way that bestiality is an aberration of nature. Where else in nature does same sex cohabit with one another?

The discussion in which I was involved on RJR's Beyond the Headlines on Wednesday, October 31, brought forth the view from a listener that because of globalization, we should be viewing homosexuality as an acceptable lifestyle because other nations are doing this. Has this now become the basis of our morality – because other nations are doing it?

Let us think back throughout history to the times when persons accepted a world view because it had become so pervasive that thinking outside of the box appeared wrong. Later, when the world view changed, many persons realized that they should have stood up and challenged the thinking of the day. Because the whole world is going one way is no indication of the rightness or the wrongness of a moral point of view. We, as a people, must think for ourselves. We must examine our belief system in light of the influences, whether religious or philosophical, which govern our lives.

The Gleaner of Thursday, October 25, reported that Singapore's parliament decided to keep a ban on sex between men, with the prime minister saying the city state should keep its conservative values and not allow special rights for homosexuals. Globalization did not cloud their thinking and neither should we have it cloud ours.

**The Cover Of 'Objectivity'**

Another view would have us believe that if we look at the matter objectively and not be hampered by our outmoded religious beliefs, then we would be able to accept the homosexual lifestyle as an alternative lifestyle. The cover of 'objectivity' is spurious, to say the least. Every view that becomes an official position in a nation or in the world originates out of a person or persons' minds. Every mind is influenced by various inputs or stimuli which help to shape their thought patterns, personalities and world view. Is there any true objectivity? Even researchers can present their findings in ways which reflect a bias in their thinking. This is certainly true in matters of morality. The issue, therefore, is: Whose agenda will we accept? Whose thinking are we going to adopt, and what are our reasons for adopting these views?

I believe that in schools, students must be made aware of what is around them in the world; we cannot leave them ignorant. I also believe that as schools in a country with a Christian world view, we need to hold up what is the ideal and what is considered to be normal according to the teachings of the Bible. Genesis 2:23-24 (NIV) tells us:

"The man said, 'This is now bone of my bones and flesh of my flesh; She shall be called 'woman', for she was taken out of man. For this reason, a man will leave his father and mother and be united to his wife, and they will become one flesh." ((NIV) Holy Bible 1984)

That is heterosexuality and that is what the Bible teaches; nothing else is acceptable or normal.

**Published November 4, 2007**

# THE GAY AGENDA AND RIGHTS OF CHRISTIANS

There is a wind blowing across our nation, Jamaica, which threatens to destabilize the Christian world view that we accept as the norm in our country. This wind has swept in from countries such as Germany, England, Sweden and North America. It brings with it the view that posits that homosexual rights must be seen as paramount at this time. This is so because it comes under the agenda of human rights. All well-thinking individuals agree that all persons must have the rights that are due to all citizens of a nation, including homosexuals, bisexuals, transgender, et al.

What the country needs to be aware of, and stand its guard against, is that in many instances, once homosexuals have been granted their rights to practice their 'alternative lifestyle' openly, along with it comes other demands which infringe on the rights of persons with a Judeo-Christian world view. This is the pattern that has been observed in nations such as United States, Canada, Germany and England. In England, according to a report at http://www.tinyurl.com/lawforcechurches, religious groups are to be forced to accept homosexual youth workers, secretaries and other staff, even if their faith holds same-sex relationships to be sinful. Christian organizations fear that the tightened legislation, which is due to come into force next year, will undermine the integrity of churches and dilute their moral message.

## Important Development

Christianity Today Australia makes an important point on this development:

"And that is just what the homosexual activists and the militant secularists have long been working towards. They have been very clever about this. They say that religious people are welcome to practice their faith, just as long as it is not done in public."

Christians in England are coming under increasing persecution because of their faith. Yet, on the other hand, the rights of other groups, such as gays, are being promoted. In 2011 in England, a Christian couple was banned from foster-parenting because of their views on homosexuality. They "were told by a court yesterday that gay rights 'should take precedence' over their religious beliefs". Owen and Eunice Johns heard that their values could conflict with the local authority's duty to 'safeguard and promote the welfare' of those in foster care. (BBC News 2011)

This shift against Christianity is taking place not only in England but in the USA. An example of this is seen in California.

(CNSNews.com) – On January 1, the California Department of Education started implementing a new law that requires all children in the state's public schools to study the "role and contributions" of "lesbian, gay, bisexual, and transgender Americans" to the "development of California and the United States of America". (CNS News 2012)

All public schools in California, from kindergarten to grade 12, will be required to actively teach students to admire the gay lifestyle, and refusal to do so will have teachers charged with discrimination. This means that Christian teachers will not be allowed to keep silent on the matter but are being put into a situation to go against their faith if they are to keep their jobs. In each of these instances, what began as the 'gay' agenda being accepted as part of human rights has resulted in the rights of Christians being eroded.

Even more far-reaching are the implications of the following report.

## NEW YORK, July 27, 2011

A high-level push at the United Nations for more contraception and abortion among the world's youths has met with resistance from over 120,000 people, including 57,000 young people, who have signed a Youth Statement that says that so-called "sexual rights" cannot trump the real rights of life and family. Campaigners at the United Nations are seeking more permissive laws and policies in support of homosexuality, drug use, explicit sexual education, contraception, and prostitution on all levels of world government, framed as advocacy for youth's sexual and reproductive health and 'rights'. (Life Site News 2011)

Persons who hold to the traditional Judeo-Christian values which form the foundation of our society's laws and practices need to become conscious that already such values are being eroded in nations that previously were seen as having the same philosophical foundations as we do in Jamaica. Furthermore, this insidious destruction is continuing, as can be seen in the report concerning the advocacy of sexual rights for children at the United Nations. The Church must be careful that while we ensure that all mankind is treated with humanity and dignity, we do not fail to see that there are many groups that are using the human-rights cover to foist upon many unsuspecting persons, laws that will have Jamaicans finding ourselves being forced to accept lifestyles alien to us.

**Threaten Economic Sanctions**

Already we see the British Prime Minister, David Cameron, threatening economic sanctions against those Commonwealth nations that do not decriminalize homosexuality and/or buggery. United States President Barack Obama is also issuing a call in support of gay rights. These calls are being promoted as a part of the human-rights agenda. Countries are now being forced to bow to the beliefs of these superpowers. Although colonialism has ended, this situation makes us aware that cultural imperialism is still alive and rampant. Our Prime Minister, Portia Simpson Miller, has promised J-FLAG – the Jamaica Forum for Lesbians, All-Sexuals and Gays – that she will review the buggery law. As a nation, we need to be aware of this process. This issue might be decided through a vote by the people. As a nation, we are not used to voting on two issues at once, so we must be careful to see that a second matter is not being decided on in any election without the electorate's full knowledge. In addition, it is very important that every Jamaican whose world view is based on the Judeo-Christian teaching become aware of this debate and make his or her contribution to it. Furthermore, all such persons need to be enumerated.

**Published February 5, 2012**

# ASSESS THE MESSAGE BEFORE SHOOTING THE MESSENGER

There are three issues that I will be commenting on in this article. First, the response to Anne Shirley's article in Sports Illustrated about her concerns with the Jamaica Anti-Doping Commission's (JADCO) testing of our athletes; (The Jamaica Gleaner 2013) second, the state of the teaching profession in Jamaica; and third, the homosexual lobby.

The basis of my knowledge of Anne Shirley has been what I have seen of her as a public figure making contributions to the development of Jamaica. Therefore, when the media released the information that Ms. Shirley had written an article about Jamaica's anti-doping procedures, I thought that it probably had to be published in the Sports Illustrated because she possibly could not get the powers to be to listen in Jamaica. Alas, how true it is that we tend to respond to pressure from the international community more readily than we do to our own.

There was, however, a maelstrom that erupted over Ms. Shirley's revelation. At first, it seems that no one was paying attention to the message but was intent on shooting the messenger. Persons declared that Ms Shirley was a traitor. Another person said she should be tried for treason. The questions I thought we should have been asking are: Was what she said true? Why did she publish those facts in an overseas magazine? These questions came later after Shirley, who has been giving of her time and talent to develop our nation, had been lambasted and her reputation buffeted by some, including a commentator who accused her of "eating sour grapes".

After all the character assassination, the message is finally being looked at and we are aware that there are serious issues to be addressed at JADCO. The organization is now being better resourced and a more diligent approach is being taken to the testing of the athletes. Aren't these the issues that Ms. Shirley addressed? Yes, she did it in a way that exposed our problems at home, but it worked, didn't it? The authorities are now seeking to address the problems.

We need, as a people, to be less ready to destroy our own before assessing carefully the message they are trying to send us. We need to value their contributions to our society and place that as the context of our responses to what we perceive to be their negative action or utterances.

**Types of Teachers**

I am a member of the teaching profession. I have had the privilege of going into various schools across Jamaica, and I have discovered teachers who are making great sacrifices to develop the minds of our children in this country. Even in schools where there are problems with the teaching practices of many teachers, I have seen pockets of excellence.

There are teachers who are more than qualified to be deemed master teachers. On the other hand, I am concerned about the number of our teachers who do not have an insatiable appetite for learning, who are satisfied to have qualified themselves with a first degree and teacher qualification and see that as being enough. The advancement in technology has made knowledge so available to us in the field of education. There are many sources of information online where teachers can find out more about teaching method-ologies and classroom management. The matter of differentiation in teaching is an approach to teaching that is being researched constantly. This is needed in our Jamaican classrooms. Yet many teachers see the suggestion that they develop themselves in this way as being simply more work.

We are willing to scramble to get some of the scarce resources the Government has and are so desperate about it that we descend to base actions in order to ensure we get our share. It probably was this mentality that inspired our teachers to elect, once again, the former (Jamaica Teachers Association) JTA president who demeaned the profession by his unprofessional conduct to the Minister of Education. This former president of the JTA later confirmed that we were not mis-judging him when he re-enacted his appalling conduct at a recent JTA conference. It is an indictment on the teaching profession that someone who is rude, obdurate and intransigent and who displays an inability to take a conciliatory approach in the impasse with the minister of education could have been chosen to lead the JTA again.

This speaks to a lack of understanding on the part of the teachers of the era in which we are operating, and the urgent changes that need to happen in the education sector.

## Education

I want to say to my colleagues that it is time that we start seeing education as the hope of Jamaica's children. It is time that we realize that we are capable of impacting the future of this nation by putting the development of our children first.

We need to look globally at the trends in education and the economy. The possibility of open schools, or schools without borders, is becoming a reality. It is a reality that will not need so many teachers. We cannot continue to have schools where the ratio of teacher to student is 1:4. It is not viable. The Ministry of Education needs to operate efficiently if we are to develop our education system. The ministry needs to be able to transfer teachers where it has proven necessary to do so. We must acknowledge that there must be a paradigm shift in how we operate in the education system. We must change to make us sustainable. If we do not do this, we will not develop, but will atrophy and become useless. Therefore, we must understand that there are other possibilities that exist to educate our children with fewer teachers.

## Homosexual Lobby's Intent

I need to point out that on February 5, 2012, I wrote an article in The Sunday Gleaner pointing out the impending danger of the homosexual lobby's intent worldwide: to have their rights become not equal to heterosexuals' but paramount, thereby marginalizing religious bodies and effectively silencing them in the public sphere. (Tyson 2012)

After one year, this is even more evident. As we debate and lobby our Government in Jamaica concerning this issue, we need to be clear on what the outcomes will bring for persons who believe that the homosexual lifestyle is wrong. It will eventually be a gag order. This is what is happening in Canada, in England, and, increasingly many states in the USA.

I abhor the murder of any person in Jamaica, and the killing of a transsexual is testimony to our increasing acceptance of violence as the solution to any conflict. I am, however, alarmed at the number of women who are being murdered by our men. Where is the outcry for all these women whose lives are being destroyed at a greater rate than any other group of persons in Jamaica? Why isn't it being equally highlighted in the national and international media?

The problem then is that we must address the murder rate in our nation. That is the bigger concern.

**Published September 8, 2013**

# ON BAIN AND CHINA VISIT

I need to make a comment on the current situation involving the firing of Professor Brendan Bain as head of The Caribbean HIV/ AIDS Regional Training (CHART), by the University of the West Indies (UWI) (V. Davidson 2014) having been out of Jamaica for almost two weeks, in addition to reflecting on the trip to China by a group of principals from the Jamaica Association of Principals of Secondary Schools (JAPSS).

In an article published in The Sunday Gleaner on February 8, 2012 titled 'The homosexual agenda and the rights of Christians', I pointed out the following:

*The Church must be careful that while we ensure that all mankind is treated with humanity and dignity, since we are all created in God's image, we do not fail to see that there are many groups that are using the human-rights cover to foist upon many unsuspecting persons laws that will have Jamaicans finding ourselves being forced to accept lifestyles and world views alien to us, as our own. (Tyson 2012)*

Already, we see the British Prime Minister threatening economic sanctions against those Commonwealth nations that do not decriminalize homosexual relations. President Obama is also issuing a call supporting gay rights. These calls are being promoted as a part of the human-rights agenda. Countries are now being forced to bow to the beliefs of these superpowers. Although colonialism has ended, this situation makes us aware that cultural imperialism is still alive and rampant.

The firing of Prof Brendan Bain by the University of the West Indies (UWI) is an indication that the tide of gay-rights advocacy has now reached Jamaica's shores. Despite the many arguments being put forward to the contrary, it seems clear that "he who pays the piper calls the tune."

**Powerful Agencies**

The powerful funding agencies that support the group known as the Caribbean Vulnerable Communities have given strength to the voice of groups such as Jamaicans for Justice, that has clearly shifted its mandate to establishing the rights of the lesbian, gay, bisexual, transgender and intersex (LGBTI) persons. The news of the victory party held by this group, rejoicing that UWI is "now theirs," simply confirms this truth which they publicly decry.

The Church in Jamaica must realize that this is a signal of things to come unless we begin to address, spiritually and socio-politically, the intention of the LGBTI groups to change our culture. The Church

398

must be the prophetic voice to point out the outcome of our nation bowing to the dictates of the LGBTI lobby.

## China Visit

A group of nine principals was invited by the Confucius Institute at UWI to participate in a visit to Beijing and Taiyuan in China. The host of this trip was the University of Technology of Taiyuan. The principals were required to pay their airfare, while all expenses related to travelling and accommodations in China were covered by the University of Taiyuan. The purpose of the trip was to expose us, principals, to the culture and education system of China. The visit was designed to broaden our appreciation for the culture behind the Mandarin language and inspire us to begin establishing Confucius classrooms in our schools where students would be taught Mandarin.

From as far back as 2008, while principal at Ardenne High, I had started to explore the possibility of establishing a Mandarin Club at the school as a co-curricular activity because I realized that China was rising to be an influential economic power in the world. My thinking was that if our students were given an opportunity to learn this language, they would have an advantage in gaining jobs when the Chinese began to expand their involvement in Jamaica.

After I retired, the club at Ardenne was started with the help of the Confucius Institute, which by that time had been established at UWI. Thanks to Rev Ellis and Carol Myers, who carried the vision to fruition.

**Linguistic Benefits**

Having visited China, I realized, even more, the need for our students to learn Mandarin. The mantra of the programme to teach Jamaican students Mandarin is, 'One more language, one more chance'. This has become a reality. We met nine students from Jamaica who are studying Mandarin for a year at the University of Technology in Taiyuan. That university had given these students scholarships after they participated in learning Mandarin at the Confucius Institute at UWI. They now have the possibility of gaining scholarships to pursue further studies after completing their first year in the programme. Indeed, acquiring the language will give them one more chance.

This summer, the Confucius Institute will be conducting a programme to teach Mandarin to students at the institute at UWI.

**What did we gain from our tour?**

We gained many things and I will only be able to comment on a few in this article. First, we gained an appreciation for a culture that values its history and uses every opportunity to engrain this in its people. In the schools we visited, there were walls and rooms set up to depict, by narrative and pictures, the history of the institutions. We need to adopt this approach to help build a sense of pride in our students for our culture and to help to solidify a sense of identity.

Second, education for the Chinese is a top priority. Its importance is valued not only by the government, but also by the people. When we were in Beijing and Taiyuan, we saw no children of school age on the streets during the week. They were all engaged in school. When we visited the schools, we observed that the students were disciplined and thoroughly engaged in the process of learning.

School began as early as 7 a.m. and students were given breaks of varying lengths throughout the day, but classes ended between 8 and 9 p.m. We learnt that students would then go home and their parents expected them to study until midnight. Is it any wonder that the students from Asia outperform others in the world?

**Published June 8, 2014**

# Part 8

# GOVERNMENT LEADERSHIP IN JAMAICA

# WHY JAMAICANS ABROAD SHOULD VOTE

Once upon a time, in a sleepy town called Chapelton in Clarendon, lived a man who was a friend to humanity. His name was Fergus Simpson. He pastored 10 churches in Northern Clarendon.

In 1989, his youngest daughter, Janeth, returned from university in the United States to work in Jamaica and to assist her father in his work. She began, with her father's encouragement, to work with a group of young people in Chapelton who felt they had no future and did not believe in themselves.

Many are now graduates of colleges and universities in the U.S. and are intent on giving back to their community. Fergus Simpson left a legacy in Clarendon when he died in October 2000.

That legacy survives in the hearts of the young and those in the community who knew him, through the work of a foundation established in his name by his youngest daughter, Janeth Simpson-Brown.

**Realizing The Vision**

The Fergus Simpson Foundation's mission is to 'Treasure the Past, Train the Future and Transform the Community' of Chapelton. This is a big vision inspired by the work and life of a man who was big in integrity and impact. In this first phase of realizing the vision, the Foundation has, for the past three years, been training the young in the community through developing a leadership-training programme, and by operating a day camp at the beginning of August. This year, over 147 children ranging from ages five to 18 attended the camp which was held at the Chapelton Primary School. The camp is run by the children and grandchildren of Fergus Simpson, persons who have benefited from his ministry, and friends both from home and abroad. The offspring of 'Parson', as he was called, travel from various areas in the U.S.A.. and London each summer to implement a plan that was formulated months before.

Janeth's vision has galvanized others who sacrifice to travel to Jamaica and bring money and materials to make the camp happen. This team is chaired by Parson's first grandchild, Kimara, and her husband, Damian Tomlin, graduates of top universities in the U.S., who are passionate to see the community revived.

Another person who has been extremely instrumental is Sybil Taylor-Barnett, who left Chapelton in 1959 and has been in the diaspora for many years. She is determined to help transform the community through using her extensive network of friends and family. Auntie Sybil, as she is called, was able to get assistance from Jamaica Broilers to support the feeding programme which allows each child to have breakfast and lunch for the entire week of camp. Other companies involved in underwriting some of the cost of the programme were National Commercial Bank, ICWI, OGM Communications, Food for the Poor and Digicel.

Driving through Chapelton during the week, you see campers and workers wearing the Digicel/Fergus Simpson T-shirts, in various colours, each representing the house in which they were placed. The houses help to perpetuate the name and work of those who have served the community.

## Commitment and Pride

There are four houses: Jackson, named for businesswoman, Evadne Jackson, who is over 100 years old and whose life has been spent in the development of Chapelton; Goodgame, after Lucy Goodgame, the kindest woman in Chapelton, who mothered more girls than she could possibly have borne; Latty, after Estriana Latty, a spiritual giant and entrepreneur who left an indelible mark on the community; and Simpson, after Fergus Simpson. Camp activities include workshops in music, art, dance, science, life skills, and sports. On the last day of the camp, there is a grand open house and concert where the community, which has embraced the camp, come to view the work of the campers.

Workers at the camp include volunteers from the community who serve with commitment and pride. Their work is acknowledged and honoured at the open house. More children want to participate than can be accommodated in one week. Therefore, next year, the plan is to have two camps running in consecutive weeks. This means more workers and more resources. It is worth it. Lives are being impacted and changed – one life at a time.

**Future Leaders**

Among the lives being changed are those young people that are a part of FLOC – the Future Leaders of Chapelton group. They are a select group who are undergoing leadership training and are given responsibility of assisting in the ongoing work of the Foundation in Chapelton under the leadership of Gareth Gordon and Taylor-Barnett. One member of that group is Fidel McCarthy, who, at 18 years of age, has caught the vision of giving back to the community. Fidel has been involved in the camp from the beginning. The first year, he received the Fergus Simpson Leadership Award. His prize was a bicycle. The following year, Fidel won the Kids Share School Prize, which was US$500 to assist with his school fees. Fidel has now developed a feeding programme for the elderly in the community using money which he and his friends have donated. He is from a poor background but he has seen a bigger vision and he is making it happen. He is transforming himself and his community.

Apart from the FLOC group, several young people are being mentored by individuals who are able to impart values and attitudes which will help them develop their potential. This is an example of how Jamaicans in the diaspora are giving back to their communities, apart from sending remittances home. Many other such examples can be found across the island.

Therefore, as a nation, we should not discard, without serious thought, the proposal that Jamaicans who live abroad and who wish to maintain their Jamaican citizenship should be allowed the right to vote to select who governs this nation.

**Published September 2, 2007**

# COURAGEOUS LEADERSHIP NEEDED

**Gordon House –Seat of Parliament**

Our new Prime Minister, the Honourable Bruce Golding, has sounded many fine words and promises in his inaugural speech. His was the voice of inclusion, of reconciliation, of challenging us as a people to begin working together for Jamaica, not party. He invited the former Prime Minister to sit down with him to talk about Jamaica and together to build a Jamaica where "equality and justice reign supreme". But as the saying goes, "talk is cheap" and "actions speak louder than words."

There are some actions which have been forthcoming, such as the promised free tuition. The Minister of Education has said that by November, schools will receive an additional 50 per cent of the tuition fees, with 25 per cent having already been disbursed by the previous administration. It needs to be pointed out, however, that we need to know when the last 25 per cent will be sent to the schools. Another promise that is being carried out is the clean-up action after Hurricane Dean. That has started and is set to continue.

## No Official Invitation

I am concerned, however, that the former Prime Minister has said that she has not received an official invitation from Mr. Golding to meet with him. I encourage the Prime Minister to make good this promise as quickly as possible, since it does not take money to do so. If Mr. Golding were serious when he said to Mrs. Simpson-Miller that, "In our two pairs of hands rests so much of the hopes of the people of Jamaica. Those hands can engage in hand-to-hand combat, or we can join those hands together to build a nation that is strong, just, peaceful and prosperous," (Campbell 2007) then the joining of hands needs to begin now.

Mr. Golding's role model is Nelson Mandela, who had the task of building a united South Africa after apartheid. The Jamaican situation however pales in comparison to South Africa's. There are lessons to be learned from the approach this great man took to nation building. Mr. Mandela said about dealing with opposing forces, "to make peace with (the opposition), one must work with that (opposition) and that (opposition) becomes one's partner." (Mandela 1995) If Mr. Golding wants a united Jamaica, he must begin to sit down with Portia now.

There is another area of concern with the talk that we have heard and the actions that have followed. No matter how well-sounding the Prime Minister's words are they will come to nothing if his party members are not acting in agreement with his stance. The incident of two JLP members of Government being hostile and abusive to the PNP member who 'dissed' the Prime Minister by not shaking his hand, is an example of the old-style politics that we need to move away from. If a senior politician such as Dwight Nelson can behave in as reprehensible a manner as was reported, how can we expect Jamaicans, who are not as educated, not as exposed as the Senator, to behave any better? Isn't this one of the main causes of violence and bloodshed in this nation, that someone is 'dissed'? Being 'dissed' seems to be the greatest crime in Jamaica. No one seems capable of walking away after being 'dissed'. Senator Nelson missed a significant opportunity of indicating, in a statesmanlike manner to the young PNP politician, the correct procedure to be observed in the situation. He missed the opportunity of showing, as an elder luminary in our government, how the young should conduct themselves in a situation of conflict. What a shame and what a wasted opportunity to change how we conduct ourselves in conflict. I commend the former Prime Minister on being the one who calmed that disturbing and shameful situation.

## Prime Minister's Role Model

Again, as a people, we need to look at the Prime Minister's role model as an example. We need to learn to be civil with each other in the most difficult of situations. Mr. Mandela, in commenting on this, said, "Freedom without civility, freedom without the ability to live in peace, was not true freedom at all." (Mandela 1995)

The Prime Minister needs to persuade Jamaicans with the political tribal mindset that if we put the good of Jamaica above the party, we will all be better for it. He needs to dismantle not only the physical garrisons, but also the garrisons in the mind. This must be acted out, not only talked about.

## Critical Juncture

As a nation, we are at a critical juncture – the results of the general election show this; the tumultuous rising complaints against police injustice show this; the ever-increasing civil society groups speaking out against the injustices in the land show this; the voices bombarding the talk-show programmes show this; the proliferation of the TV discussion programmes shows this. They have shown enough. The time has come for radical change in how we operate as a nation. The Prime Minister and his Cabinet need to put into effect every legislation, programme and strategy to effect the urgent changes that are needed.

This change will require strong, participatory, inclusive, courageous and radical leadership. We need to operate within a new paradigm. I challenge this government to be courageous to save this nation from its downward spiral. As Nelson Mandela says: "I learned that courage was not the absence of fear, but the triumph over it. The brave man is not he who does not feel afraid, but he who conquers that fear." (Mandela 1995)

Our leaders need to be courageous to change how we have functioned in the past. They need to not be afraid to step out and change the culture and ethos of our political life. Our Prime Minister began this process when he was courageous enough to be the only politician to acknowledge that he had associated with gunmen in the past. There are many others who have been involved, but who are now afraid to acknowledge this.

Let us be courageous and, like Mandela, put our nation first, above party and above self-interest. Only then can we begin to operate in a new paradigm of unity and prosperity.

**Published October 7, 2007**

# COP EXECUTED: A FATHER BUTCHERED

'No, No, not Brownie.' The wail erupted from the normally composed, externally correct demeanour of the uniformed policewoman. After the Area 1 choir rendered a heart-moving song, they clung to each other and moved to their seats. Then, "Wooh. No, not Brownie. Wooh. Ahh. Not Brownie." The grief was thick; the atmosphere of sorrow enveloped the church. You could cut it, if you tried. Coupled with this was anger. 'Enough is enough.' was the cry.

The funeral service of Sergeant Errol Brown of the St. James Area 1 Highway Patrol, who was murdered on December 5, 2007, is one that I will never forget. Forgotten, seems to be what happens to the policemen who have been executed protecting the citizens of this nation. Yet we, as a nation, need to be mindful that, in spite of the rogue cops that exist within the police force, there are many who are placing their lives on the line daily to protect our nation. There are good men and women serving in the force, and Sgt. Errol Brown was one such policeman.

In a nation where fathers are, many times, not fulfilling their roles as nurturers and examples to their children, Sergeant Brown was doing just that. He was the consummate husband and father. Mesha-Gay, his daughter, in reflecting on her father's life, painted the picture of a man who was a tribute to this nation. Sergeant Brown was married for 26 years to Doreen. This is how Mesha-Gay described her father:

"Daddy was a family man and to him, family was the core of his being. To his wife, Doreen, he was the perfect helpmate. He was a considerate and caring husband. He ensured that she was happy even when he was not ... How many fathers do you know who end each and every conversation with his children by saying, 'I love you? Well, Daddy did. He was never afraid to be affectionate with me or my brothers. We always knew that we were loved and protected. No one loved us more than our father. He was a dedicated, loving, honest and caring man."

How many of our Jamaican men would have such a tribute given to them by their children? Our society is reaping the results of fatherlessness and the irresponsible production of children, yet, here we have a man who exemplified how our Jamaican fathers should be, and he was wantonly butchered by gunmen who, more than likely, had no one to call father. Sergeant Brown taught his children Christian morals and values. He not only taught them, he lived them before his children. Mesha recounted that he taught them the value of, "humility and of living within our means". "He taught us never to compromise our integrity for anything."

**An Example**

As an example of how he lived this before them, she told how, on her coming home from university abroad, he would pick her up at the airport in his old car. She, out of embarrassment and frustration, would ask him why he didn't buy a new car. He told her he could have bought several new cars but instead, he chose to put her through the best schools and through medical school. His last line on that matter speaks to the character of this policeman who was brutally removed from us, "Mesha, I love you with all my heart, but not even you are going make me tief."

Oh, that we had many more policemen like Sergeant Brown. As a nation, we would have strong young men growing up to be valuable citizens of this great nation who would become nurturing husbands and fathers. Instead, we have produced heartless, cold-blooded murderers spawned from communities created out of the need for our people to have a shack to cover their heads, where running water does not exist, where light, if it is there, is stolen, where law and order is determined by the don. Our nation has spawned these persons who murdered Sergeant Brown, blowing off the top of his head, pumping eight bullets into his body while he was entering his home after coming off duty. He ran, but fell, and they did not spare him. Sergeant Brown's family resides in the U.S.A. and they implored him many times to join them since he had his green card. He felt that he had to stay to serve his country. It is such a man that was torn from us.

How did this come to pass? Politicians set up garrison communities to ensure their own continuity in the political arena. Guns were brought in to ensure compliance of all to the party who set up these garrisons. These places have become the breeding ground for the murderers of Sergeant Brown and for other criminals. As a nation we forget, to our own detriment.

As I have called for before, as a nation we need to set up a truth and reconciliation commission to look at our recent past and find a way to cleanse the spirit of our nation. The webpage of the Greensboro Truth and Reconciliation Commission informs us that more than 30 nations have utilised this model. (Greensboro Truth and Reconciliation Commission 2006) These include Peru, Ghana, East Timor and Sierra Leone. What has been achieved through the commission is what we, as a nation need, to start a new day as a people.

"The truth and reconciliation process seeks to heal relations between opposing sides by uncovering all pertinent facts, distinguishing truth from lies, and allowing for acknowledgement, appropriate mourning, forgiveness and healing." (Greensboro Truth and Reconciliation Commission 2006)

This is a new year; we are under a new administration. I challenge this administration to change the old paradigm. I challenge the Prime Minister to be a leader of courage, to face squarely the sense of hopelessness which has enveloped this nation and take the necessary actions to address the plague that threatens our existence.

Make Sgt. Errol Brown's murder count for something. Cause the innocent blood that has bathed and soaked this land to bring forth beauty out of its ashes.

**Published January 6, 2008**

# TRUTH-TELLING AND JAMAICA'S HEALING

**Cross Roads St. Andrew, Police Station**

"You will know the truth and the truth shall set you free," says Jesus Christ. (The Holy Bible King James Version 1993) It has been proven to be so, on a national and personal level, many times the world over. In Jamaica, truth-telling has begun with the confession of Detective Constable Carey Lyn-Sue, which was published in The Gleaner on Monday, January 21, 2008. (Frater 2008) The

*Ah Suh Me See It, Ah Suh Me Say It*

truth-telling continued in the confession of the unidentified gunman in The Sunday Gleaner of January 27, 2008. (Luton 2008) In our nation, these accounts go against the tide of what has become acceptable in Jamaica, which is to, "See no evil, hear no evil, speak no evil," which has come to mean that no matter what evil is going on, make sure that you do not speak about it. Therefore, to speak the truth in Jamaica when it involves others means that you are labelled as an 'informer'. Currently, it seems that to speak the truth to the authorities is the worst crime anyone can commit in Jamaica. This seems to be worse than rape, murder and incest because we are willing to endure these vicious acts rather than speak the truth.

**Culture of Silence**

A very sad example of how this culture of silence has twisted the thinking of our young is what was related to me by one of my teachers. He told me how, upon hearing about the murder of the Jamaica College student, he spoke to some of our boys and pointed out to them that if even one student had informed the school authorities of the conflict that was brewing between the two students, then the victim's life would have been spared. Their response was chilling. They said that they would not have told anyone, even if it meant saving a life because, "dem no informer".[78] This informer culture has probably been developed from our years of slavery when giving information against your fellow slave was a cruel, self-serving act. We need to realize that we are now our own masters and that not speaking the truth in our nation has resulted in our becoming enslaved by the ruthless criminals whose cause is served by our seeing no evil or speaking no evil.

Oppression, injustice and crime grow in this culture of secrecy and this is what has happened in Jamaica. By our silence, by our lack of truth telling, we have fed the monster of corruption, violence and extortion. We, the citizens of this nation, have agreed that this culture is what we want by our acts of silence. This includes the businessman who pays the protection money to the area dons[79], to the middle-class citizen who agrees to pay off the policeman who gives him a ticket, to the mother who gives her daughter to the don to take her virginity. It envelops us all.

Therefore, when Detective Constable Lyn-Sue spoke the truth, it was a courageous act, which will help to break this culture of silence that has fed this monster of violence, extortion and oppression in our society. I salute him for listening to the Spirit of God in him and his response of speaking the truth. I believe that for this evil monster to die in our nation, truth telling must be one of the weapons that we use. I think it is vain for us to expect the leaders to begin using this weapon of truth since they have too much vested interest in allowing things to stay as they are. They have too much to lose. We need a leader with the courage of a Mandela, a Martin Luther King, a Marcus Garvey, to do such a thing. Is there such a leader among us?

Nothing helped us to understand how much we have bought into this culture of silence and acceptance of wrong as right and right as wrong like the response of some of Carey Lyn-Sue's comrades to his speaking the truth. Some felt that Carey Lyn-Sue was breaking a "secret pact not to backtrack from a contrived storyline, regardless of the consequences." These cops felt that Lyn-Sue was a traitor because he spoke the truth. It has been reported that other cops felt that someone had paid him off to say this. They described what he did as, "duttiness".[80]

Lyn-Sue's confession, however, has started a snowballing effect, which I think will continue. The account of the unidentified gunman gives indication to this, and the self-confessed paedophile in Wednesday's Gleaner adds to the effect. The account of the unidentified gunman confirms further what is being spoken about by many Jamaicans: That there are policemen and politicians who are in league with criminals, "No ends (turf) can exist without di police help." He continues with, "How yuh tink man get rifle and money more time? One ends (turf) right now have 15 rifles and a politician mek dem reach deh."[81] More Jamaicans need to come forward and speak to their involvement in the criminal culture of our country and what they know about how this system operates. Truth-telling needs to continue to break the hold of crime over our nation.

**Revealing is Healing**

I commend Detective Constable Carey Lyn-Sue on doing what his conscience dictated and I pray that many others will have the courage to do what he did: Speak the truth. The slogan for the Truth and Reconciliation Commission in South Africa was 'Revealing is Healing'. Let us begin the revealing and thereby start the healing in our nation. We cannot hope for any economic recovery with this culture of silence which feeds crime and oppression in our midst.

We cannot expect our people to develop a culture which sees each man expecting to honestly earn a day's pay to buy what his family needs, to get justice when a wrong is done and to live in peace if we do not change this culture of see no evil, speak no evil. No matter how many initiatives are generated to jump-start our economy, if this culture doesn't change, they will all peter out to nothing. It is only the truth that shall free us as a nation, that can heal us as a people. Let's begin the healing.

**Published February 3, 2008**

# GIVE US VISION LEST WE PERISH

Jamaicans are still revelling in the glow and euphoria of the achievements of our athletes in Beijing, despite the effects of Gustav. The questions, however, are still being asked: What can be learnt from our athletes' achievements? How can we ensure that lasting value is gained from what has been accomplished in Beijing?

Certainly, one of things that we need to realize is that the secondary-schools' sports programme has been the cradle of our great athletes. We have been told that we have a particular edge as Jamaicans because we have the quick-tick muscle. We have recognized that as a tiny country, we must tap into our uniqueness in order to find and maintain a place in this global village. The potential that we have to produce world sprinters must be seen as a part of what will set us apart in this increasingly homogenized world. Doesn't it, therefore, make sense that the Government and private sector ensure that the cradle of the sprinters is well funded, organized, constantly remolded and shaped to ensure that it gives support to developing the athletes of Jamaica?

## Schools' Allocation Budget

At present, the Government does not give support to the sports programme at the secondary-school level. Schools have an allocation in the budget for physical education, not the extended sports programme. Therefore, in order to support the sports programme in the school, many boards of management and principals must find ways and means to raise the funds necessary to do this. The fact that the Inter Secondary Schools Sports Association (ISSA), the body that organizes and oversees the secondary- schools' sports competitions is made up of principals of secondary schools, speaks to the truth of this situation. The management of the Manning Cup and the DaCosta Cup Football competitions is done by ISSA; the organization of the National Boys' and Girls' Athletic Championships is done by ISSA; and we could go on.

I believe that we are at that stage of development in our nation where we need to look again at how the Government interfaces with schools with regard to sports. There is a ministry of sports that should be working at developing a broad and integrated approach to the production of world- class athletes in Jamaica. This ministry should be engaging bodies such as ISSA in conceiving and implementing such a plan. It should not only be focused on the post-secondary level, but this plan should also include corporate Jamaica. These companies that supported the athletes in Beijing benefited stupendously from their success in the Olympics.

We must lift our vision of sports to another plane. We must become intentional as a nation in developing this vast potential that the secondary schools by themselves have been struggling to do. I do not think that the sports development needed to achieve such an objective should be left to the creative genius of individual principals, as good as we are at 'tunning our hands to mek fashion'[82]. This vision needs more than us; it needs more than extortion.

Another area that needs a national and broad development plan at the secondary- school level is the performing arts. We have produced world-class musicians and we are recognized globally because of Bob Marley and our other great reggae artistes. Isn't this another area that as a small nation we should be tapping into - this creative, musical ability that seems to pulse through our Jamaican psyche? Yet, traditionally, we have one music teacher per school. This is because the Government's policy of determining the number of teachers employed to the schools is based on a ratio. Therefore, schools such as Ardenne are allowed to employ one teacher for every 20 students. When, however, you try to offer a diverse pro-gramme which includes technical and practical-based subjects that can only accommodate small classes, it limits the number of teachers that are left to be deployed to the other subject areas.

I think that the Government should be looking at schools that wish to use a poly-technic approach in their curriculum development and give them the necessary resources to support this approach. Such a programme would offer to our students, areas in which their varying abilities could be developed. Therefore, if a child has the aptitude for the performing arts, a programme should be offered that causes this to grow; if a child has the capacity for technical subjects, development should be encouraged; if a child has the potential to be a good athlete, support should be provided; if a child is curious about the world and wants to be a scientist, labs and good teachers should facilitate this; if a child is an abstract thinker and wants to explore issues, a programme in the humanities should be there to develop this ability. A secondary school is a cradle for all these potentials.

**Grammar or Technical Schools**

Whereas support is given traditionally for the grammar and technical subjects, this support is based on whether schools are categorized as grammar or technical schools. There are schools such as Ardenne that are neither grammar nor technical schools, but which seek to offer a curriculum that allows each child to find his or her niche and to excel. I am asking the Ministry of Education to shift its focus and look at how resources are allocated, based not only on a pupil-teacher ratio, but also on the programmes that are offered. For instance, to develop a performing-arts department would require not just additional teaching staff, but also resources to develop appropriate facilities, such as a small studio where students can learn about the technical support needed in recording music, among other things. This would need a shift in our traditional approach to education.

We must recognize who we are, what our strengths as a people are and seek to develop the greatness within us in order to ensure our distinct and unique identity in this homogenized world.

**Published September 9, 2008**

# A TALE OF TWO COUNTRIES

J amaica, famous for its music and sports achievement, for Bob Marley and Marcus Garvey, for Merlene Ottey and Usain Bolt, blessed with breathtaking natural beauty, its rolling hills and verdant valleys; the other Jamaica, the "byword among the nations, peoples shake their heads at us" (Psalm 44:14). ((NIV) Holy Bible 1984) We are being scorned by more and more nations because of our culture of violence and corruption.

I was speaking to a Jamaican who had visited Istanbul and she showed me a newspaper from that city, which in one day, featured two Jamaicans. On one page, it showed that in one city, a statue of Bob Marley was being erected, while on another page, Usain Bolt's achievements were being praised. We were justly proud that one "lille, bitty nation like we"[83] could have such an impact on the world that in a city far removed from us, in a culture unlike ours, our name was being lauded. Compare that report to what is being published daily in our newspapers: our constant downgrading on the international level because of our corruption and economic situation. Look at the fact that Costa Rica has now been added to the growing list of nations that do not welcome us with open arms any longer. These nations screen and investigate us before they will allow us to enter their countries because of the violence and mayhem that Jamaicans are importing into their societies.

Not only is our propensity for lawlessness, corruption and violence affecting us here in Jamaica but we are now blushing with increasing shame because of our reputation abroad. When is it going to stop? When are we going to realize that we need to take drastic and draconian steps to halt this rapid slide? I had great hopes for our Prime Minister that he would have displayed the political will and moral fortitude needed to implement laws and strategies necessary to clean up this country; however, it is not happening.

**Why can't it happen here?**

Instead, we are seeing dons running this nation. As the proverb says, "If you lie dung with dawg, yu gwine catch flea."[84] We have heard that there were leaders in New York who took measures to bring the crime rate in that city under control. It happened there. Why can't it happen here? In Colombia, where cocaine ruled and caused mayhem, drastic steps were taken to clean up that country. Why can't it happen here?

I wish to remind us of the prime minister's commitment to clean up corruption in his inaugural speech:

"Corruption in Jamaica is much too easy, too risk-free. We are going to make it more difficult, more hazardous, with stiff penalties for violations.

We intend to:

Impose criminal sanctions for breaches of the rules governing the award of government contracts.

Establish a special prosecutor to investigate and prosecute persons involved in corruption.

Enact legislation for the impeachment and removal from office of public officials guilty of misconduct, corruption, abuse of authority, or betrayal of public trust.

Introduce whistleblower legislation to protect persons who provide information on wrongdoing on the part of public officials.

Review the libel and slander law to ensure that it cannot be used as a firewall to protect wrongdoers.

The high level of crime must be tackled, not simply at the back end where it hurts, but at the front end where it originates." (Campbell 2007)

In spite of these commitments, our nation appears to be more corrupt now than two years ago, and violence increases. There is an increasing sense of hopelessness that is threatening to overtake our nation. In the Gleaner of Wednesday, December 2, I read, "Transparency International, a global anti-corruption watchdog, says Jamaica is facing the clear and present danger of succumbing to what it calls, 'state capture'." (Campbell 2009) I asked myself, "What is that?"

## Corruption

The article continued to explain that the term describes "a situation where powerful individuals, institutions, companies or groups within or outside a state use corruption to shape a nation's policies, legal environment and economy to benefit their own private interests". This seems to describe what has been happening in our nation. We need to realize that we can no longer expect that we can operate however we please, whenever we please, and expect the rest of the world to use our reputation gained through Marley and Bolt, among others, to cover our corruption and violence. We are suffering and we will continue to suffer for it.

As a people, we need to decide which Jamaica we are going to allow to grow and develop. We are now at risk of becoming a rogue state among the nations of the world. The Government and Opposition need to come together, as the Prime Minister had promised in his inaugural speech, and combine their forces and influence to redeem the situation. The tribalistic approach to life that is generated in every facet of this nation needs to change in order for us to survive as a nation. This approach needs to begin at the top. The Vale Royal Talks need to continue and become even further, The Vale Royal Actions.

Business persons need to combine forces to undo the control of the dons who demand protection money and therefore are the ones who are calling the shots. In Jamaica, there are more churches per square mile than any other country. The Church has the position to help to effect change and stop seeing itself as having no responsibility for our present situation. We all have contributed to the present condition, including the Church, either by active involvement in the corruption, or by silent acquiescence because of fear.

We need Davids in this nation to save us from the Goliath of crime, violence, lawlessness and corruption.

Mr. Prime Minister, you promised us that you would have the political will to effect change. Display that political will and fortitude now for your nation's sake. Be David. Slay Goliath.

**Published December 6, 2009**

# JAMAICA'S TIPPING POINT

**Tivoli Gardens**

T he events of Monday, May 24, and Tuesday, May 25, 2010, are of our own making. The situation in Tivoli Gardens was allowed to develop for more than 40 years. A state seemingly outside of Jamaica's laws and regulations was allowed to exist by succeeding governments. We, the people of this nation, sat by and spoke of Tivoli Gardens in hushed tones and with fear. This, the "mother of all garrisons", spawned other garrison communities around Jamaica, because in the eyes of the politicians, the pattern seemed to work.

Around our nation, enclaves of the dispossessed are committed to one political party or another, or one don or another, in an effort to gain material benefits which the State has failed to provide them. These communities spawn gangs, which are violent and become breeding grounds for criminals. We have created a monster that is now devouring us.

Not only have we allowed this pattern of garrisons to be replicated throughout Jamaica, but we have accepted it to such an extent that it is now acknowledged as a part of our culture. A part of a culture which has accepted that: politicians grant dons contracts under the guise of them being building contractors; dons are so powerful that it was being proposed to bring them to Parliament to broker peace deals; if you have 'two cents, u affi let aaf pon anodder man'[85]; anything you can do to earn a money, even if it breaks the law, is fine because 'man affi live'[86]; 'passa passa'[87] and the like are acceptable forms of entertainment for the young; mothers can teach their babies, once they can speak, to sing lewd lyrics and gyrate their young bodies to music describing how man must ... them; obscenity is an acceptable form of expression; vulgar loud music and pornographic movies can be shown on public transportation to school children; gun lyrics – once it rhymes – is good music; to be dissed[88] is a sin worthy of death; the other great sin is 'informer fi dead;'[89] the first response in a conflict is violence; to break the law is fine, as long as you can get away with it; politicians are expected to be corrupt and the police the same; morality is a bad word; decency and manners are colonial vestiges which tie us to our slave past; freedom of expression in whatever form is the highest good; sexual immorality no longer exists, apart from homosexuality, since marriage is no longer necessary, with even ministers of government 'shacking up'. The list is unending.

## Government must be Challenged

We have come to quite a state. Never again are we to allow our country to come to such a pass. We are at a tipping point in this nation. We, in civil society, must ensure that we tilt this nation in the right direction. The Government must be challenged and held accountable to act on behalf of the nation. It must now put the nation's interest first.

The anti-crime laws that need to be passed must be fast-tracked in Parliament. Enough talk, action, 'not a bag a mouth'[90]. The laws governing political campaign funding must be put in place and enforced. In fact, Fae Ellington's proposal that the private sector not contribute scarce funds to such an exercise in grandstanding is an even better plan. A plan needs to be developed to 'degarrisonise' communities supporting the Jamaica Labour Party or the People's National Party. In addition, standards of decency in the public sphere must be established and maintained. We must hold public officials to higher standards of conduct. The crude and vulgar display in Parliament is symptomatic of a culture which accepts vulgarity as the norm. It is embarrassing to watch our elected officials behave in a way which I would not condone in the classroom among students. Am I then to point the students to our parliamentarians to observe their behaviour as an example of what is expected?

The effort at having transparency and accountability in public life needs to be made a priority. We see that the USA is now focusing on wealthy Jamaicans who have amassed wealth without a known source. Why aren't there laws in our nation that would have the tax administration enforcing disclosure of such funds and its sources to them? Is it that these persons have bought out our politicians with campaign donations so that their hands and mouths have been committed to them and they have, therefore, been made incapable of acting?

Furthermore, there needs to be clear distinctions made in law between the Government and the judiciary that the politicians, even those in power, cannot use the legal system to further their own agendas. In like manner, the police certainly cannot be allowed to be investigating themselves. There must be a civil body, which even if it does not oversee the process, should certainly participate in such investigations, not only the Bureau of Special Investigations.

I want to commend the brave members of civil society who have been making their voices heard during this traumatic period in our history – persons such as Joseph Matalon, president of the Private Sector Organization of Jamaica, Carolyn Gomes of Jamaicans for Justice, and the former head of the Jamaica Constabulary Force, Rear Admiral Hardley Lewin. I want to encourage the church leaders who have been speaking out on the state of our nation to continue to do so. I commend Bishop Herro Blair on his attempts to assist the unfortunate citizens of Tivoli.

We, however, need more Jamaicans to make their voices heard. We need more Jamaicans whose lives can stand the glare of transparency to stand up and speak up in support of truth and integrity in this nation. Never again are we to be lulled into a state of complacency and fear of politicians and 'bad man'.

The Bible says, and Jamaica is a case in point, "Righteousness exalts a nation, but sin is a reproach to any people." Prov.14:34 (Bible Gateway 1993).

**Published June 6, 2010**

# CURBING THE MINDSET OF CRIMINALITY

This article represents the thoughts of the Jamaica Association of Principals of Secondary Schools (JAPSS), an organization comprising principals of high schools across Jamaica that has been in operation for decades. The current president is Sharon Reid, principal of St Andrew High School for Girls. I am vice-president, and secretary is Glennor Wilson, principal of Claude McKay High School. As principals of secondary schools, we have been faced with the impact of a society that has been decaying spiritually, morally, socially and economically. These realities need to change. So, too, must the violent nature of our society, and the corruption which is pervasive, if we are to have the chance to develop and prosper. We need to give our children the opportunity to be educated in an environment free of fear and violence.

It has been too long that dons and criminals have had the almost exclusive power of monopoly across several communities of this country, and we think it is time that the Government, the security forces and patriotic Jamaicans take back this country.

The current situation in Jamaica, whereby our security forces are seeking to challenge the status quo of dons ruling garrison communities in Jamaica and to restore our nation to the rule of law and order, calls for all Jamaicans to give their strong support to this initiative in order for these objectives to be achieved. This initiative is a war against crime and lawlessness in Jamaica. A nation must give its support to its troops when they are at war.

At its meeting on June 11, the Jamaica Association of Principals of Secondary Schools, therefore, resolved that:

1.  There is to be genuine, balanced support given to the security forces in the execution of the mandate given by the Government to bring to justice, criminals who have been inflicting terror and violence on our society. This should include granting the security forces all the necessary resources that they will need to achieve this objective effectively.

2.  The heads of the Jamaica Defence Force and the Jamaica Constabulary Force are to operate without concern for corrupt politicians who might seek to undermine their efforts in an attempt to protect their party supporters who are criminals. Every community in Jamaica must be open to be searched by the security forces to root out each and every such criminal and acts of criminality. In their effort to bring stability and civility to the country, every effort must be made and care taken to protect law-abiding citizens and give them the respect they deserve.

3. If the state of emergency provided the framework whereby the security forces were able to enter Tivoli Gardens, then it should be used judicially to provide the similar framework whereby the security forces will be able to go into every other such community that exists in Jamaica.

## 'Badmanship'

This is a matter that must be pursued and given priority because of what we are seeing in the classrooms. The mindset of criminality is affecting our youth at every level and in every part of our island. This phenomenon is no longer confined to the urban areas of Kingston and St Catherine, but has become evident in the schools across the length and breadth of Jamaica. 'Badmanship' is the behaviour that is now thought to be 'hype' by our boys and admired by our girls. The pervasive and rampant over-sexualisation of our youth is a product of this culture which sees young girls being demanded by the dons and gunmen in communities across the island. Many of our girls have accepted this view of themselves as being of value only if a man or boy wants to have sex with them. They openly and willingly buy into this belief that a girl's value is based on her sexual activity.

This criminal mindset is further evidenced in the practice of extortion being played out in the schools. Both boys and girls seek to prey upon younger students or the 'soft' ones to extort money from them for their own means. They have learnt this from what our dons have been doing in this society. In addition, because some students are not receiving love, affirmation and acceptance at home, they now look to gangs to provide these needs in their lives. Some gangs are school-based, while others are community-based. These gangs become surrogate families for these students. This is what, after all, they have been seeing in operation around them. "Children live what they learn."

As a nation, we must recommit ourselves to work together as a society to provide a positive environment within which our children can grow and develop to be adults who will benefit our nation. This can only happen if we work together as a community to build strong family support for our children. We must determine to start practicing and teaching the values and morals that will strengthen, not simply our children, but our nation.

Let us ensure that our children attend school regularly; that they are provided with the textbooks that are necessary; that they are given the nourishment needed for their brain to function optimally; that their homes be places of safety and not abuse. Let us, as a society, make sure that they are not on the streets loitering when they should be at home. Let us make sure that they are not out late at nights in places which not even adults should be.

Let us see how, as a society, we can work together, in the home, school, church, media, security forces, private sector and the Government to create a society where our children can be given a fighting chance at developing as wholesome and productive individuals and, thereby, strengthen our nation.

**Published July 4, 2010**

# COURAGEOUS LEADERSHIP NEEDED – PT 2

**Trench Town**

In an article titled "Courageous Leadership Needed" published in The Sunday Gleaner on October 7, 2007, I wrote:

"A s a nation, we are at a critical juncture – the results of the general election show this; the tumultuous rising complaints against police injustice show this; the ever-increasing civil society groups speaking out against the injustices in the land show this; the voices bombarding the talk-show programmes show this; the pro-liferation of the TV discussion programmes show this. They have shown enough. The time has come for radical change in how we operate as a nation. The prime minister and his Cabinet need to put into effect every legislation, programme and strategy to effect the urgent changes that are needed.

"This change will require strong, participatory, inclusive, coura-geous and radical leadership. We need to operate within a new par-adigm. I challenge this Government to be courageous to save this nation from its downward spiral. As Nelson Mandela says: 'I learned that courage was not the absence of fear, but the triumph over it. The brave man is not he who does not feel afraid, but he who conquers that fear'. (Tyson 2007)

"Our leaders need to be courageous to change how we have functioned in the past. They need to not be afraid to step out and change the culture and ethos of our political life. Our prime minister began this process when he was courageous enough to be the only politician to acknowledge that he had associated with gunmen in the past. There are many others who have been involved but who are now afraid to admit this.

"Let us be courageous and, like Mandela, put our nation first, above party and above self-interest. Only then can we begin to operate in a new paradigm of unity and prosperity." (Campbell 2007)

Those words were penned after the present Prime Minister assumed his leadership of this country, yet they are still relevant almost three years later because not much has changed. The political parties are still playing their games and are not seeking consensus on what is best for this nation. Three years later, what has changed is that our citizens are even more aware that politicians generally lack truth and credibility. What has changed is that we feel a sense of hopelessness concerning the leadership of our political process. What has changed is that we are in a quandary as to how to find viable alternatives to the present system to lead our nation. What has changed is that as a people, we are completely disillusioned by the present political leadership. The latest RJR poll testifies to this disillusionment. We have reached to this place because over the years, the political leaders have not held the concepts of truth and morality as being of paramount importance in determining how they function and carry out their responsibilities.

The practice of giving the country half-truths in an attempt to lull us into complacency by having us believe that we are receiving the whole truth is indicative of minds that are deceptive and lacking in integrity.

**Mired in Deception**

It seems that the political old guard, then, has been shaped in a way of operating which is mired in deception and expediency. On both sides of the fence, this way of functioning needs to change. How are we going to do this? Are we going to throw out the older politicians? If so, where are the replacements? Are the younger politicians committed to truth and integrity? I see no evidence of this. As a nation, we are in a political quagmire. It seems clear then that the members of civil society need to continue to place pressure on our political leaders to change their modus operandi. They must be held accountable for their policies and their actions. I have no doubt that this stands true whether it is the Jamaica Labour Party or People's National Party in power. As the polls show, they are not much different from each other.

There are several pieces of legislation that need to be passed and implemented to ensure that the back of criminal activities is broken in this nation. I encourage the Parliament to expedite these laws to give teeth to the attempts now being made to deal with the culture of lawlessness that is rampant in our society.

Another matter of grave concern at this present time is the dismantling of the garrisons. Let us not forget that there are garrisons on both sides of the political fence. What is being done to change these garrisoned communities? This reality in our Jamaican landscape needs to the dealt with. I am glad to see that pressure is being brought to bear on how funds for political campaigns are garnered. This, however, is not enough. We also need to change how votes are garnered.

No longer can we accept that "all politicians are liad"[91] and leave it at that. As civil society, we must put pressure on the politicians to abide by the principles of truth, honesty and integrity. They report to us, the society. We are the people who have put them there. They must understand that we have the power to take them out. If we do not maintain the pressure on the politicians to abide by the principles of truth and integrity, then they will continue the "same old, same old" practices.

I firmly believe that a people get the government that they deserve. If, then, we do not demand integrity in our leaders and remove them if they do not comply, we do deserve the corrupt, dishonest, self-serving politicians who now rule over us.

**Published August 1, 2010**

# CHAPELTON THE FORGOTTEN PLACE

Each year the Fergus Simpson Foundation hosts a day camp for the children of Chapelton and the surrounding environs. The camp is usually held from Monday to Friday in the first week of August. The camp was first held at the Chapelton All-Age School, but because it has grown in numbers, it is now held at Clarendon College. Family members of the late Rev Fergus Simpson, along with other volunteers, come from the United States and London to run this camp. Funds are usually scarce but companies such as Jamaica National, National Commercial Bank, Digicel and the Insurance Company of the West Indies have given donations at various points throughout the years to assist in making this camp a possibility. In addition, there are individuals who give sacrificially to make camp happen – one such person is Dr Rema Green.

This year, over 190 children participated in the camp where they ate breakfast and lunch each day. Meals are prepared by volunteers from the community and other young people, some of whom have benefited from the camp in the past. These young people also assisted as volunteers with the other activities throughout the day.

These activities included devotions, life skills classes, fine arts pro-grammes such as dance, drama and music, and sports. In addition, there is a sports day and a grand finale where the students perform for the community. The children of the Chapelton community look forward every year to this camp which is now in its seventh year.

Many persons who come from abroad to volunteer at camp grew up in Chapelton or visited as second-generation family members of persons originating from the area. There are others, like me, who grew up here as children and who are now living in another part of Jamaica. We are all appalled at the state of the community and its environs. The roads, in particular, are in serious disrepair. There are some roads which have no asphalt left on them at all; others have huge craters that we are forced to negotiate each time we make our way through the community. There are large water mains exposed where the water has beaten away the gravel and the asphalt in the road.

Chapelton seems to have become a forgotten place, like a home that is no longer inhabited and cared for. Driving along the roads, your vision is obstructed by overgrown wild grass. In the town, there are dilapidated, decaying buildings which seem to ready to crumble if a strong wind blows. There are only a few promising business places in operation. One wonders if the member of parliament for the area has made a recent visit to see what is happening in the com-munity since he does not live there. I remember growing up in the community as a child and hearing about Sir Donald Sangster who was the member of parliament (MP) for the area. Later, the MP was Dr Percival Broderick, who was followed by Mr. George Lyn. These persons related to the community as if it mattered to them because they were from the area or made the area their home. The present MP seems to operate like an absentee landowner, reaping the benefits of the votes without giving the care and input needed to make the area prosper.

## Income-Generating Entity

The town houses some important structures such as the historic St Paul's Anglican Church, a town centre featuring a park clock tower, a courthouse, a Collector of Taxes office, a police station, a market, along with the Chapelton All-Age School, and Clarendon College. However, the area needs a factory or other income-generating entity to bring economic benefits to the people who live in and around the community. The youth of the area are moving out to seek jobs in Kingston because there are not many opportunities for employment in the town. Chapelton deserves a chance to survive and to grow economically. The basic structure for a town remains, although those structures now need to be developed and strengthened so that once again the town which was once the capital of Clarendon will become a thriving, bustling town centre.

Even as the Fergus Simpson Foundation seeks to implement their motto to 'Treasure the Past, Train the Future and Transform the Community' by working in a small, consistent way with the youth of Chapelton, similarly we ask the political directorate that has responsibility for the development of the community to embrace the area as their own, to expand their vision of what can be accomplished and secure the future of this rural town.

## Succeeding Governments

On another note, I participated as an organizer of the conference for the Caribbean Association of Principals of Secondary Schools (CAPSS) which was held at the Sunset Jamaica Grande in Ocho Rios last month. Over 150 secondary school principals attended, 80 being from nine other English-speaking Caribbean countries. In a session in which each country gave an overview of secondary education in their country, we realized that universal secondary education has been achieved in those countries which are doing well, while a number of others, including Jamaica, have yet to achieve this goal. Barbados pointed out that the education plan in that country does not change with each new administration. Instead, there is a long-term plan which is followed consistently by succeeding governments. I hope that as a nation, we too will soon see the effects of our Ministry of Education maintaining the goals that were outlined in the Transformation in Education plan from the previous administration. The substantive programmes recommended are being followed by this administration of the Ministry of Education. The nation should therefore see the effects of the focus that has been put on early-childhood education and the increased move to improve the teaching and assessment quality at the primary level. Hopefully, we will soon be able to narrow the divide between the traditional and non-traditional high schools.

**Published August 7, 2011**

# CIVIL SOCIETY COMES OF AGE

The events of the past 18 months have shown us as a Jamaican populace that civil society has power and that such power must be used to protect the rights of our people.

For years, Jamaicans have known of the garrison politics that operates in our nation and, in particular, in Tivoli Gardens. This situation would be spoken of in hushed tones by many, but it is only in recent years that civil society has begun speaking out against this type of political arrangement. One remembers the days when in certain constituencies, more than 100 per cent voter turnout was the norm. The establishment of the Electoral Commission has helped to change some of these practices, yet still others have been deeply ingrained in the psyche of Jamaicans that it will take some time for these behaviours to become reprehensible to indoctrinated party supporters on both sides of the fence. The association of our political parties with criminal gangs is another well-known reality in the Jamaican context. In spite of the repeated denials by politicians on both sides, the man on the street is quite aware of what happens in that regard. We can recall high-powered political figures attending the funerals of acknowledged gunmen who they designated 'contractors' and 'area leaders'. These men, according to the politicians, have no police record nor had they been proven to be criminals. All of these proclamations convinced nobody but themselves, as Jamaicans are quite aware that our justice system, which depends on eyewitness reports in court, ensures that none of these accused 'dons' would be convicted since the eyewitnesses usually conveniently disappear, have loss of memory, or are killed. These realities were the background to the events of May 2010.

This culture of crime and violence and its association with the political directorate came to a head in Jamaica with the USA's request for the extradition of 'Dudus' Coke, the strongman of Tivoli Gardens. Jamaica watched as our Government defended the strongman of Tivoli. Our country was put at risk, and many of us were alarmed at what was taking place. The use of ICT enabled information to be moved around at ready speed and for important organizations in the country such as the PSOJ, the Jamaica Chamber of Commerce, and the Jamaica Umbrella Group of Churches to bring pressure to bear on the Government to cease protecting Dudus. The gunfights of last May are forever etched in the minds of all Jamaicans. It was clear that the bloody confrontation which took place when Tivoli residents barricaded the community in order to protect their leader could have been prevented had the extradition request been handled differently. Lives were lost, property destroyed, and the reputation of the nation brought into disgrace in the international arena. (The Sunday Gleaner 2010)

**Redemption for Bruce Golding?**

In any democratic nation, such happenings would result in the resignation of the head of state. This call was no different in Jamaica; however, what was different was that here, the political directorate was so arrogant in its own sense of entitlement that it saw no need any resignations to take place. It was civil society, including the man on the street, who called in to radio talk shows, wrote in the press, and communicated with the Government to advocate that the Prime Minister should resign. In response to this pressure, Mr. Golding set up the Manatt commission of enquiry. This, if nothing else, did two things: enabled the Jamaican people to have an eye, for the first time, into the intrigue of government politicizing and provided daily entertainment for a people disillusioned with, angry at and betrayed by its Government. At the end of that production, the Prime Minister was still at the helm of the Government. (Luton 2010) There was one resignation from the Government previous to the enquiry which was a token thrown to the public. It meant nothing.

Mr. Golding's announcement on Sunday that he intends to resign was shocking. It is evident, however, that Mr. Golding understands that his personal political ambitions must take second place to what is best for the nation and, may I say, for his party. For that under-standing and for taking the subsequent action of resigning, he must be commended. I recall having great hopes for Mr. Golding when he gave his swearing-in speech. He has done some good for our country, but as Antony said of Julius Caesar in Shakespeare's play, "The evil that men do lives after them, the good is oft interred with their bones." (Shakespeare, Julius Caesar 1991) I believe, however, that Jamaica will recall the good that Prime Minister Bruce Golding did for this country because he has redeemed himself by stepping down at this time.

It is civil society that has helped to bring the changes in our Jamaican political scenario. The push for greater transparency and accountability must increase. Our leaders need to remember that they are elected by the people to serve them. They must, at all times, realise that they must operate as servant-leaders and not arrogant despots. Civil society has an important part to play to ensure that this realization is kept in the forefront of the minds of our government.

Martin Henry, in The Sunday Gleaner of June 13, 2010, made the following points in his article 'Government and civil society': (Henry 2010)

"A recurring demand is for 'civic participation' in governance. One of the most powerful coalitions emerging and which includes the Private Sector Organization of Jamaica, Jamaica Manufacturers' Association, Jamaicans for Justice, Citizens Action for Free and Fair Elections, Jamaica Exporters' Association, Media Association and Bar Association, among others, has announced its intention "to demand non-partisan civic participation in the affairs of the nation going forward" and affirmed its "commitment to a process that broadens and increases public participation in and oversight of the national decision-making process".

What now needs to be carefully considered are the mechanisms which will allow orderly and productive engagement without unduly constricting the capacity of the Government to govern.

**Published October 2, 2011**

# END NOTES

Baker-Henningham Helen, Meeks-Gardner Julie , Chang Susan, Walker Susan. 2009. "Experiences of violence and deficits in academic achievement among urban primary school children in Jamaica." *Child Abuse and Neglect* (Elsevier Limited) 33: 296-306.

Barrett, Wesley. 2008. *Reggae Boyz.com Discussion Forum.* Edited by Karl. Karl. May 05. Accessed May 16, 2008. http://www.reggaeboyzsc.com/Forum06/Topic5264-8-1. aspx?PostID=5332&DisplayMode=3&#bm5332.

BBC News. 2011. *news/uk-england-derbyshire.* February 28. Accessed February 4, 2012. http://www.bbc.com/news/ uk-england-derbyshire-12598896.

Bellanfante, Dwight. 2010. "Men Want to be Responsible Fathers." *The Gleaner.* Kingston: The Gleaner Company, May 24.

Burrell, Skatta, Queen Ifrica, Mr. Vegas, Robert Livingston, Foota Hype, and Mystic, interview by Cliff Hughes. 2009. "Impact of Dancehall." *Impact.* Kingston, (October 22).

Campbell, Edmond. 2007. "Bruce Takes Charge." *The Gleaner.* Kingston: The Gleaner Company, September 12.

—. 2009. "Ja in danger of 'state capture', says watchdog." *The Gleaner.* Kingston: The Gleaner Company, December 2.

Chung, Dennis. 2014. "Social behaviour - the missing link for Jamaica's development." *The Gleaner.* Kingston: The Gleaner Company, April 25.

CNS News. 2012. "New Law in Support of LGBT Implemented in Public Schools." *News.* Reston, Virginia: Media Research Center, January 1.

Coombs, Michael Dr. 2014. "Heal the Family and Save the Nation." *Concept Paper - National Association for the Family.* Mandeville: Unpublished, May.

Davidson, Barry, and Faith Linton. 2012. *Answers to Questions Parents Ask.* Kingston: Family Life Ministries.

Davidson, Barry, and Maureen Watson. 2006. *Healthy Families: A Caribbean Perspective.* Kingston: Family Life Ministries.

Davidson, Vernon. 2014. "Gay Advocates want UWI Professor sacked." *The Jamaica Observer.* Kingston: The Jamaica Observer, May 18.

Davis, Rae. 2004. *Task Force on Educational Reform.* Research, The Ministry of Education, Kingston: The Ministry of Education.

## End Notes

Dawkins, Kuwanda. 2009. "Not so fast, Docta C." *The Gleaner, Letters to the Editor.* Kingston: The Gleaner Company, February 24.

Duckworth, Angela Lee. 2013. *Grit: The power of passion and perseverance.* TED Talk. April. Accessed July 2013. https://www.ted.com/talks/angela_lee_duckworth_grit_the_power_of_passion_and_perseverance.

Editorial. 2009. "Do Kartel and Mavado really respect their fans?" *The Gleaner.* Kingston: The Gleaner Company, September 23.

Jamaica. Ministry of Education. 2010.
"School Security and Safety Guidelines." *School Security and Safety Guidelines.* Kingston.

Elliot Institute. 1993. *Post-Abortion Review.* Elliot Institute. Accessed March 1, 2008.
fterabortion.org/1993/looking-for-advice-in-all-the-wrong-places-2/.

Family Life Ministries. 2014. "Family Life Ministries 30th Anniversary Magazine." *Family Life Ministries 30th Anniversary Magazine.* Kingston: Family Life Ministries.

Family Life Ministries, Jamaica. 2014. *family life ministries Jamaica.* Family Life Ministries. Accessed November 28, 2014. http://www.familylifeministriesjamaica.com/.

Flanagan, Caitlin. 2009. "Why Marriage Matters." *Time Magazine.*

Forbes, Marcia. 2009. "Language and Lyrics-the rampin' debate." *The Gleaner.* Kingston: The Gleaner Company, February 17.

Francis, Jermaine. 2014. "Thwaites emphasizes quality over quantity of subjects." *The Gleaner.* Kingston, March 6.

Frater, Adrian. 2008. "Cops label confessor a traitor." *The Gleaner.* Kingston: The Gleaner Company, January 21.

Frost, Robert. 1914. *poetryfoundation.org.* poetry foundation.org. Accessed October 5, 2012. https://www.poetryfoundation.org/poems/44266/mending-wall.

Fullan, Michael. 2003. *The Moral Imperative of School Leadership.* Thousand Oaks, California: Corwin Press.

Gardner, Robert B, and Nina Van Erk. 2011. "Standars for Measuring Success Not Based on Number of Victories." *High School Today.* Vol. 4. no. 4. Edited by Bruce L Howard and John C. Gillis. Indianapolis, Indiana: National Federation of State High School Associations, January 11.

Goodman, Ellen. 2015. "How to Talk about Dying." *The New York Times.* New York: The New York Times, July 1.

Graham, Lascelves. 2011. "High Schools aren't sports academies." *The Daily Gleaner.* Kingston: The Gleaner Company, January 5.

Greensboro Truth and Reconciliation Commission. 2006. *Greensboro Truth and Reconciliation Commission.* May 25. Accessed January 6, 2008. http://www.greensborotrc.org/.

Harriott, Anthony. 2002. *Crime Trends in the Caribbean and Responses.* Short, United Nations Office on Drugs and Crime, Kingston: United Nations Office on Drugs and Crime.

Henderson, Nan. 2013. "Havens of Resilience." *Educational Leadership* (ASCD) 71 (1).

Henry, Martin. 2010. "Government and civil society." *The Sunday Gleaner.* Kingston: The Gleaner Company, June 13.

Heschel, Abraham. 1967. *The Insecurity of Freedom: Essays on Human Existence.* Toronto: Ambassador book Ltd.

Hodari, Askhari Johnson, Sobers McCalla, Yvonne. 2009. *Lifelines: The Black Book of Proverbs.* Portland, Oregon: Broadway Books.

Jamaica Observer. 2014. "The argument for abortion is indeed compelling." *Jamaica Observer.* Kingston: Jamaica Observer, October 31.

Jamaica, Member of the Board of the National Gallery of, interview by Cliff Hughes. 2014. *2012 Biennial Exhibition of the National Gallery of Jamaica* Kingston, (July 1).

Jensen, Eric. 2009. *Teaching with Poverty in Mind.* Alexandria, Virginia: ASCD.

Johnes, Geraint and Johnes, Jill. 2007. *The International Handbook on the Economics of Education.* Edited by Geraint and Johnes, Jill Johnes. North hampton, Massachusetts: Edward Elgar Publishing.

Johnson, Bill. 2010. "Education System gets Grade F." *Education 2020.* The Jamaica Gleaner. Kingston: The Jamaica Gleaner, April 27.

Johnson, Jovan. 2015. *news.* The Gleaner Company. January 20. Accessed February 7, 2015. http://jamaica-gleaner.com/article/news/20150120/migrate-seek-better-opportunities-and-contribute-jamaica-advises-crawford.

Jules, Didacus. 2010. "Re-thinking Education in the Caribbean." *Caribbean Examiner*, October.

Jules, Didacus. 2010. "Rethinking Education for the Caribbean." *Caribbean Examiner* (Caribbean Examination Council) 8 (2).

Life Site News. 2011. "Youths resist United Nations push form more contraception and abortion among the world's youths." *LifeSiteNews.com.* New York: Life Site News, July 27.

Luton, Daraine. 2010. "'Dudus' enquiry." *The Gleaner.* Kingston: The Gleaner Company, October 13.

—. 2008. "Gunman bares all." *The Sunday Gleaner.* Kingston: The Gleaner Company, January 27.

—. 2014. "Prison Schools." *The Daily Gleaner.* Kingston: The Gleaner Company, January 22.

Mandela, Nelson. 1995. *Long Walk to Freedom.* New York: Back Bay Books.

Jamaica. Ministry of Health. 2007. "National HIV/STD Control Programme." Ministry of Health. October 15. Accessed December 5, 2008. http://moh.gov.jm/wp-content/uploads/2015/07/NHP_Annual_Report_2006.pdf.

Montagu Wortley, Mary. 2010. *brainy quote.com.* Accessed December 10, 2011. https://www.brainyquote.com/quotes/quotes/m/mary-wortle164237.html.

Palmer, Stacy A. 2012. "The Evolving Family." *The Sunday Gleaner.* Kingston: The Gleaner Company, December 9.

Passion and Purity. 2009. *About Passion and Purity.* Passion and Purity. Accessed September 5, 2009. http://www.passionandpurityja.com/page/about-passion-and-purity.

PBS. 2002. *Frontline Report.* January. Accessed April 2, 2013. http://www.pbs.org/wgbh/pages/frontline/shows/teenbrain/.

Planning Institute of Jamaica. 2010. "www.vision2030.gov.jm." *jis.gov.jm.* The Planning Institute of Jamaica. Accessed May 10, 2013. http://jis.gov.jm/media/vision2030_popular_versionsmallpdf.com_.pdf.

—. 2012. *www.vision2030.gov.jm.* Accessed February 6, 2015. http://www.vision2030.gov.jm/National-Development-Plan.

Pollard, Velma. 2003. *From Jamaican Creole to Standard English: A Handbook for Teachers.* Kingston: The University of the West Indies Press.

Reid, Tyrone. 2009. "New sex position?" *The Gleaner.* Kingston: The Gleaner Company, May 7.

—. 2007. "Same Sex Lessons." *The Gleaner.* Kingston: The Gleaner Company, October 31.

—. 2012. "Sex book puzzles education ministry." *The Sunday Gleaner.* Kingston: The Gleaner Company, September 16.

RJR News. 2013. "Hanna Wants Abortion Law Reviewed." *RJR News.* Kingston, June 19.

Ross, Will. 2005. "One-Minute World News." *BBC News.* April 12. Accessed December 1, 2008. http://news.bbc.co.uk/2/hi/africa/4433069.stm.

—. 2005. "One-Minute World News." *BBC News.* April 12. Accessed December 1, 2008. http://news.bbc.co.uk/2/hi/africa/4433069.stm.

Shakespeare, William. 1991. *Julius Caesar.* New York: Dover Publication.

—. 1993. *King Lear.* Jeremy Hylton. Accessed May 5, 2007. http://shakespeare.mit.edu/lear/full.html.

Simms, Glenda. 2009. "Child Sexual Abuse and Underdevelopment." *The Sunday Gleaner.* Kingston: The Gleaner Company, June 28.

Spaulding, Gary. 2015. *Lead Stories.* The Gleaner Company. January 14. Accessed February 4, 2015. http://jamaica-gleaner.com/article/lead-stories/20150114/cry-attention.

2011. "Standards for Measuring Success Not Based on Number of Victories." *High School Today.*

The Sunday Gleaner. 2010. "Crushing Coke." *The Sunday Gleaner.* Kingston: The Gleaner Company, May 30.

The Chief, Inspector. 2011. *Inspection Findings/School Reports.* National Education Inspectorate Jamaica. Accessed March 2, 2012. http://www.nei.org.jm/Inspection-Findings/School-Reports.

The Gleaner Editorial. 2008. "ReggaeBoyz.com Discussion Forum." *ReggaeBoyz.com.* The Editor. May 29. Accessed June 1, 2008. http://www.reggaeboyzsc.com/forum1/showthread.php?t=16945.

The Gleaner. 2009. "Fathers in Action Needs Your Help." *The Gleaner.* Kingston: The Gleaner Company, November 19.

—. 2011. *newspaperarchive.com.* The Gleaner. January 24. Accessed October 5, 2012. spaperarchive.com/kingston-gleaner-jan-24-2011-p-4/.

—. 2009. "Youth Group Thrilled at New Sex Position." *The Gleaner.* Kingston: The Gleaner Company, May 13.

The Jamaica Gleaner. 2013. "Jamaica-Gleaner.com." The Gleaner Company. August 22. Accessed September 6, 2013. https://newspaperarchive.com/kingston-gleaner-aug-22-2013-p-11/.

Jamaica. Ministry of Education .1980. "The Education Regulations 1980." The *Education Act.*

The Sunday Gleaner. 2009. "kingston-gleaner." *newspaperarchive.com.* The Gleaner Company. July 12. Accessed August 1, 2009. https://newspaperarchive.com/kingston-gleaner-jul-12-2009-p-1/?tag=births+unmarried+mothers&rtserp=tags/?pci=4&ndt=ex&pd=12&pm=7&py=2009&.

—. 2013. "Nuh Guh Deh-Campaign Targets Teenagers Involved in Risky Sexual Behaviour and Adults who Prey on the Youths." *The Sunday Gleaner.* Kingston: The Gleaner Company, December 1.

The Sunday Gleaner. 2011. *Poverty, income inequality on the rise in Jamaica.* Business, Business, The Gleaner Company, Kingston: The Sunday Gleaner.

Thomas, Donovan. 2002. *Confronting Suicide: Helping Teens at Risk.* Kingston: Youth House Publishers.

Thompson, Dr. Ralph. 2006. *Reggae Boyz.com Discussion Forum.* Edited by Tilla. October 01. Accessed May 21, 2008. http://www.reggaeboyzsc.com/Forum06/Topic5264-8-1. aspx?PostID=5332&DisplayMode=3&#bm5332.

Thompson, Kimone. 2013. "Family Planning Board head alarmed at number of high school parents." *The Jamaica Observer.* Kingston: The Jamaica Observer, March 24.

Thwaites, Daniel. 2013. "Nuh Bastard nuh deh Again." *The Sunday Gleaner.* Kingston: The Gleaner, October 27.

Tyson, Esther. 2007. "Courageous Leadership Needed." *The Sunday Gleaner.* Kingston: The Gleaner Company, October 7.

—. 2012. "The gay agenda and rights of Christians." *The Gleaner.* Kingston: The Gleaner Company, February 5.

UNESCO. 2011. "UNESCO AND EDUCATION." *UNESCO.org.* UNESCO. Accessed September 2, 2011. http://unesdoc.unesco. org/images/0021/002127/212715e.pdf.

*End Notes*

UNICEF. 2011. *jamaica/children*. Accessed May 5, 2012. https://www.
unicef.org/jamaica/children_1569.htm.

UWI, Academic from, interview by Dionne Jackson Miller. 2009.
"Impact of Dancehall." *All Angles*. Kingston, (October 28).

Vickerman, Marlon. 2008. *kingston-gleaner-jan-15-2008*. The Gleaner
Company. January 15. Accessed November 5, 2010. https://
newspaperarchive.com/kingston-gleaner-jan-15-2008-p-6/.

Wallis, Claudia, and Dell Kristina. 2004. "What Makes Teens Tick."
*Time Magazine*. New York, May 10.

Warshof, Allison, and Rappaport Nancy. 2013. "Staying connected
with troubled students." *Educational Leadership* (ASCD) 71 (1).

Williams, Paul H. 2010. "Dr. Herbert Gayle batting for Fathers." *The
Gleaner*. Kingston: The Gleaner Company, May 3.

Williams, Sian, and Janet Brown. 2006. "Child Rearing in the
Caribbean: Emergent Issues." *upan1.un.org*. Caribbean Child
Support Initiative (CCSI). May 25. Accessed January 2, 2009.
http://unpan1.un.org/intradoc/groups/public/documents/caricad/
unpan031672.pdf.

Yeats, William Butler. 2011. *Selected Poems and Four Plays*. New
York: Scribner.

# A GLOSSARY OF THE MEANINGS OF JAMAICAN CREOLE USED IN THE TEXT

**Part 1 Education in Jamaica**

1   Quarrels

2   Loud quarrels

3   Loud and vulgar quarrels

4   Miss, this is the same pair of shoes that you gave me. And do you know that I am still wearing it.

5   That is foolishness.

6   Has a large number of women all at once

7   Men mate like dogs

8   Making a hit song

9   Killing someone

10  You all play too much

11  Do not allow anyone to be disrespectful to you

12  Being disrespectful

13  Make a hit song

14  Make money

15  It is nothing

16  Sense of a proud identity

17  If someone disrespects you, he must die

18  Has a large number of women all at once

19  Has become an important school.

## Part 2 The State of the Family in Jamaica

20  It is nothing

21  Gyrating their pelvis in a sexually explicit manner

22  Has a large number of women all at once

23  To have a man support them financially

24  You spend too much time playing

25  Has a large number of women all at once

26  There is no more official designation for children born outside of marriage

27  It does not make a difference

28  Black people are malicious in their thinking and do not look out for one another

29  Idiot

30  Make money

31  Behaving like dogs attacking and eating each other

32  You spend too much time playing

## Part 3 – Societal Values

33   Many pieces of jewellery that are huge and sparkling, usually gold in colour worn at the same time

34   Dance in a sexually provocative manner, sometimes exposing private parts

35   You are not masculine, you are too soft

36   You are an idiot

37   Take the scissors and stab one of them in the eye

38   Disrespect

39   Be creative in coming up with solutions

40   Give the people what they desire

41    Have a number of women all at once

42    It is very attractive and should have been here from long ago. It is a first-class building

43   Saying hello and thank you will not impact you negatively

44   It is nothing

45   It is a big matter, a very big matter

46   A person has to do whatever is necessary to survive economically

47   Taking away my source of income

48    Make money

49   A person has to do what it takes to make money

50   Anyone who reports illegal activity to the authorities must die

51   Disrespect

52   Anancy is a folklore hero who is a spider, who is a trickster

53   It isn't anything, it is just sex

54   It isn't anything. I went through it too. Why can't she deal with it too? It did not kill me.
55   You are forcing me to give up my only source of income
56   The dogs are going to eat what is rightfully ours because of our bad decisions.


**Part 4 –The Impact of Dancehall on the Jamaican Culture**

57   A culture that glorifies being a criminal
58   A girl who behaves and dresses in a sexually provocative manner and is available.
59   Having many girls at once
60   Dressing in a way that exposes your body in a sexually provocative manner
61   Behaving in a sexually explicit manner
62   Publicly dancing with strong pelvic thrusts and gyrations especially with the opposite sex
63   Wearing a lot of showy clothes and jewellery
64   A Jamaican Dancehall Session held on a weekly basis
65   They tell you to go around smoking ganja and shooting guns
66   The culture that glorifies being a criminal
67   It is The Teacher
68   And it is Spice (The stage name of the female singer.)
69   A sexually loose woman and a criminal
70   Describing the action of thrusting during sexual intercourse that is so hard the woman's abdomen will begin to go into cramps.

71  Anyone who reports illegal activity to the authorities must die

72  Music that encourages dance moves that imitate sexual intercourse

73  How are you to discuss morals when you are hungry.

74  A person has to do what he must to survive economically.

## Part 6 – The Abortion Debate in Jamaica

75  Do not Go There

76  It isn't anything. It is just sex

77  Daughters

## Part 8 – Government Leadership in Jamaica

78  They do not report criminal activities to the authorities

79  Usually criminals with financial resources that provide funds to people living in a garrison community and thereby gain their loyalty.

80  A terrible betrayal

81  How do you think a man gets a gun and money most of the time? Right now, in one area there are 15 guns and it is because of a politician that they got there.

82  Know how to be creative to provide solutions when there are no resources.

83  A very small nation like we are

84  If you associate with persons of ill-repute, you will become just like them

85 You have to give someone else some of it.

86 A person has to find a way to make money

87 A Dancehall session held on a weekly basis.

88 Disrespected

89 Anyone who gives information to the authorities is to be killed.

90 Not just talk

91 All politicians are liars

Lightning Source UK Ltd.
Milton Keynes UK
UKHW010641260722
406393UK00002B/453

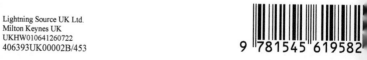